Scholastic

LITERACY PLACE

Copyright acknowledgments and credits appear at the end of this book. These pages constitute an extension of this copyright page.

Copyright © 1996 by Scholastic Inc.   All rights reserved.   Printed in the U.S.A.
ISBN 0-590-59273-4
1 2 3 4 5 6 7 8 9 10   24   02 01 00 99 98 97 96

UNIT 4

IN THE SPOTLIGHT

UNIT 5

AMERICA'S JOURNAL

Section 1

TOURING AMERICA'S CITIES

Section 2

CITY CHALLENGES

Section 3

REACHING OUT

WORKSHOP 1

WORKSHOP 2

PROJECT

IN THE SPOTLIGHT

Attend

an Actor's Workshop

We use our creativity to reach an audience.

Stories to Tell

The stories we tell connect the past to the present.

from
"HOW THE COYOTE GETS HIS NAME"
by Jerry Tello

...so all the animals gathered their young and took them back to where
they slept and as the coyote was walking up (walking motion) the hill, he was
thinking, "How can I be first...how can I be first??!!" (Make pensive face—
look at extended finger.)
By this time, the Sun (look up) had finished his cycle and touched
(tap-on-shoulder motion with index finger) the Moon on the shoulder and
Ms. Moon began sharing her brilliance.
And there sat (sitting action) the coyote on top of the hill, under a tree,
still thinking how he could be first (index finger to temple, as if thinking), when

On Stage

Through the performing arts, we entertain others.

VANESSA'S BAD GRADE
by Ross Brown
Scene Five

Vanessa is in her room when Theo walks in.

VANESSA: I got my history test back.
(She hands him the test paper.)

THEO: Whoa. This is a "D."

VANESSA: I know. I've never gotten a "D" before. I've seen them, but never next to my name.

THEO: And this one is in red. That's the worst kind to get.

VANESSA: I don't know how it happened. Robert and I studied for this.

THEO: Yeah. I saw that.
...think I should tell

Speak Out

Speeches help us persuade and inform others.

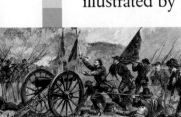

Trade Books

The following
books accompany this
In the Spotlight
SourceBook.

**Dear Dr. Bell ...
Your Friend,
Helen Keller**

by Judith
St. George

**Koya DeLaney
and the Good
Girl Blues**

by Eloise
Greenfield

AWARD WINNING Author

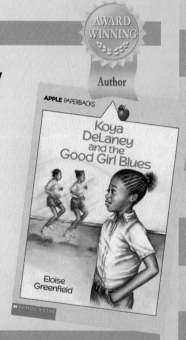

School Spirit

by Johanna
Hurwitz

AWARD WINNING Author

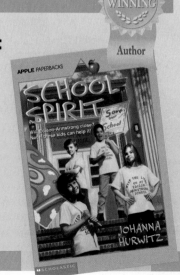

**That's a Wrap:
How Movies
Are Made**

by Ned Dowd
photographed
by Henry
Horenstein

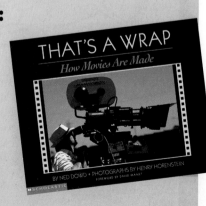

Stories to Tell

Join a young girl and her friends as they listen to real-life stories on a neighbor's porch.

Read a Chinese tale about a strange encounter in the forest. Meet three spellbinding storytellers.

WORKSHOP 1

Tell a story of your own or one that you've heard before.

from
"HOW THE COYOTE GETS HIS NAME"
by Jerry Tello

...so all the animals gathered their young and took them back to where they slept and as the coyote was walking up (walking motion) the hill, he was thinking, "How can I be first...how can I be first??!!" (Make pensive face—look at extended finger.)

By this time, the Sun (look up) had finished his cycle and touched (tap-on-the-shoulder motion with index finger) the Moon on the shoulder and Ms. Moon began sharing her brilliance.

And there sat (sitting action) the coyote on top of the hill, under a tree, still thinking how he could be first (index finger to temple, as if thinking), when he had a brilliant idea!

(Eyes wide, mouth open). "I'll just stay up all night!" That way, I'll see Mr. Sun as he awakes and I can be first!

Well, several hours passed and as hard as the coyote tried, he was still get-

9

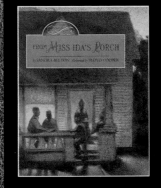

FROM MISS IDA'S PORCH

AWARD WINNING Illustrator

by SANDRA BELTON

illustrated by FLOYD COOPER

*T*here's a very best time of day on Church Street. My street. It begins when the sky and my feelings match, both kind of rosy around the edges.

You can hear all the best-time noises—Shoo Kate and Mr. Fisher laughing from their kitchen. Reginald and T-Bone slamming out their back door. Mr. Porter coming home from work in his noisy ole car, calling out to everybody he passes on the street. Netta practicing on her piano (mostly to get out of washing dinner dishes), and Mr. Willie making his just-checkin'-on call to Mrs. Jackson, his ninety-year-old mama.

The noises feel good.

Most of the big kids are getting ready to hang out somewhere, like at the drugstore down on the corner, or on the steps in front of the church. Those are some of their favorite pretending places—the boys pretending not to see the girls, and the girls pretending to ignore the boys. . . . Like my sister Sylvia pretending to ignore Peewee.

Most of the little kids are getting ready to get ready for bed. Getting ready for bed takes a long time for the little kids. Some of them can make it last all the way to the end of the best time. Especially the Tolver kids.

"Just five more minutes, Mama, please!" they say. Then after five minutes they hide somewhere in the yard for five more minutes. Then they start pleading all over again for five more minutes.

But most of the kids on Church Street are in-between kids. Like Freda and me.

Some of the best times we just sit on her porch or mine, playing jacks or reading comics. Sometimes we play statues with Rosetta and Punkin and Rodney. Sometimes T-Bone plays, too.

*M*ost of the best times, though, just about all of us end up at Miss Ida's. Sitting on her porch.

Miss Ida's house is halfway down Church Street. That's probably one reason folks end up there a lot. Another reason is Miss Ida herself. She and the best time are kind of alike. Soft, peaceful.

But the biggest reason we all end up there is that Miss Ida's porch is a telling place.

❧

Usually Mr. Fisher comes over to sit on the porch about the same time we do. It's about the time the sky is getting rosy all over. You know then that the best time is settling in.

Miss Ida calls Mr. Fisher "Poissant" because they both come from Louisiana, and that's what people there used to call him.

Mr. Fisher has been all over. It's hard to tell how old he is. But from all the stuff he's done, he could be really old. He doesn't look old at all, though. Especially when he walks. He sorta bounces. Miss Ida always says, "Poissant has a jaunty step."

Mr. Fisher has lots of memories about the places he's been and things he's seen. Almost *anything* can make him think about something he saw or heard or did a while back. He'll start out, "Puts my mind on the time . . . ," and we know what's coming.

"Tell us about that time, Poissant," Miss Ida will say to Mr. Fisher when he begins his remembering.

And he will.

Like the time Freda and Punkin were arguing about what Mrs. Jackson had said when she was over at Punkin's house, visiting Miss Esther, Punkin's aunt.

"Lena Horne ain't never visited Miz Jackson, Punkin," Freda said. "Miz Jackson was just talking outta her head, girl. You know she ninety years old. You crazy for believing her."

"You don't know nothing, Freda." Punkin was getting angry. "Just 'cause Miz Jackson's ninety don't mean she talking outta her head. Most time Miz Jackson make more sense than you!"

Punkin and T-Bone almost fell over laughing. Me, too. And this made Freda fighting mad.

"Hold on there, Miss Lady," said Mr. Fisher, taking hold of one of Freda's hands. "Don't press ugly on that pretty face. Tell me now, how come you think Lena Horne couldn't have stayed at Mrs. Jackson's house?"

"'Cause Lena Horne is famous. Why would she want to stay at Miz Jackson's?"

"Why not?" Mr. Fisher settled back in his chair.

I had a feeling that some remembering was getting started.

Used to be that most all the famous black folks who came to town stayed at somebody's house."

"How come, Mr. Fisher?" Freda sat on the stoop in front of Mr. Fisher.

"Nowhere else for them to stay! Couldn't stay in hotels. Hotels didn't allow no black guests! Famous or not. When our folk came to town to give a speech, put on a show, or whatever they came to do, we had to be the ones to give 'em a bed.

"Puts my mind on a time back in thirty-nine. I was working in West Virginia then. Working in the mines. Lived in a nice town close to where I worked. Lots of good folks there, working hard to make a life for themselves and their children."

Mr. Fisher's remembering was making him smile.

"Anyhow, a big dance took place in the town every year. Folks came from all around to go to this dance. That year, 1939, the dance was *really* going to be special. Duke Ellington was coming to town. The great bandsman himself was coming to play for the dance."

"Was Duke Ellington famous?" I bet none of us knew who Duke Ellington was. Punkin was brave enough to ask.

Mr. Fisher almost jumped out of his chair. "Don't they teach you children nothin' in school? Duke Ellington *famous*?" Mr. Fisher was almost shouting.

"Don't get bothered now, Poissant." Miss Ida put her hand on Mr. Fisher's arm. She was speaking in that peaceful way she has.

"Can't expect anybody to listen if you shouting, now can you," said Miss Ida. "Just tell the children about Duke Ellington. Tell them about the sound of that band. A sound that made your feet get a life of their own on the dance floor. Tell them how he not only led the band from his piano but also wrote most of the songs they played. How you could hum your little baby to sleep with some of those pretty songs. And how some of those songs were played by big orchestras and sung by huge choirs in halls all over the world."

Mr. Fisher had a big smile on his face. "I ain't got to tell them, Miss Ida. You doin' a fine job, a mighty fine job!"

The sky was starting to look like the never-tell blue blanket on Big Mama's bed. "Never-tell blue is light enough to still be blue but dark enough to hide the dirt," Big Mama says.

The best-time noises were still there, but they had changed. You could hear the chirping bugs. One of the Tolver kids was crying. Probably asking for something he couldn't have. Mr. Willie was playing his radio. Jazz.

Mr. Fisher was still remembering.

"Yessir. The great Duke Ellington was coming to play for us, for our dance, and there was not one hotel in the state that would put him up and take his money for doin' it. If he had a mind to rest himself in a bed, it was goin' have to be in the home of some black person."

"Did he stay with you, Mr. Fisher?" Punkin asked.

"Not with me, exactly, but in the house where I was living. Mrs. Lomax's house. Mrs. Lomax had a big, fine house, and she kept it real nice. I rented a room on the third floor."

Mr. Fisher started to grin. Like he always did when he got to a part he liked to tell.

"I was there when the great man arrived with three of his bandsmen."

"So you got to meet Duke Ellington?" T-Bone was impressed. We all were.

"I not only met him, I was there when he sat at the piano in Mrs. Lomax's parlor. Duke's playing heated up that little room. I'm telling you it did. He was some kinda good!"

Mr. Fisher grew quiet. A remembering quiet. He stopped smiling, too.

"Humph. Imagine that. A man like that. Talented, famous, everything! Not being able to pay his *own* money to sleep in a crummy little hotel room, just because he was black."

After that we were all quiet. I was wishing I knew more about what Mr. Fisher was remembering. I bet Freda was wishing so, too.

$\mathcal{E}$venin', everybody. Must be some powerful thinking over here tonight, 'cause everybody's deep into it."

Shoo Kate was climbing the steps to the porch. I hadn't even heard her coming up the walk. Nobody else must have either.

"Hey, Shoo Kate. Come over here by me." Miss Ida patted the place on the swing beside her.

Shoo Kate is Mr. Fisher's wife. Her name is really Mrs. Kate Fisher, but just about everybody calls her Shoo Kate. She told us one time that when she was little she used to tease her baby brother, telling him that their mama said he had to call her Sugar Kate 'cause she was so sweet. The name came out Shoo Kate when her baby brother said it. Then everybody started calling her that. She even told us kids to call her Shoo Kate instead of Mrs. Fisher.

After she sat down Shoo Kate reached over and poked Mr. Fisher. "What you been telling these folks, Fisher, to make everybody so quiet?"

"I ain't been tellin' them nothing you don't already know, darlin'." Mr. Fisher and Shoo Kate smiled at each other. They always seemed to be smiling and laughing together.

"Did any famous people stay in your house, Shoo Kate?" T-bone asked.

"Now I know what talking's been over here," Shoo Kate said, laughing. "Fisher, you been telling them about that time Duke Ellington came and stayed at the place in West Virginia where you were living."

"I sure was," said Mr. Fisher. "No reason to keep that fine bit of history a secret."

"So it's history now, is it, Poissant," said Miss Ida. I think she was teasing. All the grown-ups laughed.

"Well, T," said Shoo Kate, "I never made history like Fisher here, but I *was* somewhere one time when history was being made."

"Shoo Kate, I bet I know what you're talking about. Go on, tell the children." Miss Ida sounded excited.

※

The sky was really getting dark. I like the best time most of all when the sky is dark. You can imagine that almost anything is out there. You can imagine almost anything.

Shoo Kate began her story.

"Around the same time Fisher was living in West Virginia, I was living with my family in Washington, D.C. My papa worked for the railroad. He was a train-car porter, so he had to travel most of the time. All of us looked forward to Papa's days off, the days he was going to be home.

"Oh, those were the best days—the days when Papa was home. He made sure we all did something special on those days. All of us together, Papa, Mama, and each one of us kids. We didn't have much money, but we had enough. And as shut out as we were in Washington, we could still find lots of things to do."

"What do you mean 'shut out,' Shoo Kate?" Freda asked.

"Just what the words say, sugar. Black folks were shut out.

We couldn't go to the movie theaters, the big restaurants, just about anyplace you think folks ought to be able to go if the place is open to the public and folks have the inclination to go. Why, when my papa was growing up in Washington, black folks couldn't even go to the national monuments!"

Punkin looked at Shoo Kate kind of funny. "But Washington is the capital city," she said. "That's where they make laws for the whole country. How could they break the law, keeping folks from going places just 'cause they was black?"

Freda had been waiting all evening to get back at Punkin, and her chance had finally come.

"Now look who's talking outta her head! Girl, don't you know nothing? Used to be that the *law* said it was okay to keep black folks out," she said.

"Don't you two get started now. Freda's right about the laws, of course," Miss Ida said, pulling Punkin down to sit beside her. "But that's another story. A long story for another time. Go on, Shoo Kate, please."

Shoo Kate did.

"Anyhow, this one time we were all real excited because Papa was going to be home for Easter. He wasn't always able to be there for holidays. So we were all looking forward to having him home and being able to dress up in our new clothes and go to church together.

"But it wasn't Papa's plan for us to go to church that Easter Sunday. After we were all dressed and ready to leave the house, Papa said we were going to catch the trolley car.

"Then we really got excited. Catching the trolley car! We knew that Papa must be planning something special because we didn't need to catch the trolley to go to our church. We only had to walk a couple of blocks to get there."

Shoo Kate sat up straighter. It was like her remembering was pushing at her back.

"How grand we were, riding on the trolley that Easter Sunday morning. And even grander when Papa explained that we were on our way to the Lincoln Memorial. That was exciting enough. Then he went on to tell us that we were going there to hear one of the greatest voices in America!"

"Who were you going to hear, Shoo Kate?" Freda asked the question this time.

"We were going to hear Marian Anderson. A grand, grand singer—a voice more magnificent than you could *ever* imagine!

"But there was more to it than just going to hear Marian Anderson sing. Much more."

Shoo Kate wiggled down to the edge of her chair and moved her face closer to us.

"It was like this. Several months before that Easter Sunday, a concert had been arranged. It was arranged for Marian Anderson to sing at Constitution Hall. Constitution Hall was the big concert stage in Washington, where all the famous musicians appeared. People from all over the world.

"Marian Anderson was certainly famous. *And* she had sung all over the world. Didn't matter, though. Marian Anderson's concert was not going to take place in Constitution Hall. You see, Marian Anderson was black. The people who owned the hall said no black musician was going to perform on their stage!"

Shoo Kate sat back in her chair. Her eyes got narrow.

"While we rode on the trolley, Papa told us what had happened. A lot of people in Washington were furious about Miss Anderson not being able to sing at Constitution Hall. The wife of the president of the United States was one of these furious people. So she and some others got together to arrange for Miss Anderson to sing somewhere else."

Shoo Kate started moving her hands as she talked. Her smile started coming back.

"Constitution Hall with its white columns and high-up ceiling wouldn't welcome Marian Anderson. But the Lincoln Memorial would! There would be no walls to keep people out. And the sky would be the ceiling! On Easter Sunday morning just about anybody who wanted to would be able to hear and *see* Marian Anderson sing. Including my entire family!"

Shoo Kate's smile was all over her face.

"At first we thought it might rain. We had gotten there early, very early, hoping to get close enough to see. While we waited, we kept looking up at the sky, wishing for the sun to come out.

"The crowd grew and grew. So many people, all kinds of people. Black folks, white folks, standing there together in front of the Lincoln Memorial, waiting to hear Marian Anderson sing."

Mr. Fisher started grinning himself. What Shoo Kate was about to say must have been his favorite part of the story.

"It was time for the concert to start. Then, just as Marian Anderson was getting ready to walk out onto the place she was gonna sing from, the sun came out. Yes, it did!"

Shoo Kate's voice grew softer. So soft we moved closer to hear her.

"When the concert started, our papa took turns holding the little ones up so they could get a better look. When he reached down to get my baby brother Jimmy, I saw tears rolling down his cheeks.

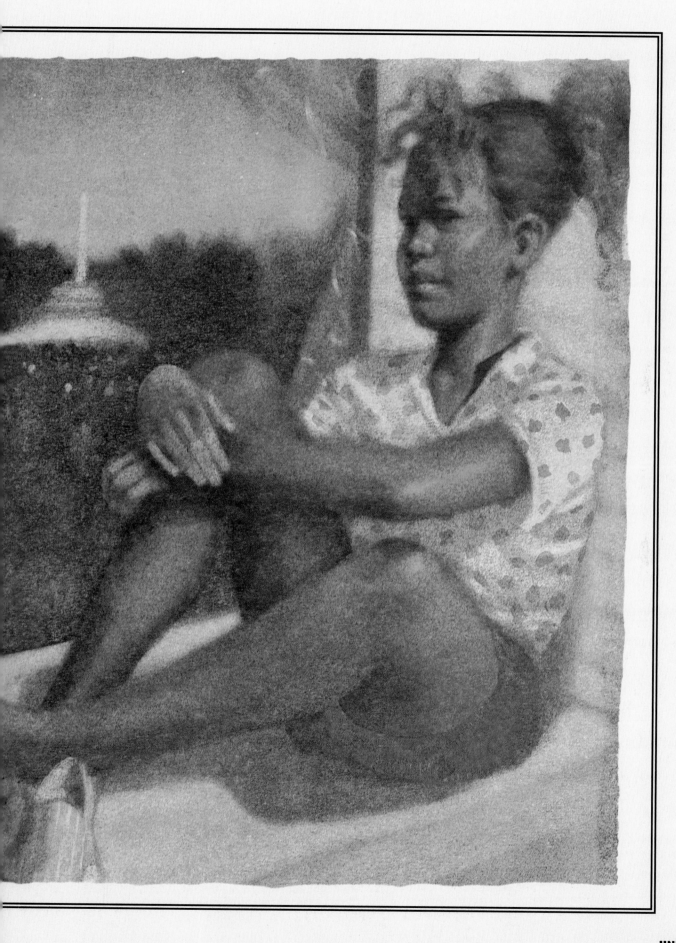

"I asked my mama if Papa was crying 'cause he was happy. This is what Mama said to us sometimes when we caught her crying. Mama said that some of Papa's tears were happy tears, but some were not. Some were tears of sadness, and maybe even anger.

"Mama said to me, 'Listen to the words she sings, Kate.' Miss Anderson was singing a song I knew, 'My Country, 'Tis of Thee.' I recognized the words:

'. . . *From every mountainside*
Let freedom ring'

" 'Your papa's thinking about those words and what they should mean,' Mama said. 'Thoughts like that might be making him feel good and bad at the same time. That's probably why there are tears on your papa's face.' "

Shoo Kate sat back in her chair. Her voice got almost regular.

"So you see, on that Easter Sunday I saw history being made there at the Lincoln Memorial. I also saw my papa cry with pride and sadness at the same time. It was a day that will live in my memory forever."

Shoo Kate's remembering had kind of put a spell on us. On everybody listening. Even Punkin was real still, and she was usually moving around like a doll on strings. When my father and my sister Sylvia walked up on the porch, we all jumped. Nobody had heard them coming.

"Goodness, you all gave me a fright." Miss Ida got up. "Hi, Sylvia. Here, take my seat, J.S.," she said to Daddy. "I'll get more chairs from the house."

"No need, Ida," Daddy said. "A few folks are going to be leaving very soon and there'll be plenty of room."

Daddy looked over at me and Freda. I knew that the very best time was about to be over for us.

"Hey, J.S., what you been up to?" Daddy and Mr. Fisher were shaking hands.

"I just been walking down to the corner to make sure Sylvia and her friends know it's time to come home."

"Sylvia don't know nothing when Peewee's around." I just had to say that. My sister thinks she's something special just 'cause bony ole Peewee said she was cute.

"Shut up!" Sylvia wanted to hit me. I just knew it.

"Don't speak that way to your sister," Daddy said to Sylvia. "And you, missy," he said pointing to me, "if you want to get your extra few minutes here, I think you'd better have kinder thoughts for Sylvia."

"There's been some wonderful thoughts on this porch tonight, folks. Let's keep the good words going." Miss Ida always makes things okay.

"J.S.," she said, "you missed a wonderful story. Shoo Kate was telling us about the time she saw Marian Anderson."

"Oh, yeah," Daddy said, like he was remembering something. "You told me a little about that, Shoo Kate. I wish I had been here to hear the whole story."

"Tell him the story, Shoo Kate. We'd love to hear it again. Right, Freda?" I wanted so much to make the best time last.

"Good try, baby, but it won't work tonight." Daddy hardly ever let my tricks work on him.

"I have another chapter for that story, however. Want to hear it?" While he was talking, Daddy winked at Shoo Kate. I thought he was fooling.

Miss Ida sat up in her seat. Like she felt the same as me. Wanting the evening to go on.

"Come on, J.S., sit down and take your turn this evening." Miss Ida motioned for us to make room for Daddy.

Then my daddy started his remembering.

"I had an uncle—Uncle Henry—who lived in Washington," Daddy began. "He taught at Howard University there, for many years.

"Uncle Henry was a big man, well over six feet tall. He had wide, full eyebrows that came together like a hairy *V* whenever he frowned. And Uncle Henry frowned easily. Especially when one of us was messin' up. His voice was like a drum—booming, deep.

"His voice, his frown, and his attitude could put the fear of God in you. Uncle Henry didn't play!"

Daddy chuckled.

"I dearly loved Uncle Henry, though. We all did. In fact, he was probably the favorite of everybody in the family. Whenever there was going to be a family gathering, we all wanted it to be at Uncle Henry's. At Uncle Henry's you knew there would be lots to do, lots to eat, and best of all, lots and lots of Uncle Henry."

Daddy has a deep voice, too. A good telling voice.

"Uncle Henry had worked hard to get where he wanted to be in life. And he was one of the lucky ones: He got there. Yep, Uncle Henry was a grand old guy. One of those people you hope will go on forever."

Daddy looked out into the darkness. I think he was seeing Uncle Henry in his mind. I think I was, too.

"Whenever us nephews and nieces were gathered around the breakfast or dinner table, Uncle Henry would claim the floor, but we didn't mind at all. Uncle Henry was a magnificent storyteller! And though we didn't know it then, his stories were like fuel for our young minds.

"Uncle Henry firmly believed that the knowledge of our history—the history of black folks—was the most important story that we could ever be told. I can just hear him now: 'You can know where you are going in this world only if you know where you've been!'"

Mr. Fisher slapped his hand on his leg. "Now that's a man after my own heart!" he said.

"*Shhhhh*, Fisher. Let J.S. go on," Shoo Kate said.

Daddy did. "Uncle Henry held us spellbound with his stories. He told us about the great civilizations of Africa that existed thousands of years ago, and—"

"Tell us about that!" T-Bone moved real close to Daddy.

"That's a story for another time, T," Daddy said. "I'll be sure to tell you, but I'd better get on with this one now.

"One of Uncle Henry's stories described how he had been there that Easter Sunday at the Lincoln Memorial. But that same story had another part, a part that told something that had happened *before* that famous Sunday.

"You see, another important event had taken place in that same spot seventeen years earlier—the dedication of the Lincoln Memorial. Uncle Henry had been there then, too."

"Wow!" said T-Bone and Punkin. I knew how they felt.

"It wasn't as much of a 'wow' as you might think, kids. At the dedication of this monument to the man known as the Great Emancipator, the black folks who came had to stand in a special section. A section off to the left of the monument. Away from the white folks, who could stand dead center, right in front."

Daddy had started breathing hard. It sounded loud. Everything else was quiet. Except Daddy's breathing.

"Anyhow, during one of our visits to Uncle Henry, Marian Anderson was going to be giving another concert. It was very important to Uncle Henry that all the nieces and nephews have a chance to go."

"So, you heard a concert at the Lincoln Memorial, too, right?" T-Bone sure was making it hard for Daddy to get on with his story. I wanted to put some tape over his mouth.

Daddy smiled. "No, as a matter of fact, I didn't. The concert I went to was held at Constitution Hall."

"What?" All of us were surprised at this twist.

"That's right," Daddy said. His breathing wasn't so loud now. "It was 1965, over twenty-five years since that concert at the Lincoln Memorial. Marian Anderson was now at the end of her career as a singer. This concert was taking place so she could say farewell to Washington audiences.

"Constitution Hall was still one of the finest concert stages in Washington, a stage now open to all performers, no matter what their color. It had been that way for years. But that concert and that magnificent singer were special. Very special."

Everybody was looking at Daddy as he went on.

"Many of the people in the hall that night were African Americans. Some of these black people had also been standing on the grass under the sky that Easter Sunday morning. And some, like Uncle Henry, had been out there on the grass for the dedication in 1922. Now these same people were sitting in the forbidden hall, some of them in the best seats in the house!

"When Marian Andersen came onto the stage, the applause of the crowd was like the roar of a thousand pounding seas. It went on and on and on. But above the noise, there was one thing I heard very clearly."

"You heard your Uncle Henry, right?" Miss Ida was smiling at Dad. And her eyes were sparkly. Like raindrops are sparkly when I can look through them on my window and see the sun.

My dad's voice was real soft. "I did, Ida. I could hear Uncle Henry. But I think I would have known what he was saying even if I hadn't heard him. Just like I can hear him right now: 'You can know where you are going in this world only if you know where you've been!'"

In the quiet after Daddy stopped talking, I looked out into the velvet black sky. I tried to imagine the sound of a thousand pounding seas. I tried to imagine some other things, too. Like how it might have been to ride on a trolley. Or to spend the night in the same house with a famous person. Or to go to a famous monument and not be able to stand where I wanted to.

My dad's story brought the end to the very best time that evening.

Like we always did, Freda, T, Punkin, and I said good-night to all the grown-ups and walked each other home. I walked Freda home and then she walked me home, and then I walked her home again. Sylvia told on us like she usually does, so I finally went home for good to go to bed.

Just before I go to sleep is the very, very last part of the very best time. After I'm in bed and my light is turned off, I can look out my bedroom window and see Miss Ida's porch.

Most of the time the grown-ups are still there. I can hear them talking and laughing, but it's soft and far away.

These sounds feel good. They keep the very best times close. So close that they're with me when my eyelids stop cooperating and just drop. I think the very best times go with me into my dreams. . . .

THE HOME

"The Homecoming," by Laurence Yep, is a story from The Rainbow People, a collection of 20 Chinese folk tales. In this book Yep retells traditional stories that were collected and translated in the 1930s by a researcher who worked with Chinese Americans living in Oakland, California.

Once there was a woodcutter who minded everyone's business but his own. If you were digging a hole, he knew a better way to grip the shovel. If you were cooking a fish, he knew a better recipe. As his village said, he knew a little of everything and most of nothing.

If his wife and children hadn't made palm leaf fans, the family would have starved. Finally his wife got tired of everyone laughing at them. "You're supposed to be a woodcutter. Go up to the hill and cut some firewood."

COMING

by Laurence Yep

illustrations by Chi Chung

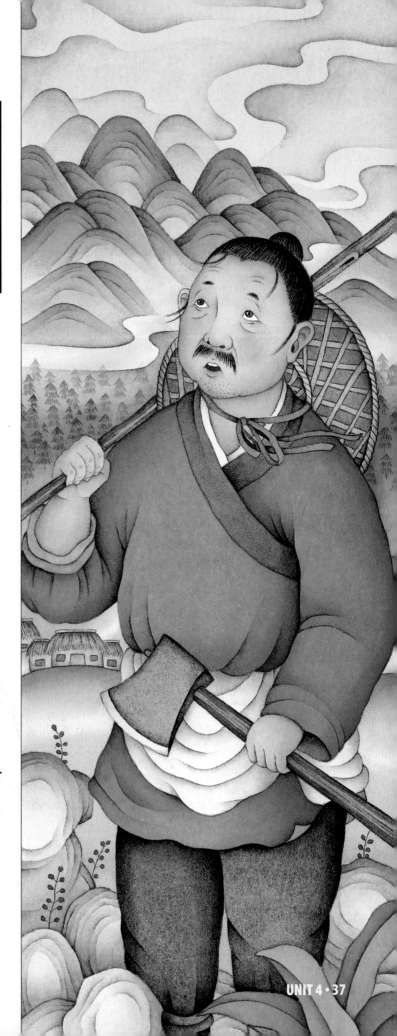

"Any fool can do that." The woodcutter picked up his hatchet. "In the mountains there's plenty of tall oak. That's what burns best."

His wife pointed out the window. "But there's a stand of pine just over the ridgetop."

Her husband looked pained. "Pine won't sell as well. I'll take my load into town, where folk are too busy to cut their own. Then I'll come back with loads of cash." With a laugh, he shouldered his long pole. After he cut the wood, he would tie it into two big bundles and place each at the end of the pole. Then he would balance the load on his shoulder.

Waving good-bye to his children, he left their house; but his wife walked right with him. "What are you doing?" he asked.

His wife folded her arms as they walked along. "Escorting you."

He slowed down by a boy who was making a kite out of paper and rice paste. "That thing will never fly. You should—"

His wife caught his arm and pulled him along. "Don't be such a busybody."

"If a neighbor's doing something wrong, it's the charitable thing to set that person straight." He tried to stop by a man who was feeding his ducks. "Say, friend. Those ducks'll get fatter if—"

His wife yanked him away and gave him a good shake. "Do I have to blindfold you? We have two children to feed."

"I'm not lazy," he grumbled.

She kept dragging him out of the village. "I never said you were. You can do the work of two people when no one else is around. You're just too easily distracted."

She went with him to the very edge of the fields and sent him on his way. "Remember," she called after him. "Don't talk to anyone."

He walked with long, steady strides through the wooded hills. "I'll show her. It isn't how often you do something, it's how you do it. I'll cut twice the wood and sell it for double the price and come back in half the time."

Complaining loudly to himself, he moved deep into the mountains. I want just the right sort of oak, he thought to himself. As he walked along, he kept an eye out for a likely tree.

He didn't see the funny old man until he bumped into him. "Oof, watch where you're going," the old man said.

The old man had a head that bulged as big as a melon. He was dressed in a yellow robe embroidered with storks and pine trees.

Playing chess with the old man was another man so fat he could not close his robe. In his hand he had a large fan painted with scenes.

The fat man wagged a finger at the old man. "Don't try to change the subject. I've got you. It's checkmate in two moves."

The funny old man looked back at the chessboard. The lines were a bright red on yellow paper, and the chess pieces were flat disks with words painted in gold on their tops.

"Is it now, is it now?" the funny old man mused.

The woodcutter remembered his wife's warning. But he said to himself, "I'm not actually talking to them. I'm advising them." So he put down his hatchet and pole. "Actually, if you moved that piece"—he jabbed at a disk—"and moved it there"—he pointed at a spot on the board—"you'd have him."

But the old man moved a different disk.

The fat man scratched the top of his bald head. "Now how'd you think of that?"

The woodcutter rubbed his chin. "Yes, how *did* you think of that?" But then he nodded his head and pointed to one of the fat man's disks. "Still, if you shifted that one, you'd win."

However, the fat man ignored him as he made another move.

"Well," the woodcutter said to the old man, "you've got him now."

But the old man paid him no more mind than the fat man. "Hmmm," he murmured, and set his chin on his fist as he studied the board.

The woodcutter became so caught up in the game that he squatted down. "I know what you have to do. I'll be right here just in case you need to ask."

Neither man said anything to the woodcutter. They just went on playing, and as they played, the woodcutter became more and more fascinated. He forgot about chopping wood. He even forgot about going home.

When it was night, the funny old man opened a big basket and lifted out a lantern covered with stars. He hung it from a tree and the game went on. Night passed on into day, but the woodcutter was as involved in the game now as the two men.

"Let's take a break." The old man slipped a peach from one big sleeve. The peach was big as the woodcutter's fist, and it filled the woods with a sweet aroma.

"You're just stalling for time," the fat man said. "Move."

"I'm hungry," the old man complained, and took a big bite. However, he shoved a piece along the board. When he held the peach out to the fat man, the fat man bit into it hungrily.

Alternating moves and bites, they went on until there was nothing left of the peach except the peach stone. "I feel much better now," the old man said, and threw the stone over his shoulder.

As the two men had eaten the peach, the woodcutter had discovered that he was famished, but the only thing was the peach stone. "Maybe I can suck on this stone and forget about being hungry. But I wish one of them would ask me for help. We could finish this game a lot quicker."

He tucked the stone into his mouth and tasted some of the peach juices. Instantly, he felt himself filled with energy. Goodness, he thought, I feel like there were lightning bolts zipping around inside me. And he went on watching the game with new energy.

After seven days, the old man stopped and stretched. "I think we're going to have to call this game a draw."

The fat man sighed. "I agree." He began to pick up the pieces.

The woodcutter spat out the stone. "But you could win easily."

The old man finally noticed him. "Are you still here?"

The woodcutter thought that this was his chance now to do a good deed. "It's been a most interesting game. However, if you—"

But the old man made shooing motions with his hands. "You should've gone home long ago."

"But I—" began the woodcutter.

The fat man rose. "Go home. It may already be too late."

That's a funny thing to say, the woodcutter thought. He turned around to get his things. But big, fat mushrooms had sprouted among the roots of the trees. A brown carpet surrounded him. He brushed the mushrooms aside until he found a rusty hatchet blade. He couldn't find a trace of the hatchet shaft or of his carrying pole.

Puzzled, he picked up the hatchet blade. "This can't be mine. My hatchet was practically new. Have you two gentlemen seen it?" He turned around again, but the two men had disappeared along with the chessboard and chess pieces.

"That's gratitude for you." Picking up the rusty hatchet blade, the woodcutter tried to make his way back through the woods; but he could not find the way he had come up. "It's like someone rearranged all the trees."

Somehow he made his way out of the mountains. However, fields and villages now stood where there had once been wooded hills. "What are you doing here?" he asked a farmer.

"What are you?" the farmer snorted, and went back to working in his field.

The woodcutter thought about telling him that he was swinging his hoe wrong, but he remembered what the two men had said. So he hurried home instead.

The woodcutter followed the river until he reached his own village, but as he walked through the fields, he didn't recognize one person. There was even a pond before the village gates. It had never been there before. He broke into a run, but there was a different house in the spot where his home had been. Even so, he burst into the place.

Two strange children looked up from the table, and a strange woman picked up a broom. "Out!"

The woodcutter raised his arms protectively. "Wait, I live here."

But the woman beat the woodcutter with a broom until he retreated into the street. By now, a crowd had gathered. The woodcutter looked around desperately. "What's happened to my village? Doesn't anyone know me?"

The village schoolteacher had come out of the school. He asked the woodcutter his name, and when the woodcutter told him, the schoolteacher pulled at his whiskers. "That name sounds familiar, but it can't be."

With the crowd following them, he led the woodcutter to the clan temple. "I collect odd, interesting stories." The schoolteacher got out a thick book. "There's a strange incident in the clan book." He leafed through the book toward the beginning and pointed to a name. "A woodcutter left the village and never came back." He added quietly. "But that was several thousand years ago."

"That's impossible," the woodcutter insisted. "I just stayed away to watch two men play a game of chess."

The schoolteacher sighed. "The two men must have been saints. Time doesn't pass for them as it does for us."

And at that moment, the woodcutter remembered his wife's warning.

But it was too late now.

SOURCE

NATIONAL
STORYTELLING
FESTIVAL

Jonesborough, Tennessee

Article

The Art of

Most traditional stories were passed along orally for generations before anyone wrote them down. Today, modern storytellers from diverse cultures continue the oral tradition. They share traditional tales and personal stories with audiences around the globe.

The National Storytelling Association, headquartered in Jonesborough, Tennessee, is dedicated to preserving and expanding the art of storytelling. Each year, the NSA holds a National Storytelling Festival. Some of the most renowned storytellers in the world perform there. You will meet some of them on these pages.

Storyteller	Childhood Home
 **DEREK BURROWS**	Burrows was born and raised in Nassau, Bahamas. He also spent a great deal of time on his grand-parents' farm on Long Island, Bahamas.
 **DONALD DAVIS**	Davis grew up in the mountains of North Carolina, in an area settled by the Scottish. His rural community had no radios, electricity, or other modern conveniences until the 1950s.
 **OLGA LOYA**	Loya grew up in a Mexican-American neighborhood in Los Angeles, California, where her neighbors spoke a lively mixture of English and Spanish.

Storytelling

Why he/she became a storyteller	Origin of his/her stories	Special Techniques
While studying music, Burrows played with a group that performed ballads based on old European stories. Learning all those old stories made him think back to the stories he had heard as a child. He began to research the stories he remembered and to collect new tales from Bahamian friends. Today, Burrows uses stories and music to share his rich cultural heritage with others.	Burrows' stories come from the Caribbean. They contain elements of African stories, as well as elements of stories told by the Arawak—the first people to live on the Bahama Islands. Many of the stories are about traditional characters called B'Anase and B'Boukee.	Burrows likes to have his audience participate in his stories. He sometimes asks the audience to add phrases to a story or to respond to "Boonday," a traditional Bahamian storyteller's chant. Burrows often includes music in his performances, playing one or more of the fifteen instruments he has learned. He sometimes teaches the audience to sing parts of the songs he plays.
Wherever he went, new acquaintances asked Davis many questions about his rather unusual childhood. He found that the best way to answer them was by sharing childhood stories. When he returned home for visits, Davis collected additional stories from friends and neighbors.	Many of Davis's stories are traditional Appalachian stories called Jack Tales, which are based on ancient Scottish tales. Davis has also crafted a number of stories based on events from his own childhood.	Davis believes that stories are made of pictures. When he tells a story, he is trying to help the audience understand the pictures inside his head. Therefore, he uses lots of body language and descriptive language to tell his stories. Davis tailors his words and gestures to the audience at hand.
During Loya's childhood, storytelling was a part of everyday life. While working as a community organizer, Loya decided to plan a storytelling festival as a fundraiser for her community. She found herself not only organizing but performing as well.	Loya uses people and books as sources for traditional stories from all over the world. She also enjoys studying history and uses storytelling to share important stories from the past.	Loya uses sound effects to add humor or suspense to a tale. She likes to use some Spanish when she tells stories to an English-speaking audience, so that listeners can appreciate the music of the language. Using Spanish also helps Loya convey the authentic voices of traditional Hispanic story characters, such as Coyote and Tía Miseria.

How to
Tell a Story

Storytellers use gestures and different expressions to help tell a story.

Storytellers' gestures are often written into their story script.

Storytelling is a tradition that began in ancient cultures. Early storytellers passed their tales down orally from generation to generation. Many of those stories still exist today.

What is a storyteller? A storyteller is someone who can tell stories in ways that make them come alive. Some storytellers change the sound of their voices, wear costumes, use props, sing, or speak in rhyme as they tell their stories.

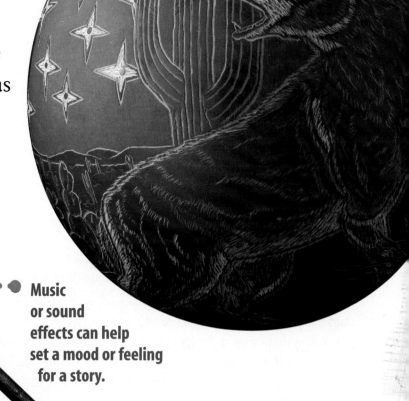

Music or sound effects can help set a mood or feeling for a story.

from
"How the Coyote Gets His Name"
by Jerry Tello

...so all the animals gathered their young and took them back to where they slept and as the coyote was walking up (walking motion) the hill, he was thinking, "How can I be first...how can I be first??!!" (Make pensive face— look at extended finger.)

By this time, the Sun (look up) had finished his cycle and touched (tap-on-the-shoulder motion with index finger) the Moon on the shoulder and Ms. Moon began sharing her brilliance.

And there sat (sitting action) the coyote on top of the hill, under a tree, still thinking how he could be first (index finger to temple, as if thinking), when he had a brilliant idea!

(Eyes wide, mouth open). "I'll just stay up all night!" That way, I'll see Mr. Sun as he awakes and I can be first!"

Well, several hours passed and as hard as the coyote tried, he was still getting tired (eyes drooping). In his struggle to keep awake, he glanced up (look up) at the tree branches and had a good idea and thought to himself, "I'll just break two small branches and put one in each eyelid to keep me awake!"

So the coyote did just that (motion of reaching up, breaking branches)... except that in a short time, the coyote was fast asleep with his eyes wide open (index finger and thumb of each hand, holding eyes wide open.)

The moon finished her cycle and several hours later, the coyote finally awoke and ran to the circle (running motion), where he saw no one except the big brown animal standing on the rock. Thinking he was first, the coyote said (stand up straight), "OK, I'm ready to pick and I want to be the Bear so I can stand on the rock and make all the announcements!"

1 Write Your Script

Choose a story that you would like to tell others. It could be a well-known fairy tale, a myth, or an experience from your own life. Create a script to help you learn your story. Organize it in a way that is useful to you. Some storytellers like to work from an outline that lists the major events of the story, then fill in the details orally. Others like to write down the whole story, using their own words. Write your first draft. Try to keep it short— about one or two pages.

TOOLS

- paper and pencil
- story to tell
- props and music (optional)

2 Plan Your Delivery

Look over your script. Think about the effect you want the story to have on your audience. Is your story happy or sad, funny or scary? You will want to create the right mood for your audience. Traditionally, storytellers have used many different methods to bring their stories to life. They make gestures, use props, change their voices, and use sound effects. Revise the first draft of your script by adding directions for yourself in the appropriate places. When you tell your story, you'll know just when to include special effects.

3 Practice Your Story

4 Tell Your Story

Practice telling your story. Refer to your script at first to make sure that you get the story right and that you know exactly when the gestures, props, music, or sound effects come into the story. Practice telling your story in front of a mirror so you can watch your movements. Tell it to a friend or a member of your family. Eventually you'll be able to tell the story from memory using all the special effects and props you've planned.

When you're happy with the way you tell the story, you will want to present it to an audience. Make arrangements to tell it to your classmates, a group of neighbors, or some of your friends. If your story is suitable for younger children, you might perform it for the kindergarteners or the first and second graders in your school. Be sure to assemble any props or costumes you will need.

If You Are Using a Computer ...

Use the Record and Playback tools to practice your story as you write it. Edit your story as you listen to how it sounds.

Tip Tape-record your special effects. Ask a helper to play the tape for you. Provide him or her with a marked script that shows when the tape should be played.

THINK
In what other situations might you use the storytelling skills you have learned?

José García
Drama Coach ▶

49

Through the performing arts, we entertain others.

On Stage

Find out what happens to Manuel when he enters the school talent show. Then read a poem about a school play.

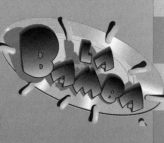

Meet Doug Funnie, who doesn't appreciate his sister's talent.

Learn how drama coach José García inspires creativity in his students.

WORKSHOP 2

Write a dialogue for characters of your own creation.

VANESSA'S BAD GRADE
by Ross Brown
Scene Five
Vanessa is in her room when Theo walks in.
VANESSA: I got my history test back.
(She hands him the test paper.)
THEO: Whoa. This is a "D."
VANESSA: I know. I've never gotten a "D" before. I've seen them, but never next to my name.
THEO: And this one is in red. That's the worst kind to get.
VANESSA: I don't know how it happened. Robert and I studied for this.
THEO: Yeah. I saw that.

51

FROM **BASEBALL IN APRIL
AND OTHER STORIES
BY GARY SOTO**

AWARD
WINNING

Author

LA BAMBA

Manuel was the fourth of seven children and looked like a lot of kids in his neighborhood: black hair, brown face, and skinny legs scuffed from summer play. But summer was giving way to fall: the trees were turning red, the lawns brown, and the pomegranate trees were heavy with fruit. Manuel walked to school in the frosty morning, kicking leaves and thinking of tomorrow's talent show. He was still amazed that he had volunteered. He was going to pretend to sing Ritchie Valens's "La Bamba" before the entire school.

Why did I raise my hand? he asked

ILLUSTRATED BY JOSÉ ORTEGA

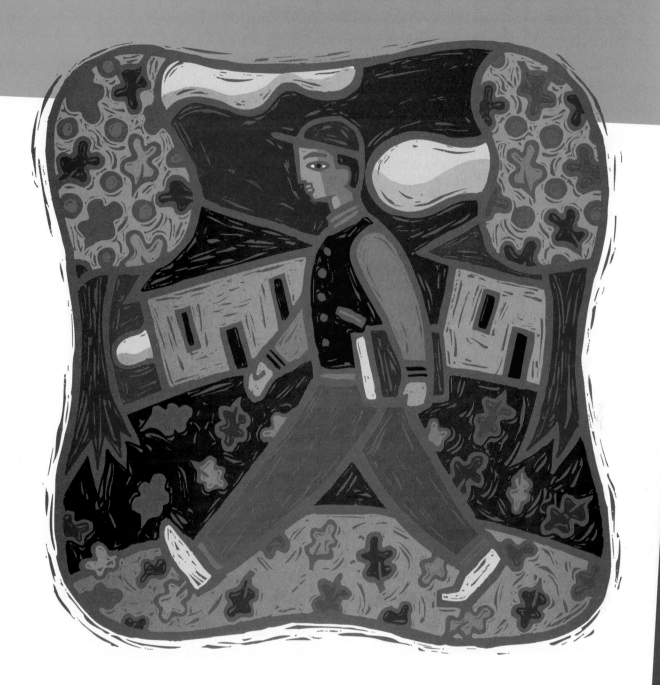

himself, but in his heart he knew the answer. He yearned for the limelight. He wanted applause as loud as a thunderstorm, and to hear his friends say, "Man, that was bad!" And he wanted to impress the girls, especially Petra Lopez, the second-prettiest girl in his class. The prettiest was already taken by his friend Ernie. Manuel knew he should be reasonable, since he himself was not great-looking, just average.

Manuel kicked through the fresh-fallen leaves. When he got to school he realized he had forgotten his math workbook. If the teacher found out, he would have to stay after school and miss practice for the talent show. But fortunately for him, they did drills that morning.

During lunch Manuel hung around with Benny, who was also in the talent show. Benny was going to play the trumpet in spite of the fat lip he had gotten playing football.

"How do I look?" Manuel asked. He cleared his throat and started moving his lips in pantomime. No words came out, just a hiss that sounded like a snake. Manuel tried to look emotional, flailing his arms on the high notes and opening his eyes and mouth as wide as he could when he came to "*Para bailar la baaaaammmba.*"

After Manuel finished, Benny said it looked all right, but suggested Manuel dance while he sang. Manuel thought for a moment and decided it was a good idea.

"Yeah, just think you're like Michael Jackson or someone like that," Benny suggested. "But don't get carried away."

During rehearsal, Mr. Roybal, nervous about his debut as the school's talent coordinator, cursed under his breath when the lever that controlled the speed on the record player jammed.

"Darn," he growled, trying to force the lever. "What's wrong with you?"

"Is it broken?" Manuel asked, bending over for a closer look. It looked all right to him.

Mr. Roybal assured Manuel that he would have a good record player at the talent show, even if it meant bringing his own stereo from home.

Manuel sat in a folding chair, twirling his record on his thumb. He watched a skit about personal hygiene, a mother-and-daughter

violin duo, five first-grade girls jumping rope, a karate kid breaking boards, three girls singing, and a skit about the pilgrims. If the record player hadn't been broken, he would have gone after the karate kid, an easy act to follow, he told himself.

As he twirled his forty-five record, Manuel thought they had a great talent show. The entire school would be amazed. His mother and father would be proud, and his brothers and sisters would be jealous and pout. It would be a night to remember.

Benny walked onto the stage, raised his trumpet to his mouth, and waited for his cue. Mr. Roybal raised his hand like a symphony conductor and let it fall dramatically. Benny inhaled and blew so loud that Manuel dropped his record, which rolled across the cafeteria floor until it hit a wall. Manuel raced after it, picked it up, and wiped it clean.

"Boy, I'm glad it didn't break," he said with a sigh.

That night Manuel had to do the dishes and a lot of homework, so he could only practice in the shower. In bed he prayed that he wouldn't mess up. He prayed that it wouldn't be like when he was a first-grader. For Science Week he had wired together a C battery and a bulb, and told everyone he had discovered how a flashlight worked. He was so pleased with himself that he practiced for hours pressing the wire to the battery, making the bulb wink a dim, orangish light. He showed it to so many kids in his neighborhood that when it was time to show his class how a flashlight worked, the battery was dead. He pressed the wire to the battery, but the bulb didn't respond. He pressed until his thumb hurt and some kids in the back started snickering.

But Manuel fell asleep confident that nothing would go wrong this time.

The next morning his father and mother beamed at him. They were proud that he was going to be in the talent show.

"I wish you would tell us what you're doing," his mother said. His father, a pharmacist who wore a blue smock with his name on a plastic rectangle, looked up from the newspaper and sided with his wife. "Yes, what are you doing in the talent show?"

"You'll see," Manuel said with his mouth full of Cheerios.

The day whizzed by, and so did his afternoon chores and dinner.

Suddenly he was dressed in his best clothes and standing next to Benny backstage, listening to the commotion as the cafeteria filled with school kids and parents. The lights dimmed, and Mr. Roybal, sweaty in a tight suit and a necktie with a large knot, wet his lips and parted the stage curtains.

"Good evening, everyone," the kids behind the curtain heard him say. "Good evening to you," some of the smart-alecky kids said back to him.

"Tonight we bring you the best John Burroughs Elementary has to offer, and I'm sure that you'll be both pleased and amazed that our little school houses so much talent. And now, without further ado, let's get on with the show." He turned and, with a swish of his hand, commanded, "Part the curtain." The curtains parted in jerks. A girl dressed as a toothbrush and a boy dressed as a dirty gray tooth walked onto the stage and sang:

> Brush, brush, brush
> Floss, floss, floss
> Gargle the germs away—
> hey! hey! hey!

After they finished singing, they turned to Mr. Roybal, who dropped his hand. The toothbrush dashed around the stage after the dirty tooth, which was laughing and having a great time until it slipped and nearly rolled off the stage.

Mr. Roybal jumped out and caught it just in time. "Are you OK?"

The dirty tooth answered, "Ask my dentist," which drew laughter and applause from the audience.

The violin duo played next, and except for one time when the girl got lost, they sounded fine. People applauded, and some even stood up. Then the first-grade girls maneuvered onto the stage while jumping rope. They were all smiles and bouncing ponytails as a hundred cameras flashed at once. Mothers "awhed" and fathers sat up proudly.

The karate kid was next. He did a few kicks, yells, and chops, and finally, when his father held up a board, punched it in two. The audience clapped and looked at each other, wide-eyed with respect. The boy bowed to the audience, and father and son ran off the stage.

Manuel remained behind the stage shivering with fear. He mouthed the words to "La Bamba" and swayed from left to right. Why did he raise his hand and volunteer? Why couldn't he

more sweaty than before, took Manuel's forty-five record and placed it on a new record player.

"You ready?" Mr. Roybal asked.

"Yeah..."

Mr. Roybal walked back on stage and announced that Manuel Gomez, a fifth-grader in Mrs. Knight's class, was going to pantomime Richie Valens's classic hit "La Bamba."

The cafeteria roared with applause. Manuel was nervous but loved the noisy crowd. He pictured his mother and father applauding loudly and his brothers and sisters also clapping, though not as energetically.

Manuel walked on stage and the song started immediately. Glassy-eyed from the shock of being in front of so many people, Manuel moved his lips and swayed in a made-up dance step. He couldn't see his parents, but he could see his brother Mario, who was a year younger, thumb-wrestling with a friend. Mario was wearing Manuel's favorite shirt; he would deal with Mario later. He saw some other kids get up and head for the drinking fountain, and a baby sitting in the middle of an aisle sucking her thumb and watching him intently.

have just sat there like the rest of the kids and not said anything? While the karate kid was on stage, Mr. Roybal,

What am I doing here? thought Manuel. This is no fun at all. Everyone was just sitting there. Some people were moving to the beat, but most were just watching him, like they would a monkey at the zoo.

But when Manuel did a fancy dance step, there was a burst of applause and some girls screamed. Manuel tried another dance step. He heard more applause and screams and started getting into the groove as he shivered and snaked like Michael Jackson around the stage. But the record got stuck, and he had to sing

> *Para bailar la bamba*
> *Para bailar la bamba*
> *Para bailar la bamba*
> *Para bailar la bamba*

again and again.

Manuel couldn't believe his bad luck. The audience began to laugh and stand up in their chairs. Manuel remembered how the forty-five record had dropped from his hand and rolled across the cafeteria floor. It probably got scratched, he thought, and now it was stuck, and he was stuck dancing and moving his lips to the same words over and over. He had never been so embarrassed. He would have to ask his parents to move the family out of town.

After Mr. Roybal ripped the needle across the record, Manuel slowed his dance steps to a halt. He didn't know what to do except bow to the audience, which applauded wildly, and scoot off the stage, on the verge of tears. This was worse than the homemade flashlight. At least no one laughed then, they just snickered.

Manuel stood alone, trying hard to hold back the tears as Benny, center stage, played his trumpet. Manuel was jealous because he sounded great, then mad as he recalled that it was Benny's loud trumpet playing that made the forty-five record fly out of his hands. But when the entire cast lined up for a curtain call, Manuel received a burst of applause that was so loud it shook the walls of the cafeteria. Later, as he mingled with the kids and parents, everyone patted him on the shoulder and told him, "Way to go. You were really funny."

Funny? Manuel thought. Did he do something funny?

Funny. Crazy. Hilarious. These were the words people said to him. He was confused, but beyond caring. All he knew was that people were paying attention to him, and his brother and sisters looked at him with a mixture of

jealousy and awe. He was going to pull Mario aside and punch him in the arm for wearing his shirt, but he cooled it. He was enjoying the limelight. A teacher brought him cookies and punch, and the popular kids who had never before given him the time of day now clustered around him. Ricardo, the editor of the school bulletin, asked him how he made the needle stick.

"It just happened," Manuel said, crunching on a star-shaped cookie.

At home that night his father, eager to undo the buttons on his shirt and ease into his La-Z-Boy recliner, asked Manuel the same thing, how he managed to make the song stick on the words "*Para bailar la bamba.*"

Manuel thought quickly and reached for scientific jargon he had read in magazines. "Easy, Dad. I used laser tracking with high optics and low functional decibels per channel." His proud but confused father told him to be quiet and go to bed.

"Ah, *que niños tan truchas,*" he said as he walked to the kitchen for a glass of milk. "I don't know how you kids nowadays get so smart."

Manuel, feeling happy, went to his bedroom, undressed, and slipped into his pajamas. He looked in the mirror and began to pantomime "La Bamba," but stopped because he was tired of the song. He crawled into bed. The sheets were as cold as the moon that stood over the peach tree in their backyard.

He was relieved that the day was over. Next year, when they asked for volunteers for the talent show, he wouldn't raise his hand. Probably.

School

from REMEMBERING AND
OTHER POEMS

BY MYRA COHN LIVINGSTON
ILLUSTRATED BY CURTIS PARKER

Play

I played the princess.
I had to stay
inside a barrel.
The prince hid away
in a keg right beside me.
Our hearts nearly sank
when the Pirate King said
we would both walk the plank.
Then our captain appeared
and he offered them gold
as a ransom, and that's when
the Pirate King told
us to come out
and plead our case,
and I climbed out and
slipped
and fell flat
on my face.

But it wasn't so bad
in the ending
because
all the audience gave us
a lot of
applause.

DouG
CAN'T DIG IT

based on a series created by Jim Jinkins
TV script by Ken Scarborough

Doug just knows his theatrical older sister Judy will do something to embarrass him at the school assembly. Worst of all, he's supposed to announce her performance! Will he step into the spotlight—or hide behind the curtains?

WIRED WORDS

Reading a TV script is different than reading a book or play. As you read, imagine that you are a director "seeing" this script come to life. Look for these directing terms as you read along:

CU: Close Up

DISSOLVE TO: The scene will fade out and change to a new scene.

INT: Interior. This refers to a specific location, like the inside of a room or building.

O.S: Off stage. A character talks from outside the scene in the picture.

SFX: Sound Effects

V.O: Voice Over. A character narrates a scene without appearing on camera.

MEET THE CAST

DOUG FUNNIE

Like any normal 11-and-a-half-year-old, Doug's main goal is to make it to junior high in one piece. Doug's daydreams help him get through sticky situations.

Porkchop
Doug's humanlike dog is his best animal friend, and Doug's advisor in times of trouble.

Skeeter
Doug's best friend is a pretty cool customer. He thinks Doug gets too worked up about things sometimes.

Roger
Smart-mouthed Roger's favorite hobby is giving Doug a hard time.

Judy Funnie
Doug's older sister has a different goal — to be the most famous actress of all time. Performing is her life!

Mrs. Wingo
Doug's teacher has every confidence in Judy's talent. If only Doug did, too.

Mr. Bone
Bluffington Elementary's Vice Principal will make sure that Doug is at that assembly.

Doug and its characters are created by Jim Jinkins.

Fade in: Int. Doug's Room—Night. Doug sits at his desk, writing.

Doug

Dear Journal: me again. Doug. Sorry I didn't write yesterday—I was too busy having a heart attack. It all started...

Int. Kitchen—Morning. Doug and Porkchop having breakfast.

Doug (V.O.)

...yesterday morning.

SFX: Loud Opera Music (Carmen—"Toreador Song")
Suddenly, Judy bursts in, wearing matador regalia and swinging a stick like a sword. She stalks Doug.

Judy

(sings)
"Toreador, en ga-a-a-rde!"
Take that!

Doug

Hey! Mom, Judy's doing that bullfighter thing again.

Judy plops down opposite Doug and stares at him.

Judy

I know something you don-hon't.

Doug

What?

Judy

"Toreador..."

She grins at him, and then, suddenly, springs up and leaves, singing.

Doug

(to Porkchop)
You know, Porkchop, sometimes I'm really glad Judy goes to her own school instead of ours.

Doug (V.O.)

Then, in class, Mrs. Wingo made the announcement...

Dissolve to: Int. Classroom—Day. Mrs. Wingo stands in front of the class.

Mrs. Wingo

Tomorrow afternoon, there will be a special school assembly, and it's going to be introduced by Doug.

Doug smiles to himself.

Dissolve to: Fantasy. A spotlight appears on a deep red curtain. Doug pops through the curtain, dressed in a snappy tuxedo. He steps up to the microphone.

Doug

Good afternoon, everybody. I'm really happy to be here. Of course I'm really happy to be anywhere except class.

SFX: Rimshot, Enormous Laughter

Doug
But seriously—

Mrs. Wingo (O.S.)
Doug?

Dissolve to: Back to reality. Angle on Mrs. Wingo.

Mrs. Wingo
Doug? Don't you want to know who you're introducing? She
asked for you especially.

Doug
Who?

Mrs. Wingo
Your sister. Judy. She's going to perform for all of us.

CU Doug. Pure terror—perhaps the picture rotates a little, with a
weirdly distorted classroom around him.

Doug
Judy?

Dissolve to: Fantasy. Int. Auditorium Stage
Judy is dressed like a beatnik. There are large projections of her every place. She bangs the bongoes in counterpoint to her words.

Judy
My *soul* throbs!
I am...your washing machine!

(brightly)
Red towel!

(sinister hush)
Pink underwear.

(loud)
Buzzzz! Unbalanced load!

Suddenly she leaps up! She caws like a chicken and flaps her wings.

Angle on the audience. Doug is in the middle, reddening in embarrassment.

Angle on Judy. She clutches her brow and bows her head as the lights flick to a single spotlight from above.

Judy
Doug loves Patti.

A gigantic backdrop drops in behind her, showing Doug and Patti in a big heart.

Angle on Doug. The audience around him is laughing hideously. We zoom in on Doug's face, frozen in fear.

Dissolve to: Int. Honker Burger. Doug and Skeeter are sitting across from each other in the same booth. They are both slumped over shakes.

Skeeter
Maybe it won't be so bad, Doug. Maybe it'll be neat.

Doug glares at Skeeter.

Skeeter

I mean...awful. Did I say neat? Terrible, I meant.

Suddenly Judy and about three of her friends burst in the front door of the restaurant, and barge up to the counter.

Friend #1

(sings)

Give us shakes, chocolate and ta-a-sty. With some fries, but don't be ha-a-sty.

Judy

Catsup, mustard, mayo, lettuce, just make sure you don't forget us!

Angle on Doug and Skeeter.

Skeeter

I think I see what you mean.

Roger (O.S.)

Hey, Funnie!

Doug looks over to where Roger, Willy, Ned and Boomer are sitting.

Roger

This is a preview of tomorrow's show? I can't wait to see it!

They all laugh.

CU Doug. Trying to smile along, he looks toward another table. Judy and her friends are just sitting down. Judy steps up into the booth, puts one foot on the table, holding aloft a milkshake.

Judy

Alas, poor Strawberry!

Her friends applaud.

Angle on Doug and Skeeter.

Doug

I have to stop her. For her own sake.

Skeeter

How can you do that?

Doug

Maybe if I get on her good side. Maybe if...I use a little psychology.

Angle on Judy's booth. Doug approaches.

Doug

Hey, Judy—

Judy turns coolly/calmly to Doug.

Judy

Yes-I'm-performing-at-your-school-tomorrow-and-no-there's-nothing-you-can-do-to-change-my-mind.

Doug

Oh, okay, see you later.

Angle on Skeeter's table. Doug slumps back.

Skeeter

Did you use psychology on her, Doug?

Doug

This is going to be harder than I thought.

Skeeter

I think I have an idea.

Skeeter stands up and whispers in Doug's ear.
Int. Judy's room—Day. CU Judy.

Judy

I hate you! I hate you! I hate hate *hate...*

SFX: Phone ringing. Judy immediately drops her character and picks up the phone.

Judy

(sweetly)

Hel*lo*?

Voice

Hello, is this Judy Funnie the actress?

Judy

Yes, it is. Who is this please?

Voice

Oh, you don't know me, but I'm a very famous producer.

Cut to: Int. Den—Day. Doug is talking into the handkerchief-covered phone. Skeeter is crouched across the desk from him.

Skeeter

J.B. Hunkamunca.

Doug

J.B. Hunkamunca.

Doug covers the mouthpiece.

Doug

(hisses)

She'll never buy that! (into phone) You what? You say you've *heard of me?* Well, I called to tell you you shouldn't do that show tomorrow.

Judy (O.S.)

Really?

Skeeter looks up. His mouth drops open. He starts trying to signal Doug.

Wider Angle revealing Judy, who's just come in the door.

Doug

It's not right for you...I feel like it's the wrong...well, just don't do it!

Judy moves from the door to the desk.

Judy

Really, Mr. Hunkamunca? Well, I suppose I'll just have to cancel it, then.

Skeeter starts poking Doug and pointing to Judy. Doug brushes him away, and Skeeter, in despair, buries his head in his hands.

Doug

Really? Great! Well, goodbye!

Doug hangs up.

Doug
She bought it, Skeet!
(bewildered)
... *Skeet?*

Doug turns to Judy.

Doug
What'samatter with Skeeter?

Judy
I haven't the faintest.

Doug
You haven't the—
(getting it)
Uh-oh.

Judy
Doug, why can't you dig it?

Doug
Huh?

Judy
You know, this is exactly why you need me to perform at your school.

She stomps to the door, throws it open and makes a theatrical exit.

Judy
Tomorrow you'll thank me, Mr. Hunkamunca.

She goes, slamming the door. Doug sighs and turns to Skeeter.

Doug
No—tomorrow I'm going to have a heart attack. Judy's never performed anything that made me want to thank her. I'll never forget the last time we were on stage together. It was a disaster.

Dissolve to: Flashback. Int. Auditorium—Day. The set is the inside of a mouth. A bunch of kids are dressed as teeth. Judy is dressed as plaque, and is attacking them.

Doug (V.O.)

It was the Dental Hygiene play. I was the toothbrush—Judy was plaque.

Judy

Here are the teeth that wouldn't brush. Now I will come and turn them to mush!

All Teeth

Help! Help, save us Mr. Toothbrush!

Doug enters, dressed as a toothbrush complete with superhero cape. He brushes Judy.

Doug

Here I am and plaque I will crush! Take that and that!

Judy begins to die elaborately.

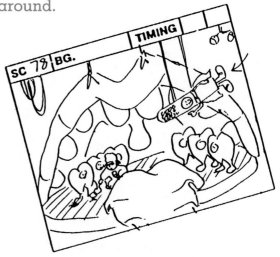

Doug

And now all plaque is gone.

Judy

Uhhhhhh....

Doug notices Judy is still staggering around.

Doug

(louder)

And now plaque is gone!

Judy

Uhhhhh....

SFX: Audience snickers

Doug

Judy!

Doug reddens in embarrassment. He goes over and tries to brush her off stage. Flats fall down, Teeth run everywhere. General hub-bub.

SFX: Audience laughs

CU Doug, reddening in extreme embarrassment.

Doug
Yup, that play just about killed me.

Cut to: Int. School Hallway. The class moves along the hallway toward the door to the auditorium.

Doug (V.O.)
So there I was faced with another of Judy's performances, only problem was, I couldn't think of one good reason to get me out of it.

Roger comes up next to Doug.

Roger
Hey, Funnie! I can't believe it! You're really gonna go through with it?

The class files into the auditorium door. Roger pushes in in front of Doug.

Roger
Well, Funnie, I hope you and your goofy sister have fun—it's your funeral! Ha ha ha.

Doug hesitates. He looks around and keeps walking down the corridor. Porkchop follows. Doug, looking behind him, comes into this corridor and closes the door behind Porkchop.

Doug (V.O.)
I just needed a minute to think.

Cut to: Int. Auditorium Stage. Lamarr Bone confronts Mrs. Wingo behind the curtain.

Bone

Where's Funnie? We got a show to do!

Cut to: Int. Corridor. Doug is still pacing. He stops and looks at Porkchop.

Doug

What do you think, Porkchop? Should I go in front of everyone and introduce Judy?

Porkchop

(whines)

Doug

You're right. It could be the Dental Hygiene Play all over again.

Doug stops pacing in front of the door he came in through— the one that goes back out to the hallway. He considers it. Then Doug turns away from the door.

Doug

Boy, sure could use a little fresh air, Porkchop. How about you?

Another angle. Doug is at the other end of the corridor and is confronted with three unmarked doors. He hesitates, then chooses one and goes through it.

Doug

This way, I think.

Cut to: Int. Stage

Angle on Doug. It is very dark. Doug blinks. He reacts with surprise.

Doug (V.O.)

And there she was.

Judy, in beatnik garb, nervously peeks through the curtains at the audience. Mrs. Wingo stands next to her.

Judy

This could be a very important performance for me. Shakespeare did his first performance for his brother's grade school. Did you know that?

Angle on Doug. He turns to the curtain next to him and peeks out. Roger and some of his friends are laughing.

Angle on Judy and Bone

Bone

Well, can't find him. Let's get this show on the road. (shouts offscreen)
Dim the lights!

Judy

But you told Doug I wanted him to introduce me, right?

SFX: Kids cheer

Angle on Doug, nervously looking from Judy to the door next to him labelled "Exit."

Mrs. Wingo (O.S.)
Now, dear, we have to start.

Judy

But, we have to wait for Doug. I—I wanted him to see this.

Bone

Now listen, young lady...

Doug

Wait! I'm here.

Dissolve to: Int. Auditorium. Doug is at the microphone, quieting the applause.

SFX: Applause, Whistles

Doug

Hello, everyone, I'm Doug Funnie and here's someone I've known

all of my life and most of hers, my sister, performance artist
Judy Funnie.

SFX: Applause, Hoots, Whistles

Cut to: Int. Hallway Outside of Auditorium—Day.

Doug paces nervously.

Doug (V.O.)
So in the end I stood up for Judy's act. But that didn't mean I
wanted to sit down and actually watch it.

He hears something and stops pacing.

Doug (V.O.)
But then I heard something I never expected.

SFX: Muffled laughter, then scattered light applause

Doug, curious, creeps over to the auditorium door and opens
it a crack. He sees a few people clapping. As Doug turns
away from the door in some confusion to consider this,
suddenly, BLAM! The door flies open and kids pour out,
knocking Doug left and right in their hurry. All around him
he hears the comments of his schoolmates.

Kids

—Wow! It was great!

—I didn't get it.

—I hated it, but I liked her hair.

—Very symbolic.

A hand comes in and pulls Doug out of the crowd. Doug finds himself face-to-face with Roger.

Roger

Hey, Funnie, you want to know what I thought of that show?

Doug

Well...

Roger

I *loved* it! It was *great*.

Doug

Really?

Roger throws his arm around Doug.

Roger

Yeah. It completely got me out of having to take a math test! Ha ha ha. Tell your sister she can come back anytime she likes.

Doug looks at Roger in amazement.

Dissolve to: Int. Auditorium—Later. Doug walks through the door at the back of the deserted auditorium. There is a group gathered around Judy on the stage. Doug walks up and stands by the sidelines.

Photographer

Can we get a picture for the Daily Honk, Judy?

Judy

Sure, just a second.

She breaks away from the group and goes over to Doug.

Judy
(quietly)
Come on, Doug.

Doug
Awww....

Wider angle. Judy drags a showily reluctant Doug to center stage. They pose. With a flash they freeze; the colors bleed out until it's black and white.

Doug (V.O.)
So I guess it turned out all right.

Angle on Judy and Doug

Dissolve to: Int. Doug's Room—Night. We Pull Out from the picture, which is tacked to the bulletin board behind Doug's head. Doug is writing in his diary.

SFX: Opera music from other room

Doug (V.O.)
I didn't need to have a heart attack after all. Not only was it not embarrassing, but I think Judy's actually quite...good. No: quite... sisterly. No: quite...

Suddenly the door bursts open. The music and Judy (dressed as a toreador) and Porkchop (dressed as a bull) all blast in, taking over Doug's room.

Doug
...*embarrassing*. She's quite embarrassing.

Ext. House—Night.

Doug (V.O.)
Juuuudyyyy!

Fade out.

José García

Drama Coach

This coach *teaches* kids how to *act up!*

When you watch a movie, TV show, or play, the actors' performances often seem perfect. How do actors learn the tricks of their trade? If they're lucky, they have the help of a good drama coach like José García. García works with professional actors. He also teaches young people about acting and helps them prepare to give school presentations.

80 **UNIT 4**

PROFILE

Name: José García

Occupation: drama coach

Previous jobs: substitute teacher, actor, set designer, maskmaker

Favorite actors: James Caan and Geraldine Page

Favorite play: *The Blood Wedding* by Federico García Lorca

Favorite story as a fifth grader: *The Lord of the Rings* by J.R.R. Tolkien

Most embarrassing moment on stage: "While showing off during a high school singing concert, I pushed my voice so much that I went flat."

QUESTIONS
for José García

Here's how drama coach **José García** *trains* performers to *exercise* their **creativity.**

Q **When did you first become interested in acting?**

A I created my own skits with friends as early as second grade. I even won the sixth-grade talent show at my school!

Q **Who attends your acting workshops?**

A I coach professional actors preparing for roles. I also work with kids who want to learn about acting, or who are preparing for school plays or other presentations.

Q **Do all actors need coaches?**

A Like any skill, acting is easier for some people than for others, but training is always important.

Q **Many of your students have no acting experience. How do you get them started?**

A I put them through a lot of exercises. I want them to be able to work with their whole bodies, from the tips of their toes to their hair follicles! Actors cannot work effectively unless their whole bodies are loose.

Q **What kinds of exercises do you do?**

A One favorite exercise involves masks. The students and I put on masks and move our faces and bodies silently. We try to convey the feeling of the masks through body language. As time goes on, we add sound, and eventually speech.

How do you help students prepare to perform in plays?

 We begin by reading through the script. We spend time analyzing the characters. Actors need to know their characters inside and out. Then they can begin to "play" with the roles and make them their own.

 What's the most important skill an actor can have?

 I'd have to say sincerity. You have to believe in the role you are playing. If you are sincere, you will win over your audience.

 Many people worry about stage fright. What is it?

Butterflies in the stomach, trembling, anxiety, and fear of failure. It can be scary, but without it you don't have the edge. It's that excitement that allows an artist to work on a heightened level.

 Besides working with actors, what things might you do in a typical day?

I write plays and screenplays, and I spend time researching them. I also have to promote myself as an actor and drama coach. It takes a lot of work to get work! When I have time left over, I design masks and drama sets.

José García's
Tips **for Young Performers**

1 Learn everything you can about your craft. There's always room to learn and improve.

2 Discover your own natural talents and strive to expand them. Don't try to be like someone else.

3 Don't allow others to discourage you. Believe in yourself.

How to Write a Dialogue

When a movie, play, or TV show is written, the writer must decide what the characters will say to each other. He writes down their words, or dialogue, in script form for the actors to learn. **What is a dialogue?** A dialogue is a conversation between two or more characters or people. When you talk with a friend, your conversation is called a dialogue.

A dialogue script has a title. The author's name goes beneath the title.

A brief description sets the scene of the dialogue.

Character names are written in capital letters so that they will not be confused with the lines of dialogue.

Photo courtesy of NBC

● Stage directions are written in parentheses.

VANESSA'S BAD GRADE
by Ross Brown
Scene Five

Vanessa is in her room when Theo walks in.

VANESSA: I got my history test back. (She hands him the test paper.)

THEO: Whoa. This is a "D."

VANESSA: I know. I've never gotten a "D" before. I've seen them, but never next to my name.

THEO: And this one is in red. That's the worst kind to get.

VANESSA: I don't know how it happened. Robert and I studied for this.

THEO: Yeah, I saw that.

VANESSA: When do you think I should tell Mom and Dad?

THEO: The sooner the better.

VANESSA: But if I tell them now, they might not let me go to the dance with Robert.

THEO: Vanessa, there is a chance that you may never dance again.

VANESSA: But how can they get angry? I've been getting "A's" all along. This is one little "D."

THEO: When it comes to Mom and Dad, there are no little "D's."

1 Create Your Characters

The first step in writing a dialogue is to create the characters who will do the talking. Knowing your characters will help you to decide what type of dialogue to write. For example, a conversation between a grandmother and her grandson will be different from an argument between two friends.

TOOLS

- Paper and a pencil
- Colored pencils

Write a short description of each character. Include physical characteristics (height, hair color, etc.), as well as personality traits. As you write the dialogue, your descriptions will remind you of what your characters are like. Later, they will help your readers to "get in character" for their roles.

2 Choose a Topic

Now that you have created characters, you need to decide what they will talk about. They could be doing something as simple as walking through their neighborhood, talking about what they see. Or perhaps they're at home, discussing something that happened to them earlier in the day. Write down a brief description of the topic to go with your character descriptions.

3 Write Your Dialogue

Review your character descriptions and topic of conversation. Decide how you want the conversation to begin. Start writing! Think about the way a real conversation begins and how it builds. Think about what each of your characters would say and how he or she would say it. Try to make your dialogue sound like a real conversation between real people. Write down the conversation. Each time a different character begins to speak, you should write his or her name followed by a colon. (Use the dialogue on page 85 as a guide.)

Tip Once you've written a dialogue, read it aloud. Does it sound natural—like a real conversation? If not, make some changes and read it aloud again.

4 Perform Your Dialogue

Invite some friends or classmates to play the characters in your dialogue. You may want to take on one of the roles yourself, or be the "director" and help your "actors" to get in character and read the parts as you had envisioned them. Read through the dialogue a few times. When you and your fellow actors are satisfied with the way it sounds, you might want to perform it for your class.

If You Are Using a Computer ...

Use the Record and Playback tools to practice your story as you write it. Edit your story as you listen to how it sounds.

THINK

What did writing a dialogue show you about the way that we express ourselves through ordinary conversation?

José García
Drama Coach ▶

87

Speeches help us persuade
and inform others.

Speak Out

Meet Dinah Seabrooke,
who hopes to persuade
her classmates to vote
for her. Find out how to
give a great speech.

Read about the
Gettysburg
Address and
other famous
speeches.

Study famous
quotations on a
time line of historic
speeches in the
United States.

PROJECT

Prepare and deliver the stage
presentation of your choice.

89

from

DINAH
for President

by Claudia Mills
illustrated by Michael Steirnagle

*Ever since Dinah Seabrooke entered the race for sixth grade president,
she's been trying to get across her campaign message—recycling. She's got to
convince the students of JFK Middle School how important it is to recycle the
school's trash.*

*The election is only a few days away, and Dinah has to think of some
creative ways to make her point. So far, she's made posters, and even worn
a recycling bucket on her head. How will she manage to top that?*

Benjamin was crawling. The Seabrookes spent most of Sunday
afternoon out in their backyard watching him inch his way forward
across an old quilt spread on the grass.

"Of course, it's not true crawling yet," Dinah's mother explained to
her. "With true crawling he'd be up on his hands and knees. This is what
you'd call creeping."

"But it counts," Dinah said. "For his baby book."

"You bet," her father said. He crouched down at the edge of the
quilt. "Come on, little guy! Come to Daddy."

With a big, drooly smile, Benjamin headed over to his father. He
propelled himself with his elbows, like an infant Marine dragging his
way across a patchwork jungle.

"Way to go, Benjamin!" His father grabbed him up for a tickling
hug, then set him down on the quilt again.

"Okay, Benjamin." Dinah took the next turn. "Come to me. Come to Dinah!" Sure enough, he crept in her direction.

Dinah was happy. For no reason at all, she was happy. Maybe it was the autumn sky, the newly washed blueness of it, bright and hard like the glaze on a porcelain bowl. The maple tree in the Harmons' yard was beginning to turn color, catching fire at the tips of the branches. The sun was warm, but the breeze had in it the sharp freshness of fall, Dinah's favorite season.

"I love the world," Dinah told Benjamin, flopping down on the quilt next to him. "Do you know how lucky you are to live here? In a world like this?"

"It'll do," her father said.

Flat on her back, Dinah gazed up at the sky. Maybe if more people lay on the grass and looked up, they wouldn't want to turn their world into a giant landfill. Or litter, or pollute. When Dinah was a famous actress she would use her fame to help environmental causes. She'd make television commercials for recycling, and people would say, "If a big movie star like Dinah Seabrooke believes in recycling, maybe we should, too." And if she were elected president of the United States someday, she'd make a law that everyone had to recycle, and she herself would use recycled paper for the invitations to her inaugural ball.

Dinah sat up. "The election is this coming Friday," she said. "That's just five days away. We'll have the debate in social studies on Wednesday, but only twenty-five people will be there to hear it. I have my two-minute speech at the assembly on Thursday, but two minutes isn't very long. I have to do something else, one more thing, so that every single sixth grader will know how much our school needs a recycling program."

"I suppose you could try wearing one of our trash cans on your head," Dinah's father suggested.

"Daddy! You're not being serious. I can't wear anything else on my head. It's against the dress code." All Dinah needed now was to be nicknamed Trash Can Head. Besides, wearing the bucket on her head hadn't really made the others understand anything about the importance of recycling. It had been a publicity stunt for Dinah herself, rather than a serious demonstration of the merits of her platform.

"I think you're doing enough," her mother said. "Your speech is sure to be wonderful, if I know my daughter."

That much was true. Dinah had already begun practicing her speech, and in her opinion it was every bit as good as Lincoln's Gettysburg Address. But the nagging doubts raised by Greg's poll refused to go away.

"No," she said. "I need one more thing."

Her parents exchanged glances.

"If you say so," her mother said. "But try not to get into any more trouble."

"I'll try," Dinah promised. But sometimes, despite her best intentions, trouble just *happened*.

On Monday morning, Dinah took the box of big plastic trash bags from the kitchen drawer and tucked it into her backpack. She had a plan. She'd stay after school and collect all the wastepaper thrown away that day, or as much of it as she could, and she'd carry it around with her throughout the day on Tuesday. Not on her head, just in a couple of trash bags she could drag behind her as she changed classes. *Look*, she'd say, *all of this was thrown away in one single day*. What more clear and dramatic way of showing the need for a schoolwide recycling program?

As soon as the 3:18 bell sounded, Dinah darted from room to room, eager to empty as many wastepaper baskets as she could in an hour. After half a dozen classrooms, her first trash bag was full almost to bursting. She left it next to her locker and started on another. In a few minutes, the second bag was full, as well.

On she raced down the long, silent halls of JFK Middle School, dumping basket after basket into her bags. The janitors would be surprised to find that some elf had arrived before them and spirited all the trash away.

By a quarter past four, Dinah was exhausted. She would never have guessed it was so much work to empty one school's trash baskets. Nor had she guessed one school could produce so much trash. Ten bulging sacks full of wastepaper stood in front of her locker.

Now what? Suddenly Dinah realized a fatal flaw in her plan. She couldn't fit even one trash bag into her narrow locker, let alone ten. There was no way she could haul all ten bags home with her on the crowded bus. But if she left them by her locker overnight, the janitors would cart them away.

"Curly Top!" Dinah turned to find Miss Brady staring down at her. "What on earth do you have in those bags?"

Pirate's treasure. Canned goods for the needy. Freshly washed gym wear. Dinah rapidly ran through a series of lies, then said in a voice that came out smaller and squeakier than she meant it to, "Trash."

"And what, may I ask, are you doing with ten bags of trash?"

Wearily, Dinah explained. How many points would Brady take off for unauthorized trash collection?

"Where do you think you're going to put them now that you've collected them?" Brady's voice kept jabbing at Dinah like a long, bony finger. "I don't suppose you thought of that, did you?"

"No," Dinah admitted. "I was thinking about it just now, when you found me."

"Well, how about the gym locker room?" Brady suggested crisply. "There's plenty of room there. I'll leave a note for the cleaning staff not to remove them. You can stop by and pick them up first thing in the morning."

Dinah's eyes widened. She opened her mouth and then shut it again.

"Well, don't stand there gaping like a goldfish," Miss Brady snapped at her. "Let's take them there before you miss the 4:30 bus."

Brady hoisted four of the bags, two in each hand, and strode down the hall with them. Dinah made herself follow with another two. Together they came back to collect the rest.

"You'd better go now," Brady told Dinah when all ten bags were lined up against the rear wall of the gym locker room. "Mind you, I want these out of here by the start of first period tomorrow, no ifs, ands, or buts."

"But—" Dinah had to know. "Why are you helping me?"

"You think you kids are the only ones who care about recycling?" Brady asked. "I think it's a crime what this school throws away. I've said so time and time again at faculty meetings."

"What happened?"

"Nothing. Maybe something will now. I doubt it, but it's worth a try. Okay, Curly Top, out of here."

"Thank you," Dinah managed to say.

Brady brushed it away with the back of her hand. "Go!" she boomed.

Dinah dashed for the bus.

The next morning Dinah ran to the gym locker room as soon as the school doors opened. Miss Brady helped her tie the bags together with the thick twine Dinah had brought from the utility room at home. Then, dragging the bags behind her like a mule pulling a barge down the Erie Canal, Dinah made her slow, laborious way to homeroom.

No one had noticed when Dinah caught her skirt in her locker door the first day. But everyone noticed someone pulling ten trash bags down the hall. They had to notice, or they'd trip and go sprawling.

"Hey, kid, get out of my way!" an eighth grader shouted at her. But he was the one who ended up getting out of the way.

Luckily Dinah had thought to hang a sign around her neck, so she didn't have to waste any precious breath on explanations.

THIS TRASH WAS COLLECTED

IN ONE DAY AT YOUR SCHOOL.

SHOULDN'T IT BE RECYCLED?

DINAH SEABROOKE SAYS YES!

DINAH SEABROOKE

FOR SIXTH-GRADE PRESIDENT!

"Dinah Seabrooke for sixth-grade janitor!" one boy jeered, but Dinah was too tired to respond. The hall stretched out before her endlessly. *Bumpity, bumpity, bumpity, bump.* She dragged her load up the long flight of middle-school stairs.

Another boy chanted, "Jason's in the White House, waiting to be elected. Dinah's in the garbage can, waiting to be collected!"

Very funny. On Dinah trudged, pulling the weight of the world behind her.

Homeroom at last. Dinah left her load just outside the door and sank into her seat.

"What do you have in those bags, Seabrooke?" Jason asked her. He paused, obviously trying to think of a hilarious answer to his own question. Then his face lit up. "Deodorant!" he said loudly. "Dinah just bought a week's supply of deodorant!"

"Oh, shut up," Blaine told him. Blaine? "At least Dinah cares about something. At least there's something she *believes* in."

"That's right, Dinah believes in deodorant!" Jason was laughing so hard he had trouble getting the last word out.

"You are so juvenile, I can't believe it," Blaine said. "Just ignore him, Dinah."

Dinah threw Blaine a grateful smile. These days she was certainly receiving assistance from unexpected quarters.

"No," Mr. Prensky said as Dinah began dragging her ten trash bags down the aisle to her seat. "No. I won't stand for it. No."

"No, what?" Dinah asked, but she knew.

"I will not permit you to disrupt this class another time with your ridiculous campaign, or whatever you call it."

"I'm just trying to save the planet," Dinah said coldly.

"Well, go save it in Mr. Roemer's office. Go. Now."

Dinah obeyed. She and her trash bags made their grand exit from first-period English.

"You again," Mr. Roemer said when the secretary ushered her into his office. "What is it this time?"

Dinah told him.

"I thought we had agreed that you weren't going to cause any more disturbances," Mr. Roemer said.

Dinah doubted that she had agreed to any such thing. When Dynamite Dinah was around, disturbances were only to be expected. And this time was different. How were people going to realize the enormity of the trash problem in their school if Dinah didn't make them actually *see* how much trash there was?

"I didn't wear anything on my head this time."

"I suppose we can be grateful for that," Mr. Roemer said. He studied the ten trash bags. "You really collected all that paper in one day?"

Dinah nodded. "This isn't even all of it."

"Well, if one of this year's class officers wants to take the initiative for a recycling program, I guess I'd look into it."

Dinah's heart soared. If Mr. Roemer looked into a recycling program, he'd have to see what a good idea it was. Now all she had to do was get herself elected president so that he'd look into it.

"All right, Dinah, go sit out by Mrs. MacDonald's desk for the rest of the period."

"What about my bags?"

"You'll have to leave them here."

"But I *need* them. People *should* be disturbed by them. I *want* them to be." Dinah's rush of joy was perilously close to becoming misery.

"Look," Mr. Roemer said, "suppose we leave them outside the main office, just for today, with your sign taped to the wall next to them. How would that be?"

"That would be wonderful." Dinah thought about hugging Mr. Roemer, but decided against it.

He walked to the door with her. "Remember, Dinah, the squeaky wheel may get the most grease, but it doesn't necessarily get the most votes."

But Mr. Roemer didn't understand. Dinah had to get the most votes. She just had to.

"**K**ids!" Mr. Dixon bellowed at the start of sixth period on Wednesday afternoon. "Clear your desks! Clear your minds! Today's the day we've been waiting for. Illustrious candidates, take your places."

Mr. Dixon set three chairs at the front of the room, facing the rows of desks. Dinah picked the chair farthest from Mr. Dixon.

She liked to go last when she had a presentation to make. The last speech had the greatest impact.

"Each candidate will give a two-minute speech, then each will get two minutes to respond to the speeches made by the others. After that we'll open the floor for questions. Winfield, you're on."

Jason stood up. He looked tan and athletic and sure of himself.

"Why should you elect me president of your class? Because I have a proven record of leadership in sports. I was captain of my youth-league baseball team last year, and it came in second in the whole city. Being a team captain taught me a lot about getting along with people and getting them to work together toward a common goal. I learned how to make hard decisions and how to stick by them afterward.

"Right now I'm on the football team, and I'm the only sixth grader who's gotten to play in a game so far this fall. I plan to go out for the basketball and baseball teams, too.

"My dad says that sports are like life, and life is like sports. Don't you want a *winner* to lead your class as president? If you elect me as president, I'll work hard all year to turn JFK into a school of champions."

Some of the boys began to cheer, but Dixon rapped on his desk with the pointer. "Hold your applause. You'll get your say at the polls on Friday. Yarborough."

Blaine took her place. She looked pale, but composed.

"The greatest problem our school faces today—" Blaine paused for emphasis "—is apathy. A lot of people in this school just don't care about their schoolwork, about extracurricular activities, about their *school*. Less than half of all sixth graders attended the activities fair in September, and of those who did attend, less than half joined any club.

"The right to attend JFK Middle School goes hand in hand with certain responsibilities. Responsibilities to study, to obey school rules, to support school activities. There won't *be* any school activities unless we, the students, support them. No sports." Blaine nodded at Jason. "No Environmental Action Club." She nodded at Dinah. "No drama or music, no science fair, no school newspaper.

"Our school is named after the thirty-fifth president of the United States, John Fitzgerald Kennedy. In his inaugural address, Kennedy said, 'Ask not what your country can do for you; ask what you can do for your country.' I say, 'Ask not what your school can do for you, but what you can do for your school.' Get involved. Join a club. Try out for a team. Make a difference. All of us working together can make JFK the best school in the state. I'm ready. Are you?"

Blaine sat down. It was all Dinah could do not to burst into applause herself. Blaine made Dinah feel proud she had joined the Drama Club, guilty she hadn't joined the Environmental Action Club, sorry she had ever made fun of the Girls' Athletic Association. *Ask not what your school can do for you; ask what you can do for your school.* Dinah could have used a line like that herself: Ask not what your planet can do for you; ask what you can do for your planet.

"Seabrooke. Earth to Dinah Seabrooke," Dixon called out.

Dinah jumped. It was her turn. She walked slowly to the same spot where Jason and Blaine had stood. Then she began.

"I stand before you today as the only candidate for sixth-grade president who will bring a recycling program to your school. Every person in this country throws away four hundred and eighty-one pounds of paper every year. Every day in this country, thousands of trees are chopped down to make paper, thousands of living, breathing, growing trees. Every day more acres of land become a landfill—a garbage dump, crammed full of waste that could have been recycled, that *should* have been recycled.

"The average school throws away tons of paper every year. On Monday I collected ten whole trash bags full of paper other kids had thrown away.

"Look," Dinah said. "Look around you. Lie down on the grass under a tree and look up at its branches. In spring they're covered with fragrant flowers; in summer with cool, green leaves; in autumn with fiery foliage; in winter with soft, white snow. It makes me sick to think of cutting down a beautiful, magnificent tree to make a bunch of Dittos." Scattered applause. "A tree is like a poem. Or a prayer. Or a symphony. It deserves to be saved, and loved.

"We have a chance to keep our planet green and growing. We can chop down more trees and dig more landfills, or we can save trees and recycle. The choice is ours. The choice, this Friday, is yours."

If that didn't make them want to save trees—and vote for Dinah—nothing on earth possibly could.

"Rebuttals. Winfield, two minutes."

Jason faced the class. "I don't really disagree with anything Blaine said. Nobody's more involved in school activities than I am. But I can't go along with Dinah's big thing about saving trees. First of all, even if we recycled paper, nobody else does. If there're a million schools, and one recycles paper and the rest don't, I don't see how that helps anything. Besides, that's what trees are *for*—to use to make things people need. As far as I'm concerned, recycling is a dumb waste of time. About as dumb as wearing a bucket on your head to the cafeteria."

Jason grinned at Dinah. She made herself wait for her turn to reply.

"Yarborough."

"Jason tells us that *he's* involved in school activities. Good. I congratulate him for setting that example. But we need a president who's not only involved himself but will try to get others involved, too. And I want to see kids getting involved not just in sports, but in every school activity.

"Including recycling. Recycling is *not* dumb. I think Dinah's absolutely right about the need for a recycling program in our school. I would have made it part of my platform, except, well, Dinah thought of it first, so it belongs to her. But if I win, I will work to set up a program like Dinah talked about. *We* can do what's right even if everybody else doesn't."

"Seabrooke."

Dinah leaped to her feet, still as furious as she had been two minutes ago.

"What's dumb isn't wearing a bucket on your head. What's dumb is laughing at someone who's trying to make a difference. What's dumb is littering, and throwing away things that could be recycled, and cutting down trees instead of planting new ones. What's dumb is not even noticing that we've just been given one planet, and one chance to take care of it."

Dinah struggled to pull herself together. She wanted to say something as nice about Blaine's speech as Blaine had about hers. She took a deep breath and went on.

"Blaine is right. We *can* make a difference, in all kinds of ways we don't even dream about. Blaine's right that we should ask what we can do for our school. And what we can do for our school is set up a recycling program. What we can do for our planet is save it."

Dinah sat down. Her hands were shaking and she felt close to tears. But she had said what she wanted to say.

"Class. Questions. One at a time. Levine."

"This is for Blaine. I mean, it sounds good to get people involved in school activities, but how are you actually going to do it?"

Blaine had her answer ready. "I have a couple of ideas. One is that I think a different activity should be featured every week on morning announcements. That same week there can be a display all about that activity on the bulletin board in front of the main office. The school newspaper can print more stories about some of the clubs kids don't know much about, instead of writing all the time about sports. And sometimes kids should get out of class to work on a club activity. Everybody wants to get out of class, right?"

The others laughed. Then Mr. Dixon called on the next kid. "Foster."

"This is for Jason. Can you give us any specific example to show how being in sports has given you leadership experience?" Alex Foster was a friend of Jason's; they had obviously planned the question together.

"Good question," Jason said. "Here's one. When I was captain of my baseball team last year, the coach and I had to make decisions about which kids would get to play and which kids would have to sit on the bench. Sometimes good friends of mine ended up sitting on the bench, but I couldn't let them play just because they were my friends. I had to do what was best for the team. If I were president of our class, it would be the same way. I'd do what was best for everybody."

"Adams."

"This is for Dinah." The smirk on Artie's face gave the question away before he even asked it. "In general, do you like to wear strange things on your head?"

"Let's not waste time with jokes, Adams," Mr. Dixon warned.

"Okay, I have another question. Dinah, is it true you love trees so much you want to marry one?"

"Okay, Adams, out of here. One chance is all I give."

Artie cheerfully collected his things and left for Mr. Roemer's office. But the damage was already done. Dinah felt her cheeks flaming. She'd certainly rather marry a tree than a boy.

"Does anyone have a *serious* question for Dinah?"

One girl put up her hand. "Do you really think you can get the school administration to adopt a recycling program?"

"Mr. Roemer told me himself that if one of the new officers took the initiative for a recycling program, he'd look into it."

It was a good answer. But Dinah could tell most kids weren't listening. From somewhere in the back of the room she heard again the familiar chant, "Dinah's in the garbage can, waiting to be collected!"

There were a few other questions, all for Blaine and Jason. Then Mr. Dixon rapped on his desk again. "That's it for today, folks. With the exception of our dear departed friend, Mr. Adams, you came up with some great questions. In the last U.S. presidential election, less than half of the eligible voters chose to exercise their right to vote. I hope all of you vote on Friday. It's up to you to choose one of these three candidates to lead your class through this academic year."

Silently he tapped the pointer against each of the three names he had written on the chalkboard at the beginning of the class period.

Winfield.

Yarborough.

Seabrooke.

"Which one will it be?"

From

You Mean I Have To Stand Up And Say Something?

by Joan Detz
illustrated by David Carner

How to Figure Out What You Want to Say

Okay, you've just gotten an assignment to give a five-to-ten minute speech in English class next Friday.

Now what do you do? Do you race home and start writing your speech? Do you start making lots of charts to illustrate your talk? Do you run to the library to get some facts? No! The first thing you should do is to ask yourself, "What do I really want to say?"

You know, you can't include everything in one speech. If you try to include everything, your audience will become bored and confused.

Do you remember those times when a math teacher tried to put too much material in her lesson and you got confused trying to understand all those complicated formulas?

Or, do you remember when your older brother talked too much at the dinner table and you just wished he'd shut his mouth and give you some peace and quiet?

Well, that's how your audience will feel if you try to put too much stuff in one speech.

So whenever you get a speaking assignment, start by asking yourself, "What do I really want to say?" Limit yourself to one topic. Don't try to include everything you have ever learned.

For example, suppose you must give a speech about *yourself*. Wow—that's a big topic! You can't possibly tell your audience everything about yourself in five to ten minutes—or even five to ten hours, or five to ten days.

So, start by asking yourself, "Gee, what do I really want to tell these people about me?"

See what I mean? You have *lots* of things to tell people about yourself. Now you must choose the one area that you think will be the most interesting, or the most helpful, or the most unusual.

Remember, if you try to tell the audience everything about yourself, you will just bore them or confuse them—and they won't get a good understanding of who you really are.

Make a list of all the things you could talk about:

- how you love animals and always take care of stray cats and dogs that wander into your neighborhood
- what it was like growing up in a foreign country
- how you got to be so interested in tennis
- the way you always want to try new adventures (camping, backpacking, canoeing—and now a ten-day wilderness hike with your father)
- why you've developed such a good sense of humor

said, "The best time for planning a book is while you're doing the dishes." That can also apply to speeches.

Who knows what wonderful ideas you'll get while you're doing the dishes or making your bed or walking the dog? If it's a good idea, grab it . . . and move on to the next step.

What if you can't think of anything to say?

Can't think of anything to talk about? Don't panic. Just ask yourself, "What's the one subject that always catches my attention? What do I really care about? What topic would I like to hear more about?"

If *you're* interested in the topic of your speech, that enthusiasm will probably rub off on your audience.

Once you get a good idea for a speech, stick with it. *Don't* keep switching topics or trying something else. Commit yourself to that topic, and move ahead with your preparations.

And don't be too fussy about when you get your good ideas. The mystery writer Agatha Christie once

SOURCE

the history magazine for young people
COBBLESTONE

Magazine

A FEW
APPROPRIATE
'REMARKS'

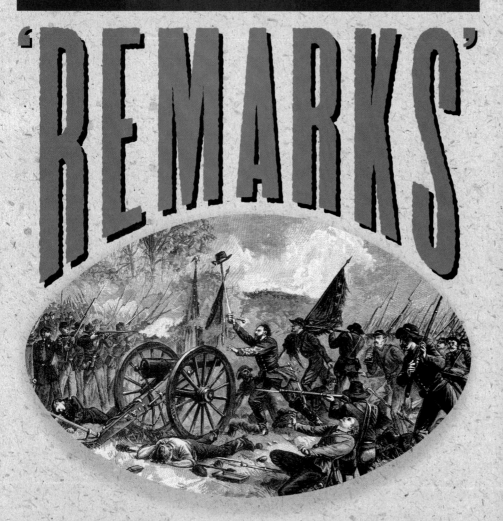

BY
HAROLD HOLTZER

ILLUSTRATED BY
STEPHEN ALCORN

As Union and Confederate forces battled ferociously at Gettysburg, the Union's Commander in Chief, Abraham Lincoln, waited in Washington for news from the front.

Hour after hour during those anxious days and nights, an eyewitness remembered, Lincoln's tall form could be found at the War Department, bent over stacks of telegrams from the battle. On the third day, his burden grew even heavier: His fragile wife, Mary, was thrown from her carriage in a freak accident and suffered a head injury.

Finally, after seventy-two hours of unrelieved tension, Lincoln learned that the North had prevailed at Gettysburg. Privately, he was disappointed that his generals did not follow up their victory by pursuing the Confederates as they fled south. Publicly, he sent the army the "highest honors" for their "great success." He seemed to sense that, flawed or not, the Battle of Gettysburg would be a turning point in the Civil War.

The citizens of Pennsylvania, also aware of their new place in history, moved quickly to create a national cemetery for the thousands of casualties at Gettysburg. A dedication ceremony was planned, and Lincoln received an invitation to attend. He was not, however, asked to deliver the major speech of the day. That

Edward Everett gave a two-hour oratory before Lincoln's speech.

honor was given to a New England statesman and professional orator named Edward Everett. Lincoln, one organizer worried, was incapable of speaking "upon such a great and solemn occasion." The president was asked merely to give "a few appropriate remarks." Yet aware that the event was momentous, Lincoln accepted the halfhearted invitation.

As the day grew near, Lincoln's wife urged him to reconsider. Their young son, Tad, had fallen ill, and Mrs. Lincoln was near hysteria. (Only a year earlier, their middle child, Willie, had died.) On the morning of his father's departure, Tad was so sick he could not eat breakfast. Lincoln himself felt unwell, but he decided to go anyway. With little fanfare, he boarded a train for the slow journey to Gettysburg.

The legend that the president waited until he was on the train to prepare his speech and then scribbled it on the back of an envelope is untrue. Lincoln carefully wrote at least one version of his speech on White House stationery before he left and probably rewrote it in his bedroom in Gettysburg the night before delivering it.

On Thursday, November 19, a balmy, Indian summer day, the six-feet-four Lincoln mounted an

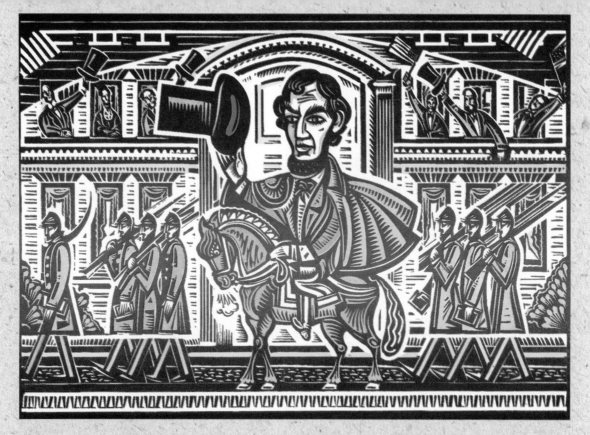

Lincoln rides to the cemetery on an undersized horse.

undersized horse and joined a mournful procession through the town and toward the new cemetery near the battlefield. An immense throng had gathered there, and as Lincoln arrived on the speakers' platform, every man in the crowd respectfully removed his hat. The president was greeted with "a perfect silence."

For two hours, Edward Everett held the spectators spellbound with his rich voice and soaring words. A hymn followed, then Lincoln rose to speak. "Four score and seven years ago," Lincoln began in a high-pitched voice. He spoke for barely three minutes, ending with the words "government of the people, by the people, for the people, shall not perish from the earth."

Almost as soon as he had begun, he sat down. Some eyewitnesses recalled a smattering of applause, but others heard "not a word, not a cheer, not a shout." A stenographer leaned over to Lincoln and asked, "Is that all?" Embarrassed, Lincoln replied, "Yes—for the present." A photographer in the crowd, fussing with his camera, had not even had time to take a picture.

Lincoln thought his speech was a failure. "People are disappointed," he grimly told the man who had introduced him. To add to his misery, he came down with a mild case of smallpox on the trip back to Washington.

Lincoln addresses the crowd at Gettysburg.

Many who listened to the speech felt differently, however. While some newspapers dismissed the speech as "silly," "dull," and "commonplace," another correctly predicted the Gettysburg Address would "live among the annals of man." Perhaps the best compliment of all came from Edward Everett. A few days after they both had spoken at Gettysburg, he wrote to Lincoln, saying he wished he had come "as close to the central idea of the occasion, in two hours, as you did in two minutes." Lincoln replied, telling Everett how pleased he was that "the little I did say was not entirely a failure."

Today, one hundred twenty-five years later, Abraham Lincoln's Gettysburg Address is remembered as one of the great speeches of all time.

Address Delivered at the Dedication of the Cemetery at Gettysburg

Four score and seven years ago our fathers brought forth on this continent, a new nation, conceived in liberty, and dedicated to the proposition that all men are created equal.

Now we are engaged in a great civil war, testing whether that nation or any nation so conceived, and so dedicated, can long endure. We are met on a great battle field of that war. We have come to dedicate a portion of that field, as a final resting place for those who here gave their lives, that that nation might live. It is altogether fitting and proper that we should do this.

But, in a larger sense, we can not dedicate—we can not consecrate—we can not hallow—this ground. The brave men, living and dead, who struggled here, have consecrated it, far above our poor power to add or detract. The world will little note, nor long remember what we say here, but it can never forget what they did here. It is for us the living, rather, to be dedicated here to the unfinished work which they who fought here have thus far so nobly advanced. It is rather for us to be here dedicated to the great task remaining before us—that from these honored dead we take increased devotion to that cause for which they gave the last full measure of devotion—that we here highly resolve that these dead shall not have died in vain—that this nation, under God, shall have a new birth of freedom—and that government of the people, by the people, for the people, shall not perish from the earth.

Abraham Lincoln
November 19, 1863

History Preserved

President Lincoln hand wrote and autographed a total of five copies of his Gettysburg Address. Photographed here is one of two copies that historian George Bancroft requested from Lincoln. Bancroft had the copies reproduced for the Soldiers' and Sailors' Fair held in Baltimore, MD, in April, 1864. This copy is the best preserved of the five existing handwritten copies.

Four score and seven years ago our fathers brought forth, on this continent, a new nation, conceived in Liberty, and dedicated to the proposition that all men are created equal.

Now we are engaged in a great civil war, testing whether that nation, or any nation so conceived, and so dedicated, can long endure. We are met on a great battle-field of that war. We have come to dedicate a portion of that field, as a final resting-place for those who here gave their lives, that that nation might live. It is altogether fitting and proper that we should do this.

But, in a larger sense, we can not dedicate— we can not consecrate— we can not hallow— this ground. The brave men, living and dead, who struggled here, have consecrated it, far above our poor power to add or detract. The world will little note, nor long remember what we say here, but it can never forget what they did here. It is for us the living, rather, to be dedicated here to the unfinished work which they who fought here have thus far so nobly advanced. It is rather for us to be here dedicated to the great task remaining be-

fore us— that from these honored dead we take in=
creased devotion to that cause for which they here gave
the last full measure of devotion— that we here highly resolve that these dead shall not have died in
vain— that this nation, under God, shall have
a new birth of freedom— and that government
of the people, by the people, for the people, shall
not perish from the earth.

Portrait of Abraham
by Matthew Brady,
circa 1862

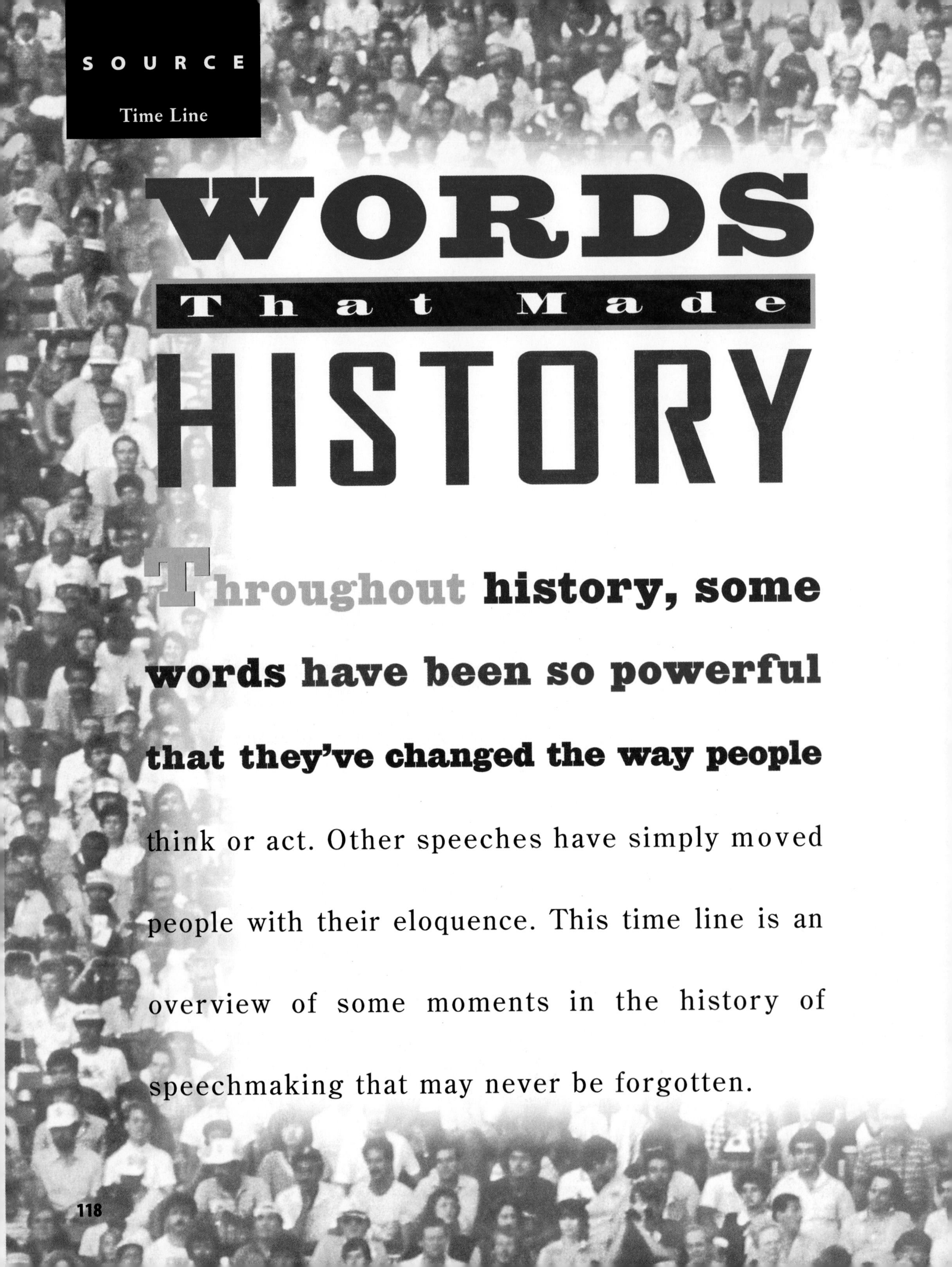

WORDS That Made HISTORY

Throughout **history, some words have been so powerful that they've changed the way people** think or act. Other speeches have simply moved people with their eloquence. This time line is an overview of some moments in the history of speechmaking that may never be forgotten.

1775

"Give me liberty, or give me death!" Revolutionary War hero **Patrick Henry's** famous statement helped convince colonists to fight in the American war for independence.

1848

"We hold these truths to be self-evident: that all men and women *are created equal."* **Elizabeth Cady Stanton** stirred the crowd at the first women's rights convention by reading her own version of the Declaration of Independence.

1851

"This man...says that women need to be helped into carriages, and lifted over ditches, and to have the best place everywhere. Nobody ever helps me into carriages, or over mud puddles, or gives me the best place, and ain't I a woman?...I have plowed, and planted, and gathered into barns, and no man could help me...and ain't I a woman?"

A former slave named **Sojourner Truth** was a passionate speaker on the issue of equal rights for women and all African Americans.

1855

"What is man without the beasts? If all the beasts are gone, men would die from great loneliness of spirit, for whatever happens to

the beasts also happens to the man." As settlers moved across the United States, they forced Native Americans off of their lands. When **Chief Seattle** surrendered his tribe's lands, he spoke about the different ways that Native Americans and the settlers showed their respect for the earth.

1912

"I shall ask you to be as quiet as possible. I don't know whether you fully understand that I have just been shot; but it takes more than that to kill a Bull Moose."

Teddy Roosevelt was campaigning for president as the Bull Moose candidate when he delivered a death-defying speech. As Roosevelt was about to begin speaking, a man stepped out of the crowd and shot him in the chest. That didn't stop Roosevelt! He insisted on giving his speech before agreeing to go to a hospital.

1961

"And so my fellow Americans, ask not what your country can do for you; ask what you can do for your country."

John F. Kennedy gave an inaugural speech in which his words made an impact on the mood of the entire country. Kennedy wanted people to understand what it meant to be an American citizen.

1963

"I have a dream that my four little children will one day live in a country where they will not be judged by the color of their skin but by the content of their character."

These words from **Martin Luther King, Jr.'s** famous speech at the civil rights March on Washington expressed hope for a better future for everyone.

1969

"That's one small step for a man; one giant leap for mankind." **Astronaut Neil Armstrong** spoke these famous words after taking the first step ever on the moon!

1991

"As female students today, your challenges will come not so much in breaking new paths — as your mothers, grandmothers and I have done — but in deciding which to choose among the many paths now open to you." When **Sandra Day O'Connor** became the first woman justice appointed to the U.S. Supreme Court she became an inspiration to many young women, including the graduates she addressed at Widener University.

1993

"Here on the pulse of this new day/You may have the grace to look up and out/And into your sister's eyes,/And into your brother's face,/Your country,/And say simply/With hope — /Good morning." **Maya Angelou** composed a poem, "On the Pulse of the Morning" for President Bill Clinton's inauguration. Millions watched on television as she read.

How to Give a Stage Presentation

It's your turn *to be* in the *spotlight!*

"**A**ll the world's a stage," wrote the famous playwright William Shakespeare. Though you may not be a performer, you'll probably be called "on stage" at some time in your life. You might have to make a speech or give an oral report. Here's an opportunity to give a stage presentation about something you know well or really care about. The format you choose for your presentation might be a monologue, a report, a speech, or a song.

Be expressive.

Make eye contact

Smile

Wait for laughs

1 Choose Your Topic and Format

Begin by deciding what you want your presentation to be about. Aim for a presentation that's about five to ten minutes long. That can seem like a long time when you're on stage by yourself, so be sure the topic you pick is something you're interested in! You might want to focus on something happening in the news. Or you might choose to focus on a hobby, a person who inspires you, or something you consider yourself an expert in.

Once you have picked your topic, think creatively about the best way to get your message across. For example, if your topic is a hot news story, you might deliver the information as if you were a newscaster.

If telling jokes is your hobby, you may want to organize a comedy routine. Here are some additional ideas for formats for your presentation. Can you think of any others?

- song
- oral report
- poem
- speech

TOOLS

- Paper and a pencil
- Props, costumes, and sound effects

HUMOROUS MONOLOGUES

BY MARTHA BOLTON

PICTURES BY JOYCE BEHR
FOREWORD BY BOB HOPE

2 Write Your Script

Whatever your presentation is, you'll need to write a script for it. If you're creating your own monologue or comedy routine, or reading some of your own poems, you'll need to spend some time writing and organizing your material. If you're giving a report or a speech on a favorite topic, you'll need to write out what you'll say.

You might want to outline the main points you'll cover first and then fill in the details.

How Am I Doing?

Before you stage your presentation, take a few minutes to ask yourself these questions:

- Did I choose a topic that interests me and suits my audience?

- Do I know (or can I find out) 5–10 minutes worth of pertinent information about my topic?

- Have I chosen an appropriate format for my topic and audience?

Tip You might want to reread "You Mean I Have to Stand Up and Say Something?" in this SourceBook for advice on how to choose a topic.

Scholastic 0-590-45828-0 / $1.95

The Abraham Lincoln Joke Book

By
Beatrice Schenk de Regniers

Illustrations by
William Lahey Cummings

3 Prepare Your Presentation

It takes more than a good script to give your presentation pizzazz. If you did the storytelling workshop, you've learned how to make a presentation exciting. Think about using props, costumes, music, or visual aids to spice up your act. Mark up your script with any ideas you want to include.

Your presentation will be most successful if it's well-rehearsed. Have a friend or family member observe a rehearsal. They can tell you whether you're speaking clearly, and whether your props and other devices make sense to the audience. Refer to your script when you need to, but try to rely on it less the more you practice.

If You Are Using A Computer

Use the Sign format on your computer to make programs and banners for the performance. Illustrate them with clip-art or create your own drawings.

4 Stage Your Performance

Here are some suggestions for making your presentation a success.

- Monitor your voice. Speak loudly and clearly so that even the people in the back can hear you. To help your voice carry, keep your head up and try to face the audience.

- Use body language. Your gestures help to create drama and excitement! Move your face, hands, and body in ways that reinforce what you are saying.

- Organize your material so that the presentation goes smoothly.

- Finally, you might invite a parent or your school media specialist to videotape your presentation. You can watch the tape afterward and evaluate your performance.

CONGRATULATIONS

Now you know what it's like to share your creative voice with an audience. You'll use your creativity in many different situations.

José García
Drama Coach ▶

Glossary

ap·plause (ə plôz′) *noun*
A way of showing appreciation for something, especially by clapping.

applause

au·di·ence
(ô′ dē əns) *noun*
A group of people who have gathered to watch a play, speech, or other public performance.

bal·lads
(bal′ əds) *noun*
Simple poems or stories that tell a song in short verses. ▲ **ballad**

cam·paign
(kam pān′) *noun*
A series of planned actions taken to reach a goal.

chant (chant) *noun*
A manner of singing or speaking in a musical monotone.

can·di·dates
(kan′ di dāts′) *noun*
People who seek a particular position or high honor. All *candidates* for class president must give speeches. ▲ **candidate**

cau·ses (kô′ zəz) *noun*
Ideas or principles that people actively support. ▲ **cause**

coach (kōch) *noun*
A person who trains or instructs performers.

con·ven·tion
(kən ven′shən) *noun*
A group of people who get together to discuss a particular idea or belief.

de·but
(dā byoo′) *noun*
A first public appearance by a performer.

audience

ded·i·ca·tion
(ded´i kā´shən) *noun*
The act of setting aside for a special purpose.

dra·mat·i·cal·ly
(drə ma´ tik lē´) *adverb*
Vividly, in an exciting or suspenseful way.

el·o·quence
(el´ə kwens) *noun*
The ability to speak in a way that stirs people's emotions.

Word History

The word **eloquence** comes from the Latin word *eloquens* meaning "to put into words."

eye·wit·ness
(ī´ wit´nis) *noun*
A person who sees an act or event and can give a firsthand account of it.

fas·ci·nat·ed
(fas´ ə nā´ təd) *verb*
Captured the interest of.
▲ fascinate

folk tales
(fōk tāls) *noun*
Stories that were passed along by word of mouth before being written down.
▲ folk tale

im·pressed
(im prest´) *adjective*
Positively influenced or affected. Having a strong, positive opinion of.

in·ci·dent
(in´ si dənt) *noun*
A distinct event or piece of action, as in a story. John told me about a funny *incident* that happened on the school playground.

Thesaurus

incident
episode
event
occurrence

lime·light
(līm´ līt´) *noun*
The center of public attention.

Fact File

The *lime* in **limelight** isn't the kind you pick off a tree. It's a chemical substance that, when heated, gives off a brilliant white light. Scottish inventor Thomas Drummond, born in 1797, used lime to create a lighting device that was later used to illuminate lighthouses and, eventually, theatrical stages.

a	add	o͝o	took	ə =	
ā	ace	o͞o	pool		ə in *above*
â	care	u	up		e in *sicken*
ä	palm	û	burn		i in *possible*
e	end	yo͞o	fuse		o in *melon*
ē	equal	oi	oil		u in *circus*
i	it	ou	pout		
ī	ice	ng	ring		
o	odd	th	thin		
ō	open	t͟h	this		
ô	order	zh	vision		

Glossary

me·mo·ri·al
(mə môr′ē əl) *noun*
Something designed to keep a memory alive; a monument.

mon·u·ment
(mon′yə mənt) *noun*
A structure that commemorates a person or event.

Word History

The word **monument** is from the Latin word *monumentum* meaning "to remind."

mused
(myo͞ozd) *verb*
Said with extended or contemplative thought. Ellen *mused* about why her sister seemed so sad.
▲ **muse**

or·a·tor (ôr′ ə tər) *noun*
A person who is known to be a good public speaker.

Fact File

One of the most famous **orators** of all time was Roman statesman Mark Antony. The funeral speech, or **oration**, he made for Julius Caesar is considered to be a masterpiece, and is still quoted today.

orator

pan·to·mime
(pan′ tə mīm′) *noun*
A performance in which a story is told through movement and gestures, not words.

Word History

The word **pantomime** comes from two Greek words, *panto*, meaning "all," and *mimos*, meaning "imitator." Panto + mime = someone who can imitate anything.

plat·form
(plat′ fôrm) *noun*
Ideas and causes adopted by a person running for political office.

poll (pōl) *noun*
A record of people's opinions or votes on a given subject.

pre·serv·ing
(pri zûrv′ing) *verb*
Keeping safe; maintaining.
▲ **preserve**

pre·view
(prē′ vyo͞o′) *noun*
An early showing or performance.

pro·duc·er
(prə do͞o′ sər) *noun*
The person who raises the money for a performance.

pro·jec·tions
(prə jek′ shənz) *noun*
Pictures or images that appear on a screen.
▲ **projection**

pub·lic·ly
(pub′ lik lē) *adverb*
In a public or open manner or place.

pub·lic·i·ty stunt
(pu blis′ i tē stunt) *noun*
An event staged to gain public attention for a person or thing.

re·but·tals
(ri but′ lz) *noun*
Answers that disagree with what has been said. After your opponents have stated their opinions, you will have time to make your *rebuttals.* ▲ **rebuttal**

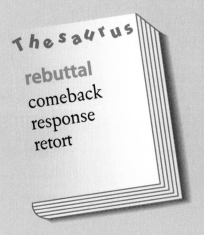

Thesaurus

rebuttal
comeback
response
retort

re·hears·al
(ri hûr′ səl) *noun*
A practice run of a performance, speech, play, or other public program.

spell·bound
(spel′ bound′) *adjective*
Fascinated or enchanted by something.

spot·light
(spot′ līt′) *noun*
Strong beam of light used to highlight performers on stage.

> ## Word Study
> The word **spotlight** can also mean "to make conspicuous; to draw attention to."

sym·bol·ic
(sim bol′ ik) *adjective*
Serving as a sign or representation of something.

the·at·ri·cal
(thē a′ tri kəl) *adjective*
Of or pertaining to dramatic presentations.

throng (thrông) *noun*
A large number of people crowded together.

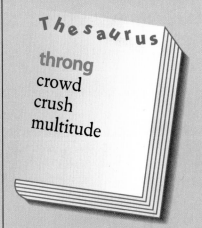

Thesaurus

throng
crowd
crush
multitude

tra·di·tion·al
(trə dish′ ə nl) *adjective*
Relating to beliefs and customs passed from one generation to the next by word of mouth or by example.

a	add	o͝o	took	ə =
ā	ace	o͞o	pool	a in *above*
â	care	u	up	e in *sicken*
ä	palm	û	burn	i in *possible*
e	end	yo͞o	fuse	o in *melon*
ē	equal	oi	oil	u in *circus*
i	it	ou	pout	
ī	ice	ng	ring	
o	odd	th	thin	
ō	open	th	this	
ô	order	zh	vision	

Authors & Illustrators

Floyd Cooper *pages 10–35*

This award-winning illustrator is known for expressive paintings that seem to draw the reader into the characters' worlds. The paintings in *From Miss Ida's Porch* were inspired by Floyd Cooper's childhood memories of neighborhood storytelling.

Myra Cohn Livingston *pages 60–61*

Today, she is one of the best-known writers of children's poetry, but Myra Cohn Livingston began her career as a professional musician. Now she creates music with words. "I think poetry must have music," Livingston says. She has composed hundreds of poems on subjects including animals, ocean life, and outer space.

Claudia Mills *pages 90–105*

This author published her first novel for young readers in 1981, but she began writing as a child. At fourteen, Claudia Mills wrote her autobiography. Called *T Is for Tarzan*, it was a big hit at her junior high school. Today, Mills lives in Maryland, where she is a college professor.

José Ortega *pages 52–59*

Born in Ecuador, this illustrator moved to New York City when he was five. José Ortega says he has always loved to draw. After high school, he attended the School of Visual Arts and became a professional artist. When illustrating "La Bamba," Ortega tried to match Gary Soto's humorous story twists in his drawings, which he created on a computer.

Gary Soto *pages 52–59*

This author says that his childhood inspired a great deal of his poems, short stories, and novels. Gary Soto has vivid memories of growing up in a predominantly Mexican-American neighborhood in Fresno, California. While attending college, Soto discovered poetry. He decided to become a writer and began putting the stories in his head down on paper. Soto hopes his work will inspire his readers the way other writers have inspired him.

Laurence Yep *pages 36–43*

Born in San Francisco, this author grew up reading science-fiction and fantasy stories. When he first started writing children's books, he began with these genres. Later, Laurence Yep explored folk tales from his Chinese heritage. Yep has won numerous awards, including the Newbery Honor Book award for *Dragonwings*.

Books &

More by Laurence Yep

Dragonwings
It's the early 1900s and Moonshadow has just come to San Francisco from China to live with his father. Read about his experiences in his new home.

The Lost Garden
Here, Laurence Yep tells the story of his own life. Find out how the writer got his start.

Tongues of Jade
In this collection, master storyteller Laurence Yep retells 17 Chinese-American tales.

Laurence Yep

Dynamite Dinah
by Claudia Mills
Dinah's new baby brother is monopolizing her parents' attention and her best friend has won the lead role in the school play. What can Dinah do to make her feel like a star again?

Radio Fifth Grade
by Gordon Korman
Benjy is the disc jockey for Kidsview, the fifth grade's school radio show, and he's determined to do everything he can to make people listen!

**Thank You,
Dr. Martin Luther King, Jr.**
by Eleanora Tate
When two storytellers visit her school, Mary Elouise discovers that performing is one way to proclaim her pride in herself and her African-American heritage.

Bard of Avon: The Story of William Shakespeare
by Diane Stanley and Peter Vennema
The great playwright and his times are brought to life in words and pictures in this lively biography.

**Sojourner Truth:
Ain't I a Woman?**
by Patricia and Fredrick McKissack
The courageous and eloquent Sojourner Truth spoke out in the fight to abolish slavery, and later became a pioneer women's-rights activist.

Theater Magic: Behind the Scenes at a Children's Theater
by Cheryl Walsh Bellville
Learning lines, building sets, sewing costumes— so many things go into putting on a stage production! This photo essay traces the process from start to finish, using an actual production of *The Nightingale* as a model.

xMedia

Videos

Software

Magazines

The Girl Who Spelled Freedom
Disney

Based on a true story, this video focuses on a family who leaves Cambodia to begin a new life in America. As their daughter begins to learn English, she develops a passion for spelling that leads her to win an important spelling bee. (90 minutes)

Voices of Sarafina
PBS/Pacific Arts Video

This documentary tells the story of a group of young South Africans who performed in a powerful anti-apartheid musical. (60 minutes)

Storyteller
Multimeanings
(IBM CD-ROM)

Storytellers can help pass on their cultural histories. This interactive video includes music, games, and lots of information. Choose the language you want to use: English or Spanish.

Video Jam
EA Kids
(Mac, IBM)

Choose from over 50 musical works, a variety of characters, special effects, and background scenes, to create your very own music videos.

Plays
Plays

This magazine is a source for all kinds of plays suitable for classroom and school productions.

Storyworks
Scholastic Inc.

This entertaining magazine includes stories and interviews, and has a play in every issue!

A Place to Write

Toastmasters International
2200 North Grand Avenue
Santa Ana, CA 92711

Write for information about a program that can help you become a better public speaker.

AMERICA'S

JOURNAL

Tour
a Historical Museum

Considering different points of view gives us a fuller understanding of history.

Many Sources

We use a variety of sources to learn about history.

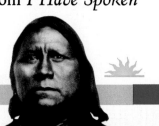

Robert Gard

Professor of Drama, University of Wisconsin

I SET OUT for the University of Kansas on a September morning with $30 that I'd borrowed from my local bank. I had one suit and one necktie and one pair of shoes. My mother had spent several days putting together a couple of wooden cases of canned fruits and vegetables. My father, a country lawyer, had taken as a legal fee a 1915 Buick touring car. It was not in particularly good condition, but it was good enough to get me there. I fell to pieces and it never got back home anymore.
I had no idea how long the $30 would last, but it sure would have to go a long way because I had nothing else. The semester fee was $22, so that low...

A Story Well Told

History can be retold in vivid ways.

THE TOP NEWS EVENTS
OF 1993–1994

OLYMPICS
PROVE
GOLDEN

In February, the world was
treated to two exciting weeks
of sport during the Winter
Olympics. The games were
held in or near the
Norwegian town of
Lillehammer. The U.S.
Winter Olympic team
collected 13 medals, its
highest total ever.

UNREST IN
RUSSIA

Fears continue that Russia
may be in for more
upheavals. President Boris
Yeltsin's reforms have created many enemies. Rising
prices, crime, and other
problems have fueled growing dissatisfaction among
political opponents as well as
the Russian public.

Many Voices

Historians compare many sources.

Trade Books

The following
trade books accompany this
America's Journal
SourceBook.

Fiction

Ben and Me

by Robert
Lawson

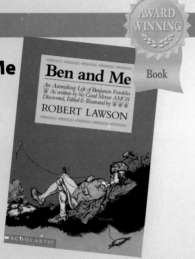

AWARD WINNING Book

Realistic Fiction

The Captive

by Joyce Hansen

AWARD WINNING Book

Historical Nonfiction

Children of the Wild West

by Russell
Freedman

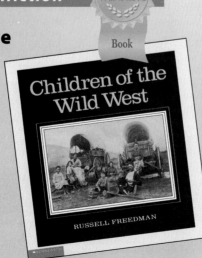

AWARD WINNING Book

Historical Fiction

Morning Girl

by Michael
Dorris

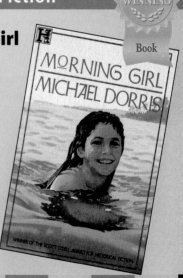

AWARD WINNING Book

Many Sources

Travel the Oregon Trail as you read the journal of a pioneer woman. Then follow the trail on a map.

See westward expansion through the eyes of a Native American chief.

Take a ride with cowboys of the Old West. Sing a song of the *vaqueros*.

WORKSHOP 1

Learn about the past from an eyewitness when you compile an oral history.

Robert Gard

Professor of Drama, University of Wisconsin

I SET OUT for the University of Kansas on a September morning with $30 that I'd borrowed from my local bank. I had one suit and one necktie and one pair of shoes. My mother had spent several days putting together a couple of wooden cases of canned fruits and vegetables. My father, a country lawyer, had taken as a legal fee a 1915 Buick touring car. It was not in particularly good condition, but it was good enough to get me there. It fell to pieces and it never got back home anymore. I had no idea how long the $30 would last, but it sure would have to go a long way because I had nothing else. The semester fee was $22, so that left me $8 to go. Fortunately, I got a job driving a car for the dean of the law school. That's how I ... the first year ... was to get a pound of hamburg-... about five cents, take ... and

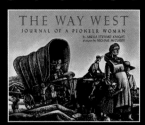

AWARD
WINNING

Book

THE W

JOURNAL OF A PIONEER

AY WEST

WOMAN   by AMELIA STEWART KNIGHT
pictures by MICHAEL McCURDY

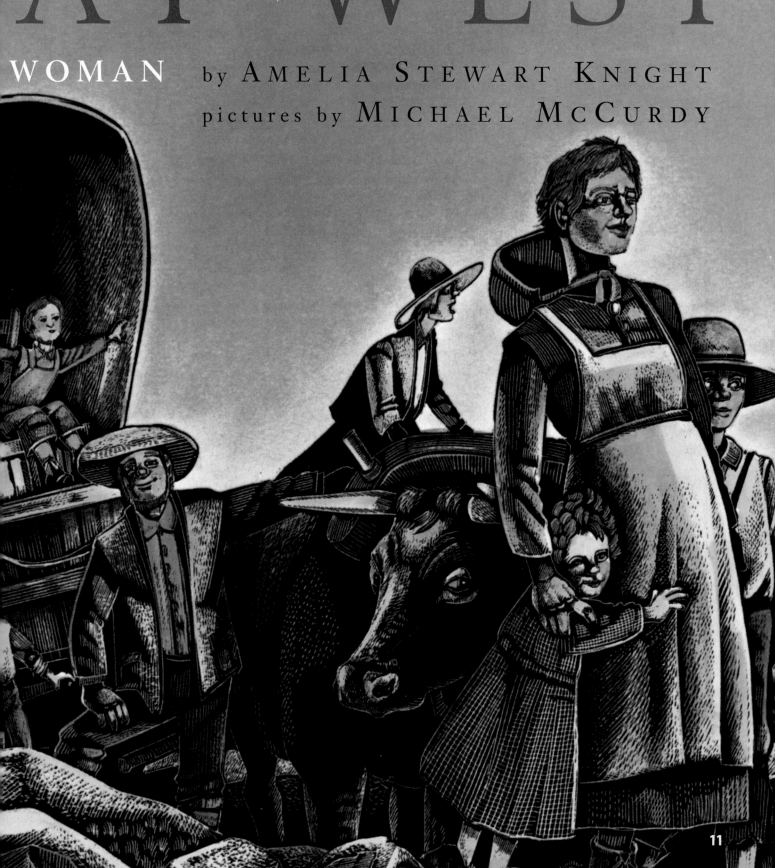

INTRODUCTION

This is the true story of Amelia Stewart Knight, her husband, and their seven children, who set out from Monroe County, Iowa, for the Oregon Territory in 1853. The boys were named Jefferson, Seneca, Plutarch, and Chatfield. The girls were Lucy, Frances, and Almira. The Knights started their journey in Iowa. Other families started in little towns along the Missouri River called jumping-off places because the travelers were leaving the United States and setting out through Indian Territory.

The overlanders traveled in big wagons pulled by yokes of six or eight oxen. Mrs. Knight cooked with "buffalo chips" over dusty fires. She rolled her pie dough on the wagon seat. If a family took their cows and dogs with them, the animals had to walk beside the wagons for more than a thousand miles.

A big wagon heavy with supplies could travel only ten or fifteen miles a day. It might take four to six months for a family to reach the Pacific coast. Only a few places existed on the long road where they could stop for repairs or more food. When the oxen got tired, or when the road got too rough, families lightened their loads by throwing away things they loved—rocking chairs, cradles, and even a piano might be left at the side of the road.

There were many rivers to cross on the long journey. But the people were ingenious; they painted the sides of their wagons with tar to keep water out. Then they lifted the wagon right off the flatbed and floated it across the river like a boat. They piled their belongings on the wagon bed and pushed that across the river like a raft. Indians helped the overlanders, warning them against quicksand, and trading salmon, deer meat, and moccasins for cloth and money.

When the overlanders came to the mountains, the work was different. The men pulled the wagons up to the mountaintops with winches and chains, and the women and children set rocks at the back wheels to keep the wagons from sliding down. Once they got to the top, the men tied strong rope around the wagons and pulled hard to keep them from smashing on the way down the other side.

Rain soaked through the canvas covers of the wagons, and people often became ill. Children were injured climbing on and off the moving wagons, and sometimes got lost when they strayed.

Mrs. Knight does not tell you until the very end that she is expecting another baby. You must remember her secret as you read.

LILLIAN SCHLISSEL

SATURDAY, APRIL 9, 1853. STARTED FROM HOME about eleven o'clock and traveled eight miles and camped in an old house; night cold and frosty.

MONDAY, APRIL 11, 1853. Jefferson and Lucy have the mumps. Poor cattle bawled all night.

THURSDAY, APRIL 14, 1853. Sixteen wagons all getting ready to cross the creek. Hurrah boys, all ready. Gee up Tip and Tyler, and away we go, the sun just rising.
(evening) The men have pitched the tent and are hunting something to make a fire to get supper.

SATURDAY, APRIL 16, 1853. Made our beds down in the tent in the wet and mud. Bed clothes nearly spoiled. Cold and cloudy this morning, and everybody out of humour. Seneca is half sick. Plutarch has broke his saddle girth. Husband is scolding and hurrying all hands and Almira says she wished she was home and I say ditto. "Home, Sweet Home."

THURSDAY, APRIL 21, 1853. Rained all night; is still raining. I have just counted seventeen wagons traveling ahead of us in the mud and water. No feed for our poor stock to be got at any price. Have to feed them flour and meal.

SATURDAY, APRIL 23, 1853. Still in camp. It rained hard all night, and blew a hurricane almost. All the tents were blown down, and some wagons capsized…. Dreary times, wet and muddy and crowded in the tent, cold and wet and uncomfortable in the wagon. No place for the poor children.

MONDAY, MAY 2, 1853. Pleasant evening. Threw away several jars, some wooden buckets, and all our pickles. Too unhandy to carry. Indians come to our camp every day, begging money and something to eat. Children are getting used to them.

SATURDAY, MAY 7, 1853. We have crossed a small creek, with a narrow Indian bridge across it. Paid the Indians seventy-five cents toll.

SUNDAY, MAY 8, 1853. There are three hundred or more wagons in sight and as far as the eye can reach, the land is covered, on each side of the river, with cattle and horses. There is no ferry here and the men will have to make one out of the tightest wagon bed. Everything must now be hauled out of the wagons, then the wagons must be all taken to pieces, and then by means of a strong rope stretched across the river, with a tight wagon bed attached to the middle of it, the rope must be long enough to pull from one side to the other, with men on each side of the river to pull it. In this way we have to cross everything a little at a time. Women and children last, and then swim the cattle and horses. There were three horses and some cattle drowned while crossing this place yesterday.

WEDNESDAY, MAY 11, 1853. It has been very dusty yesterday and today. The men all have their false eyes (goggles) on to keep the dust out.

FRIDAY, MAY 13, 1853. It is thundering and bids fair for rain. Crossed the river very early this morning before breakfast. Got breakfast over after a fashion. Sand all around ankle deep; wind blowing; no matter, hurry it over. Them that eat the most breakfast eat the most sand.

MONDAY, MAY 16, 1853. This afternoon it rained, hailed, and the wind was very high. Have been traveling all the afternoon in mud and water up to our hubs. Broke chains and stuck in the mud several times. The men and boys are all wet and muddy.

TUESDAY, MAY 17, 1853. I never saw such a storm. The wind was so high I thought it would tear the wagons to pieces. All had to crowd into the wagons and sleep in wet beds with their wet clothes on, without supper.

MONDAY, MAY 23, 1853. The road is covered with droves of cattle and wagons—no end to them.

TUESDAY, MAY 24, 1853. Husband went back a piece this morning in search of our dog, which he found with some rascals who were trying to keep him.

SATURDAY, MAY 28, 1853. Passed a lot of men skinning a buffalo. We got a mess and cooked some of it for supper. It was very good and tender. It is the first we have seen dead or alive.

TUESDAY, MAY 31, 1853. When we started this morning there were two large droves of cattle and about fifty wagons ahead of us, and we either had to stay poking behind them in the dust or hurry up and drive past them. It was no fool of a job to be mixed up with several hundred head of cattle, and only one road to travel in, and the drovers threatening to drive their cattle over you if you attempted to pass them. They even took out their pistols. Husband drove our team out of the road entirely, and the cattle seemed to understand it all, for they went into a trot most of the way. The rest of the boys followed with their teams and the rest of the stock. It was a rather rough ride to be sure, but was glad to get away from such a lawless set…. We left some swearing men behind us.

TUESDAY, JUNE 7, 1853. Just passed Fort Laramie and a large village of Sioux Indians. Numbers of them came around our wagons. Some of the women had moccasins and beads, which they wanted to trade for bread. I gave the women and children all the cakes I had baked. Husband traded a big Indian a lot of hard crackers for a pair of moccasins, [but when they] had eaten the crackers he wanted the moccasins back. We handed the moccasins to him in a hurry and drove away as soon as possible.

SATURDAY, JUNE 11, 1853. The last of the Black Hills we crossed this afternoon, over the roughest and most desolate piece of ground that was ever made (called by some the Devil's Crater). Not a drop of water, nor a spear of grass, nothing but barren hills.
—We reached Platte River about noon, and our cattle were so crazy for water that some of them plunged headlong into the river with their yokes on.

WEDNESDAY, JUNE 15, 1853. Passed Independence Rock this afternoon, and crossed Sweetwater River on a bridge. Paid three dollars a wagon and swam the stock across. The river is very high and swift. There are cattle and horses drowned there every day; there was one cow went under the bridge and was drowned, while we were crossing. The bridge is very rickety and must soon break down.

TUESDAY, JUNE 21, 1853. We have traveled over mountains close to banks of snow. Had plenty of snow water to drink. (Mr. Knight) brought me a large bucket of snow and one of our hands brought me a beautiful bunch of flowers which he said was growing close to the snow which was about six feet deep.

WEDNESDAY, JUNE 22, 1853. Very cold. Water froze over in the buckets; the boys have on their overcoats and mittens.

SUNDAY, JUNE 26, 1853. All hands come into camp tired and out of heart. Husband and myself sick. No feed for the stock. One ox lame. Camp on the bank of Big Sandy again.

MONDAY, JUNE 27, 1853. It is all hurry and bustle to get things in order. It's children milk the cows, all hands help yoke these cattle, the d– – –l's in them. Plutarch answers, "I can't, I must hold the tent up, it's blowing away." Hurrah boys. Who tied these horses? "Seneca, don't stand there with your hands in your pockets. Get your saddles and be ready."

WEDNESDAY, JUNE 29, 1853. The wagons are all crowded at the ferry waiting with impatience to cross. There are thirty or more to cross before us. Have to cross one at a time. Have to pay [the Indians] eight dollars for a wagon; one dollar for a horse or a cow. We swim all our stock.

SUNDAY, JULY 3, 1853. Two of our oxen are quite lame.

MONDAY, JULY 4, 1853. Chatfield has been sick all day with fever partly caused by mosquito bites.

THURSDAY, JULY 7, 1853. Our poor dog gave out with the heat so that he could not travel. The boys have gone back after him.

THURSDAY, JULY 14, 1853. It is dust from morning until night, with now and then a sprinkling of gnats and mosquitoes, and as far as the eye can reach there is nothing but a sandy desert, covered with wild sagebrush, dried up with the heat. I have ridden in the wagon and taken care of Chatfield till I got tired, then I got out and walked in the sand and through stinking sagebrush till I gave out.

SUNDAY, JULY 17, 1853. Travel over some rocky ground. Chat fell out of the wagon, but did not get hurt much.

FRIDAY, JULY 22, 1853. Here Chat had a very narrow escape from being run over. Just as we were all getting ready to start, Chatfield, the rascal, came around the forward wheel to get into the wagon, and at that moment the cattle started and he fell under the wagon. Somehow he kept from under the wheels, and escaped with only a good, or I should say, a bad scare. I never was so much frightened in my life.

SATURDAY, JULY 23, 1853. The empty wagons, cattle, and horses have to be taken further up the river and crossed by means of chains and ropes. The way we cross this branch is to climb down about six feet on the rocks, and then a wagon bed bottom will just reach across from rocks to rocks. It must then be fastened at each end with ropes or chains, so that you can cross on it, and then we climb up the rocks on the other side, and in this way everything has to be taken across. Some take their wagons to pieces and take them over in that way.

MONDAY, JULY 25, 1853. We have got on to a place in the road that is full of rattlesnakes.

THURSDAY, JULY 28, 1853. Have traveled twelve miles today and have camped in the prairie five or six miles from water. Chat is quite sick with scarlet fever.

FRIDAY, JULY 29, 1853. Chat is some better.

THURSDAY, AUGUST 4, 1853. Have seen a good many Indians and bought fish of them. They all seem peaceable and friendly.

FRIDAY, AUGUST 5, 1853. Tomorrow we will cross the Snake River. Our worst trouble at these large rivers is swimming the stock over. Often after swimming half the way over, the poor things will turn and come out again. At this place, however, there are Indians who swim the river from morning till night. There is many a drove of cattle that could not be got over without their help. By paying a small sum, they will take a horse by the bridle or halter and swim over with him. The rest of the horses all follow and the cattle will almost always follow the horses.

MONDAY, AUGUST 8, 1853. We left, unknowingly, our Lucy behind. Not a soul had missed her until we had gone some miles, when we stopped awhile to rest the cattle. Just then another train drove up behind with Lucy. She was terribly frightened and so were some more of us when we found out what a narrow escape she had run. She said she was sitting under the bank of the river when we started and did not know we were ready. And I supposed she was in Carl's wagon, as he always took charge of Frances and Lucy.... He supposed she was with me. It was a lesson to all of us.

FRIDAY, AUGUST 12, 1853. We were traveling slowly when one of our oxen dropped dead in the yoke. We unyoked and turned out the odd ox, and drove around the dead one.... I could hardly help shedding tears, and shame on the man who has no pity for the poor dumb brutes that have to travel and toil month after month on this desolate road.

WEDNESDAY, AUGUST 17, 1853. There are fifty or more wagons camped around us. Lucy and Almira have their feet and legs (covered with poison ivy).
—Bought some fresh salmon of the Indians this evening, which is quite a treat to us. It is the first we have seen.

WEDNESDAY, AUGUST 31, 1853. It is still raining this morning. The air cold and chilly. It blew so hard last night as to blow our buckets and pans from under the wagons, and this morning we found them scattered all over the valley.

THURSDAY, SEPTEMBER 1, 1853. After traveling eleven miles and ascending a long hill, we have encamped not far from the Columbia River and made a nice dinner of fried salmon. Quite a number of Indians were camped around us, for the purpose of selling salmon to the emigrants.

SATURDAY, SEPTEMBER 3, 1853. Here husband (being out of money) sold his sorrell mare (Fan) for a hundred and twenty-five dollars.

MONDAY, SEPTEMBER 5, 1853. Ascended a long steep hill this morning which was very hard on the cattle and also on myself, as I thought I never should get to the top.

FRIDAY, SEPTEMBER 9, 1853. There is a great deal of laurel growing here, which will poison the stock if they eat it. There is no end to the wagons, buggies, yokes, chains, etc., that are lying all along this road. Some splendid good wagons, just left standing, perhaps with the owners' names on them; and many are the poor horses, mules, oxen, cows, etc., that are lying dead in these mountains.

SATURDAY, SEPTEMBER 10, 1853. It would be useless for me to describe the awful road we have just passed over…. It is very rocky all the way, quite steep, winding, sideling, deep down, slippery and muddy…and this road is cut down so deep that at times the cattle and wagons are almost out of sight…the poor cattle all straining to hold back the heavy wagons on the slippery road.

TUESDAY, SEPTEMBER 13, 1853. We are in Oregon, with no home, except our wagons and tent.

SATURDAY, SEPTEMBER 17, 1853. A few days later my eighth child was born. We picked up and ferried across the Columbia River, utilizing skiff, canoes, and flatboat to get across, taking three days to complete. Husband traded two yoke of oxen for a half section of land with one half acre planted to potatoes, and a small log cabin and lean-to with no windows.

THIS IS THE JOURNEY'S END.

OREGON

Stories of rich farmland in Oregon gave many Easterners "Oregon Fever." The rugged trail that led them there was the longest of the great overland routes used in the westward expansion of the United States. Pioneers traveled the 2,000-mile trail one step at a time.

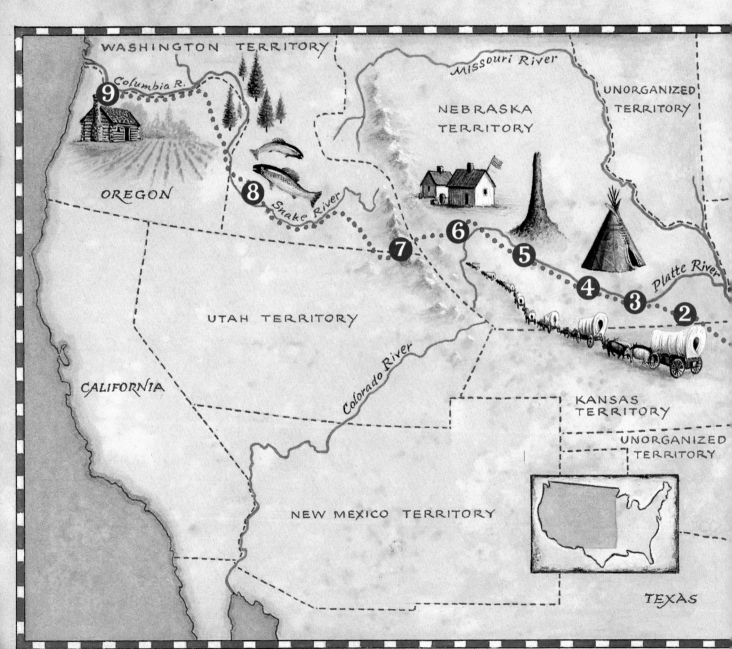

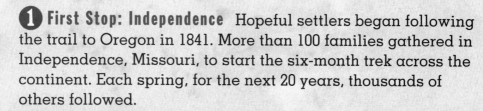

FEVER

1 First Stop: Independence Hopeful settlers began following the trail to Oregon in 1841. More than 100 families gathered in Independence, Missouri, to start the six-month trek across the continent. Each spring, for the next 20 years, thousands of others followed.

2 Wagons, Ho! The settlers joined together in wagon trains to cross the treeless plains. Wagon trains stretched for five miles and included three times more cattle and horses than people!

3 Follow the Platte Nebraska's chief river, the Platte, was too shallow for navigation, but settlers were able to follow its banks upstream.

4 Native Lands The land settlers crossed belonged to the Pawnee, Sioux, Arapaho, Cheyenne, and Crow. These Native Americans hoped the pioneers would pass through their land quickly.

5 Chimney Rock When settlers reached this 500-foot column of rock in the Nebraska Territory, they knew they had traveled about 550 miles. (But they still had a long way to go!)

6 Fort Laramie Fort Laramie was a trading post filled with useful goods such as flour, blankets, tools, rope, and water. After three months on the long trail, some people found it hard to leave.

7 South Pass Crossing the Rocky Mountains through South Pass was one of the most difficult parts of the trek. Stubborn cattle, plus heavy wagons, had to be hauled through treacherous ravines.

8 The Snake River By the fourth month, most wagon trains reached the Snake River. Its salmon-filled waters and surrounding green forests gave settlers renewed hope.

9 Journey's End! For most settlers arriving in the 1840s and 1850s, the journey's end was the beautiful and fertile Willamette River Valley.

Map of the Oregon Trail, circa 1853

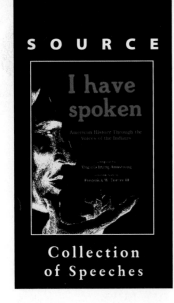
from I HAVE SPOKEN

Orator of the Plains

by

Satanta,

KIOWA CHIEF

I love the land and the buffalo and will not part with it. I want you to understand well what I say. Write it on paper....I hear a great deal of good talk from the gentlemen, but they never do what they say. I don't want any of the medicine lodges [schools and churches] within the country. I want the children raised as I was....

I have heard that you intend to settle us on a reservation near the mountains. I don't want to settle. I love to roam over the prairies. There I feel free and happy, but when we settle down we grow pale and die. I have laid aside my lance, bow, and shield, and yet I feel safe in your presence. I have told you the truth. I have no little lies hid about me, but I don't know how it is with the commissioners. Are they as clear as I am? A long time ago this land belonged to our fathers; but when I go up the river I see camps of soldiers on its banks. These soldiers cut down my timber; they kill my buffalo; and when I see that, my heart feels like bursting; I feel sorry. I have spoken.

Satanta, the "Orator of the Plains"

from

A LIBRARY OF CONGRESS BOOK

COWBOYS

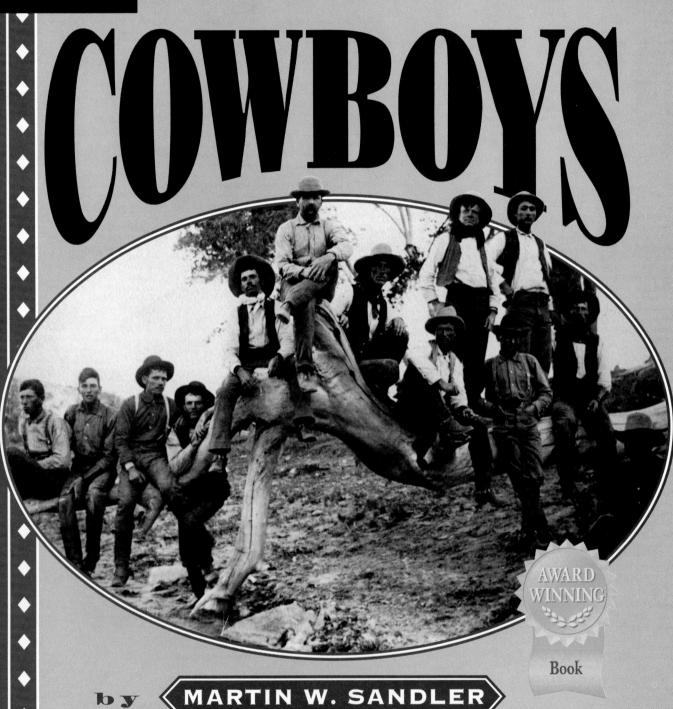

AWARD
WINNING

Book

by MARTIN W. SANDLER

An
American Hero

He is perhaps the greatest of all our heroes. More songs have been written about him and more movies have been made about him than about any other figure in American history.

Since he first came on the scene, magazines and books have been filled with stories about him. Some of the stories are true. Many are not, but they add to the myths that surround him.

e is the American cowboy, and he needs no invented myths to celebrate him.

The real story is heroic enough. It is a story of men and women on horseback who turned hard work, open spaces and brave deeds into a much-envied way of life.

A Cowboy's Life

The cowboy has a tough job to do. He is in the saddle ten to fourteen hours a day. Much of his time is spent on the range tending the cattle, chasing stray steers and calves and mending fences. Each spring he is involved in rounding up the cattle, branding the calves and then leading the herds over long trails to distant markets. Most of the cowpunchers are young—in their twenties. Many are teenagers.

Everything a cowboy wears has a purpose. His wide-brimmed hat shields him from the sun and the rain. The chaps he wears over his trousers protect him from the prickly underbrush through which he rides. His high-heeled boots keep his feet from pushing through the saddle's stirrups. On the ground, his boots allow him to get a firm footing while he brings a roped steer to a halt.

The cowhand is at the center of the giant American cattle industry. Between the late 1860's and the late 1890's, the cattle he raises will supply much of the meat that will help feed a rapidly growing nation. In that brief time, more than 40,000 cowboys will raise over nine million cattle and herd them overland to far-off railroad centers. There they will be shipped to even more distant slaughterhouses and meat-packing plants.

The cowboy is a special kind of person. He is in love with nature, particularly with the great open spaces of the American West. He has a deep respect and caring for the animals around him. Above all, he places personal freedom before everything else. His way of life becomes the envy of millions of his fellow Americans, who live in crowded cities and work in stifling factories.

> *Any cowboy who says he ain't never been throwed is a liar.*
>
> —Cowboy saying

Cowboys spend most of their time on horseback, and they need to change to a fresh horse three or four times a day. Ranch owners supply the animals, but they are wild and need to be broken in. It takes several weeks and many bone-jarring sessions to tame a bucking bronco, a task that tests the courage and skill of every cowboy who attempts it.

Breaking horses is a dangerous job. On the large ranches, men called broncobusters are hired to break in the wild horses. But even these specially trained cowboys often meet with disaster. Over the years, far more cowpunchers will be seriously injured or even killed in accidents on horseback than in the more romantic gunfights that will later fill movie and television screens.

Over the years, many myths will grow up around the American cowboy. In truth, most cowboys will never see a Native American, let alone fight one. Very few will have the chance to rescue beautiful women. But one fact will not be exaggerated: The cowboys will spend their days in the saddle, and their fame as horsemen will be well deserved.

Most of the horses that the cowboys ride are descendants of animals brought to America by the Spanish. In fact, almost everything cowboys wear or use is borrowed from Spanish-speaking cattlemen called *vaqueros* who, in the late 1700's, brought their horses, cattle and skills from Mexico into Texas. It is the *vaquero* who is the true ancestor of the American cowboy.

The cowboys come from many different backgrounds. Some are veterans of the Civil War. Many are young men from the East looking for adventure, and almost all are seeking a new way of life. Many of them are African Americans. At the height of the cattle trade, more than 5,000 African-American cowboys will work on ranches, large and small, throughout the West.

Many of the African-American cowboys are ex-slaves from Texas. During their days in slavery they broke horses and herded cattle. They are excellent horsemen. Some work the ranches for a while and then find a new occupation: They become members of all-black units in the United States cavalry, where they carve out a proud record.

Many African-American cowboys are freemen from the North. Several of these cowpunchers will become famous for their riding, roping and broncobusting skills. The most famous of all will be Bill Pickett, who develops a brand-new method of throwing and holding a steer by biting into its lower lip as a bulldog might do. Thanks to him, the term "bull-dogging" becomes an important part of the cowboys' language.

I never hankered for to plow or hoe,
And punching steers is all I know.
With my knees in the saddle and
*   a-hanging to the sky,*
Herding dogies up in heaven in the
*   sweet by-and-by.*

—From song, "The Old Chisholm Trail"

*Last night as I lay on the prairie
And looked at the stars in the sky,
I wondered if ever a Cowgirl
Could get to that "Sweet By-and-By."*

—From song, "The Cowgirl's Dream"

Not all the cowpunchers are men or boys; some are women. Throughout the West there are cowgirls who work the range and take part in cattle drives. Many are the wives and daughters of ranch owners. A few own their own ranches.

Cowgirls live in a man's world. They have to prove themselves every day. Those who are successful learn to ride, rope and shoot as well as their male counterparts do.

In fact, some cowgirls become even more skilled than most of the men. Before their days on the range are over, many cowgirls will be hired to show off their talents in the wild west shows that will become so popular around the world. One of the great stars of several of these shows will be Annie Oakley, who demonstrates that she can outshoot almost any man in the West. Audiences everywhere applaud the skill and daring of these hard-shooting, hard-riding women.

PAWNEE BILL'S HISTORIC WILD WEST
AMERICA'S NATIONAL ENTERTAINMENT

BEAUTIFUL DARING WESTERN GIRLS AND MEXICAN SEÑORITAS IN A CONTEST OF EQUINE SKILL.

Cielito Lindo

The generations of easterners (and perhaps even some modern westerners) who grew up watching William S. Hart, Tom Mix, Gene Autry, Roy Rogers, and John Wayne in the movies and on television may find it difficult to see cowboys as anything other than blue-eyed men with names like McCoy, Murphy, and Jones. In fact, the pedigree of all cowboys—black, white, brown, red—is found not in the freedom of the plains but in the slavery of Spanish America.

When the cattle herds of the early Spanish missions had grown too large for the priests to manage, they trained mission Native Americans—who under Spanish colonial law were free, but for all practical purposes were enslaved to the mission and its surrounding ranches—as horsemen. These early cowboys were called *vaqueros*—from the the Spanish word *vaca*, meaning "cow." To this day, a cowboy who likes to wear fancy duds and ornaments is called a buckaroo, which is how *vaquero* sounded to Anglo ears.

By the eighteenth century, most *vaqueros* were of mixed Native American and Spanish ancestry. They roped steers with a loop of braided rawhide called *la reata* (the later cowboy's lariat) and wore leather leggings, called *chaparreras* (chaps) to protect themselves from razor-sharp chaparral.

The "singing cowboy" of films and television could also trace his pedigree back to the Hispanic *vaquero*. While "Cielito Lindo," a traditional Spanish song, might have been too emotional for the stoic Anglo buckaroo, even he would have appreciated the message of its familiar chorus: "Sing and don't cry."

Singing Vaquero
Emanuel Wyttenbach, American, 1857–1894
Brown and gray wash heightened with white

Brightly

A pronunciation guide for the Spanish lyrics appears in italics.

De la Sie - rra Mo - re - na, Cie - li - to
Day lah See-ay - rah Moe - ray - nah, See-ay - lee - toe

Lin - do vie - nen ba - jan - do.
Leen - doe bee-ay - nen bah - han - doe.

Un par de o - ji - tos ne - gros, Cie - li - to
Oon pahr day oh - hee - tohs nay - grohs, See-ay - lee - to

Lin - do, de con - tra - ban - do.
Leen - doe, day cone - trah - bahn - doe.

ENGLISH TRANSLATION:

From the Sierra Morena, Cielito Lindo, they come softly stealing.
Laughing eyes, black and roguish, Cielito Lindo, their beauty revealing.

CIELITO LINDO *(Continued)*

Ay, Ay, Ay, Ay! ... Can-
Eye, eye, eye, eye! ... *Cahn-*

ta y no llo - res, ... Por - que can - tan - do se a -
tah ee no yo - rays, ... *Pore - kay cahn - tahn - doe say ah -*

le - gran Cie - li - to Lin - do los co - ra -
lay - grahn See - ay - lee - toe Leen - doe lohs coe - rah -

1.
zo - nes.
so - nays.

2.
zo - nes.
so - nays.

Ay, ay, ay, ay! Sing and don't cry,
Because singing raises the spirits, Cielito Lindo, and gladdens the heart.

How to Conduct an Oral History

In some societies, history is passed down almost entirely through the spoken word. Collecting oral histories is one way that historians learn about the past.

What is an oral history? An oral history is the spoken recollections of one person. It is information about past events that has been passed on by word of mouth.

Robert Gard

Professor of Drama, University of Wisconsin

I SET OUT for the University of Kansas on a September morning with $30 that I'd borrowed from my local bank. I had one suit and one necktie and one pair of shoes. My mother had spent several days putting together a couple of wooden cases of canned fruits and vegetables. My father, a country lawyer, had taken as a legal fee a 1915 Buick touring car. It was not in particularly good condition, but it was good enough to get me there. It fell to pieces and it never got back home anymore.

I had no idea how long the $30 would last, but it sure would have to go a long way because I had nothing else. The semester fee was $22, so that left me $8 to go. Fortunately, I got a job driving a car for the dean of the law school. That's how I got through the first year.

What a pleasure it was to get a pound of hamburger, which you could buy for about five cents, take it up to the Union Pacific Railroad tracks and have a cookout. And some excellent conversation. And maybe swim in the Kaw River. One friend of mine came to college equipped. He had an old Model T Ford Sedan, about a 1919 model. He had this thing fitted up as a house. He lived in it all year long. He cooked and slept and studied inside that Model T Sedan. How he managed I will never know. I once went there for dinner. He cooked a pretty good one on a little stove he had in this thing. He was a brilliant student. I don't know where he is now, but I shouldn't be surprised if he's the head of some big corporation. (Laughs.)

1 Choose a Topic

Decide on an event or a time period that you would like to know more about. Perhaps you are interested in the first moon landing, or maybe you're curious about the 1960s in general. Make sure your topic is something that someone you know has lived through. For example, you can't record an oral history about the Civil War, which ended about 130 years ago.

Once you've chosen a topic, find a friend or family member who remembers it and would like to talk to you about it!

TOOLS

- paper and pencil

- cassette recorder or video camera (optional)

2 Prepare Questions

What do you want to know about the topic you've chosen? Make a list of the questions you'd like to have answered. Leave plenty of space after each question to jot down the answer. You may want to find out a few basic facts, such as how old your subject was during the event or era you're researching, where he or she lived, and what he or she felt was most exciting or important about the topic you chose.

3 Conduct an Interview

Collect an oral history by conducting an interview with the person you've chosen. Get the ball rolling by asking some basic questions such as those suggested in Step 2. Be sure to write down (and ask!) any new questions you think of during the interview.

Some questions may prompt long, complicated answers. Don't worry about writing them down word for word. Make note of the main points and fill in the gaps when the interview is over.

Tip Ask your subject to show you artifacts such as school yearbooks, sports memorabilia, magazines, newspaper clippings, letters, and photographs from the period you are investigating.

4 Present Your Work

Write your oral history using a question-and-answer format. Feel free to leave out any questions and answers, or parts of answers, that you feel are uninteresting or unimportant.

Share your oral history with your class. Find out if any of your classmates collected an oral history on the same event or era you chose. Compare the two histories to find out how they are alike and how they are different.

If You Are Using a Computer …

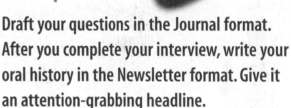

Draft your questions in the Journal format. After you complete your interview, write your oral history in the Newsletter format. Give it an attention-grabbing headline.

THINK

How are oral histories different from the stories you read in most history books?

Russell Freedman
Historian/Author ▶

A Story Well Told

Experience immigrant life in New York City at the turn of the century.

Read about Russell Freedman, a writer who brings history to life.

Meet Ellen Toliver, a fictional heroine of the American Revolution. Read a famous poem about a real-life hero.

WORKSHOP 2

Make history come alive when you compile a Year in Review.

THE TOP NEWS EVENTS OF 1993–1994

OLYMPICS PROVE GOLDEN
In February, the world was treated to two exciting weeks of sport during the Winter Olympics. The games were held in or near the Norwegian town of Lillehammer. The U.S. Winter Olympic team collected 13 medals, its highest total ever.

UNREST IN RUSSIA
Fears continue that Russia may be in for more upheavals. President Boris Yeltsin's reforms have created many enemies. Rising prices, crime, and other problems have fueled growing dissatisfaction among political opponents as well as the Russian public.

ALL SOUTH

MIDDLE EAST PEACE

At Home

from IMMIGRANT KIDS

by

Russell Freedman

Most turn-of-the-century immigrants settled in America's big cities. The immigrants needed jobs. The cities were growing fast and offered the best chances to find work. By 1910, three out of four people in New York City were immigrants and the children of immigrants. The same thing was true in Boston, Cleveland, Chicago, and Detroit.

Many immigrants could not speak English when they arrived. They knew little about American laws and customs. And so they clustered together, living in ethnic neighborhoods where they could mingle with their countrymen and speak their native languages. Almost every major city had its German and Irish neighborhoods, its Polish, Italian, Jewish, and Greek districts. People from the same village in Europe might wind up living as neighbors on the same street in America.

In most cities, immigrants moved into old, run-down neighborhoods. As newcomers, struggling to gain a foothold in America, they occupied the poorest and most congested districts. New York City absorbed more immigrants than any other city. Manhattan's Lower East Side, where so many immigrants settled, became one of the most densely populated places on earth.

Bargaining with a pushcart vendor

A walk through a crowded immigrant neighborhood was like a visit to the old country. The streets were noisy open-air markets. Pushcarts lined the pavements, offering fruit, vegetables, poultry, fish, eggs, soda water, and anything else you could think of—old coats for fifty cents, eyeglasses for thirty-five cents, hats for a quarter, ribbons for a penny. Peddlers hawked their wares in a dozen different dialects. Women wearing kerchiefs and shawls haggled for the best prices. Everyone except the kids seemed to be speaking a foreign language. Looking down upon these streets were the brick tenement buildings, where millions of immigrants began their lives in America.

Orchard Street on New York City's Lower East Side, 1898 (photo by Byron)

**Room in an immigrant family's tenement apartment, 1910
(photo by Jessie Tarbox Beals)**

Tenements were jammed with immigrants living in small, cramped apartments. The family shown above used a single makeshift room for cooking and eating, and as a bedroom for the kids. The parents slept in a tiny bedroom to the rear.

Family supper in a tenement kitchen (photo by Lewis Hine)

A more prosperous family might have three rooms: a parlor (or living room); a kitchen; and a dark, windowless bedroom in between. The parlor often doubled as an extra bedroom, while the kitchen became the family's social center. In all tenements, the toilet (or water closet) was outside the apartment, in the hallway of the building. It was used by at least two families.

Community water faucet in a tenement hallway (photo by Lewis Hine)

In older tenements, the individual apartments had no running water. Tenants fetched their water from a community faucet in the hallway on each floor. And yet many immigrants had grown up in the old country carrying water from a well. To them, an inside faucet with running water seemed wonderful.

Leonard Covello has described his family's first American home and his mother's reaction to running water in the hallway:

> Our first home in America was a tenement flat near the East River at 112th Street.... The sunlight and fresh air of our mountain home in Lucania [southern Italy] were replaced by four walls and people over and under and on all sides of us, until it seemed that humanity from all corners of the world had congregated in this section of New York City....
>
> The cobbled streets. The endless, monotonous rows of tenement buildings that shut out the sky.... The clanging of bells and the screeching of sirens as a fire broke out somewhere in the neighborhood. Dank hallways. Long flights of wooden stairs and the toilet in the hall. And the water, which to my mother was one of the great wonders of America—water with just the twist of a handle, and only a few paces from the kitchen. It took her a long time to get used to this luxury....
>
> It was Carmelo Accurso who made ready the tenement flat and arranged the welcoming party with relatives and friends to greet us upon our arrival. During this celebration my mother sat dazed, unable to realize that at last the torment of the trip was over and that here was America. It was Mrs. Accurso who put her arm comfortingly about my mother's shoulder and led her away from the party and into the hall and showed her the water faucet. "Courage! You will get used to it here. See! Isn't it wonderful how that water comes out?"
>
> Through her tears my mother managed a smile.

In newer tenements, running water came from a convenient faucet above the kitchen sink. This sink was used to wash dishes, clothes, and kids. Water had to be heated on the kitchen stove. Since bathing was difficult at home, most immigrants went regularly to public bath houses.

Tenement apartments had no refrigeration, and supermarkets had not yet been invented. Kids were sent on daily errands to the baker, the fishmonger, the dairyman, or the produce stall. They would rush down rickety tenement stairs, a few pennies clutched tightly in their hands. Since there were no shopping bags or fancy wrappings either, they would carry the bread home in their arms, the herring in a big pan from mother's kitchen.

Carrying home the groceries (photo by Lewis Hine)

Some immigrants had big families. (photo by Augustus F. Sherman)

Many immigrants had to take in roomers or boarders to help pay the rent. Five or six people might sleep in one crowded room. Children were commonly tucked three and four to a bed. Privacy was unknown, and a room of one's own was a luxury beyond reach. When an immigrant family could occupy a three-room apartment without taking in boarders, they were considered a success.

On hot summer days, the stifling tenement rooms became unbearable. Whole families spilled out of their apartments, seeking relief up on the roof or down in the street, where there was some hope of catching a cooling breeze. Kids took over fire escapes and turned them into open-air clubhouses. They put up sleeping tents of sheets and bedspreads, and spent summer nights outside, as elevated trains roared past a few feet away.

Camping out on the fire escape, August, 1916

Russell Freedman

Historian/Author

History writers manage *information* about the past.

Russell Freedman is crazy about history. He studies it, he reads about it, and he has written many nonfiction books about United States history.

"History isn't just a bunch of dates and facts," Freedman says. "History is the stories of real people in real situations."

In his books, Russell Freedman brings those stories to life. How does he do it?

PROFILE

Name:
Russell
Freedman

Occupation: historian/author

Education: University of
California at Berkeley

Favorite subjects in school:
English and history

Favorite person from history:
Abraham Lincoln

Favorite childhood books:
*Treasure Island,
Call It Courage*

Favorite library: the
Donnell Library in
New York City

Pet: Sybil, a white cat
he rescued from the
streets of New York

QUESTIONS

for Russell Freedman

Here's how **Russell Freedman** **uncovers** the *real stories* about **past** events.

 What are the steps you take when putting together a book?

 First, I research my subject. Then, I write a table of contents so that I have a clear idea of where to start and where I'm going. Next, I write five drafts of the book: a rough draft to get my ideas down, a second draft to organize the book, a third draft to cut unnecessary material, and fourth and fifth drafts' to polish my writing.

 What do you look for when you research?

When I was researching *Cowboys of the Wild West*, for example, I relied on memoirs and diaries of cowboys. Librarians helped me find books on the subject that I hadn't read before. I also search for interesting and informative photos to illustrate my books.

 Does your research take you to interesting places?

 Frequently. Right now, I'm writing a book about Crazy Horse, a Native American chief. I've already been to Montana, to the Little Big Horn National Monument, where Crazy Horse led a famous battle against U.S. troops. I've also traveled to his homeland in the Black Hills of South Dakota.

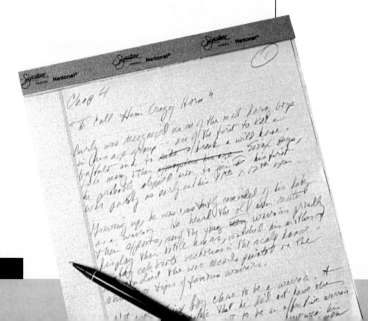

How do you choose the subjects of your biographies?

 It has to be somebody that I have a compelling interest in, and that I admire for some reason. The subject's life has to really mean something.

 Have kids ever inspired you to write a book?

 Well, I never intended to research the Wright Brothers until so many kids asked me questions about them. That's when I decided to do a little probing. The rest is history.

 How do you get readers interested in your topics?

 I focus on the details of the events or people I'm writing about so they seem as real as possible.

 Is it difficult to find the real story about some events in history?

 Yes. The book I'm writing about Crazy Horse has been my toughest project yet. His life isn't well documented, and there are contradictory stories about how he lived.

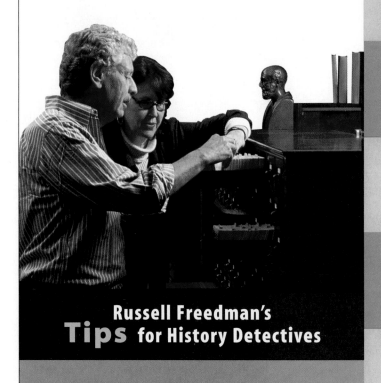

Russell Freedman's
Tips for History Detectives

1 Get interested. Never write about anything you don't care about.

2 Get current. Find the newest and most authoritative books on the subject.

3 Search for details. They'll give the reader a clearer sense of what you're writing about.

4 Be suspicious. Never have fewer than three different sources for the same event.

Toliver's Secret

AWARD
WINNING

Book

TOLIVER'S SECRET

by **Esther Wood Brady**

illustrations by **Paul Schmid**

Ten-year-old Ellen Toliver knows that the American war for independence isn't an easy one. Her father has been killed in battle against the British, and her older brother is still away fighting for the Patriots. Ellen and her mother live in New York with her grandfather, a Patriot who fights against the British in his own way. He's about to carry an important message to an agent of General George Washington, when he falls and sprains his ankle. Now it's up to Ellen to deliver the message into safe hands.

"I will explain to you what this is all about," said Grandfather, "and then you can decide what to do, Ellen. I hear a lot of talk among the British officers in my shop. I hear a lot in the Tavern, too. I have information that must get to General Washington by tomorrow night at the latest. It must get there without fail. That's why I have hidden it in a loaf of bread. The bread won't attract attention, and it can be passed from one messenger to another until it gets to headquarters."

With a frown on her face, Mother jumped up from her chair and stood in front of him. "How could a message be that important, now?" she protested. "It is only two weeks until Christmas! And the officers are planning to stop the war for Christmas. I know they are."

Grandfather scowled at her. "And how could you know that, pray tell?"

"Why," said Mother, "people all over New York are having parties and balls for the officers. I hear that hundreds of fruitcakes have been made already—and thousands of candles. That's what I heard when I went to the candle shop."

Grandfather shook his head. His face, usually so pink cheeked and jolly, looked gray and drawn.

"And General Howe loves parties," Mother pressed on eagerly. "They all love parties. I know there won't be any fighting at Christmastime!"

Grandfather's eyes were grim. "Nevertheless, this message is very important! Our army has been defeated time and time again for months!" He pulled his foot from the pot of water and sat up. "Why," he exclaimed, "the British brought thirty thousand men— three times as many as Washington had!" He swung his leg over the side of the couch as if, in his eagerness to do something for Washington's army, he was ready to start.

"Whatever information we Patriots here in New York can send him about the British is important! The only way we can win is by using surprise and cunning and determination." He started to get up, but his foot touched the floor, and he groaned and fell back on the couch.

He looked at Ellen intently. "Can you understand what I have been telling you?"

"I think so."

Ellen could see that Grandfather was very serious about the need to send his message. She, too, had been worried about all the news of lost battles and retreats, especially since Ezra was with that army. She remembered how joyous everyone had been last July when they heard about the Declaration of Independence. There had been bonfires on the village green and singing and dancing in the streets. And then the British army came to New York and there had been three months of defeat.

"If you understand how important it is to take the message, Ellen, I'll tell you how it can be done. And then you are to decide."

Ellen listened and didn't say a word.

"You walk down to the docks near the Market-house and get on a farmer's boat—or an oysterman's. They come over early every morning and they go back to Elizabeth-town at eleven o'clock. Elizabeth is a very small town. When you get off the boat, you'll find the Jolly Fox Tavern without any trouble. My good friend Mr. Shannon runs the tavern, and you give the loaf of bread to him. That's all there is for you to do, Ellen. The Shannons will welcome you and take good care of you."

Sailing across the Bay didn't seem so hard. It was finding a boat here in New York and asking a stranger for a ride that worried her.

"How could I find the right boat to take me?" she asked. She didn't intend to go, but she thought she'd ask anyway.

"The docks are right near Front Street where we walked on Sunday afternoon. The farmers and the oystermen tie up their boats near the Market-house. They are friendly people and they often take passengers back to Elizabeth-town since the ferryboat stopped running. I'll give you money to pay."

"And how would I get home again—if I should decide to go?" she said in a very low voice.

"Oh, the Shannons will put you on a boat early in the morning. You'll be back here by ten o'clock."

"Does Mr. Shannon take the bread to General Washington?" she asked.

"No, he takes it to a courier who will ride part of the way. Then he'll give it to another courier who will ride through the night with it. And finally a third man will carry it to the General in Pennsylvania."

Ellen thought about the messengers riding alone through the countryside to carry the secret message. She wondered how it felt to be all alone among the British soldiers.

Mother interrupted. "It's too much to ask of her, Father. She's only ten."

Her father reached out and squeezed her hand. "Abby, dear," he said, "I know you are distressed because of all that has happened this fall. But don't make the child timid. We all have to learn to do things that seem hard at first. A child can't start too early to learn that."

Ellen knew her grandfather wouldn't send her if he thought she couldn't do it. Now that she thought it over she knew that if she walked carefully she could remember the way to Front Street. And she would have money to pay for the boat. She had liked sailing across the East River when she and Mother had taken the ferryboat from Brooklyn to New York last November. Perhaps it wouldn't be too hard. "But what would I do if I got lost?"

"If you lose your way, just speak up and ask someone for directions," said Grandfather.

"You're sure there is no one else to take it for you, Grandfather?"

"With this bad ankle I can't walk around New York to find one of my friends—and I wouldn't know where to send you or your mother to look. Besides, there isn't time. I need your help, Ellen."

Ellen was quiet for a long time.

"Very well," she said finally. "I'll do it—if you are really sure I can."

"I know you can, Ellen. And Abby," he said, "this is nothing too hard for a child of ten. The Shannons will take good care of her, you may be sure of that. In that chest in the kitchen are clothes that Ezra left here years ago. Go out and see what you find, Ellen."

Now that she had decided to go, Ellen ran quickly to the kitchen and poked around among the blankets and old clothes in the chest that sat near the fireplace. She was eager to see what was there. "Here's a striped cap," she exclaimed. "And here's that old blue jacket with the holes in the elbows. I remember these brass buttons." Grandfather had bought Ezra all new clothes when he had come to New York to visit several years ago.

Ellen put on a red knitted shirt that was too small and the blue wool jacket that was too big. The brass buttons made her think of Ezra's grin. She put on heavy gray stockings before she pulled up the short breeches. The leather breeches were so old and stiff they could almost stand alone. She kicked up her legs to make them soften up.

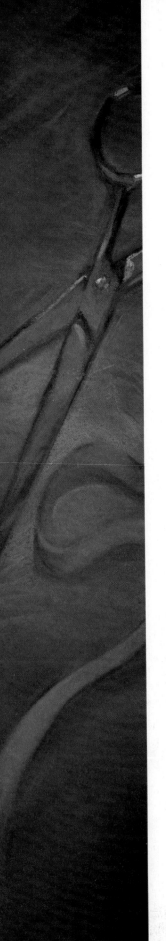

Not since she was a small child had she known what fun it was to kick her legs as high as she could. She tried to kick the skillet that hung beside the fireplace.

"These will be better for walking than petticoats," she said as she pranced about the kitchen. "Why can't girls wear these, too?"

"Ellen Toliver," said her mother primly. "It would be unseemly."

After trying on Ezra's boots, which were too big for her, she decided she would wear her own leather shoes to make walking easier. Certainly it would be easier to jump out of the way of horses and wheelbarrows and it would be better for climbing on the boat.

She ran into the shop to show her grandfather how she looked. For the first time since he fell on the ice, Grandfather laughed. "You look like a ragged little urchin all right," he said, "with those holes in your elbows. But all the better. No one will even notice you. And now we must cut your hair."

Mother picked up the scissors and stroked Ellen's long brown hair. "Couldn't we just tuck her hair under the cap?" she asked.

"No," said Ellen firmly. "I might forget and take it off! That would be dreadful. Besides, it might look bunchy beneath a cap." Better to have it short and not worry about it. She remembered her friend Lucinda who had short hair with a band of ribbon around her head. Lucinda looked very pretty with short hair. "Cut it off!" she said impatiently.

Grandfather smiled from his couch. "You'll do right well, Ellen," he said. "Tie a pigtail in back with a cord and then just snip off the part that is too long."

Ellen could feel her mother's hands tremble as she tied back the hair and snipped at the long pigtail.

"It will grow back," Ellen said to her. "How do I look?" Jumping up from the chair she stepped over the hair on the floor and stared at herself in the mirror.

"Why, I favor my father with my hair tied back!" she exclaimed. Her brown eyes were just like her father's eyes although not stern like his. Her face was thin like his, too. She stared at herself. Suddenly the person staring back at her didn't look like Ellen Toliver, and for a minute it frightened her to look so changed. Glancing sideways she could see her grandfather smiling his old cheerful smile.

Mother had given him the loaf of bread which he was wrapping in a blue kerchief and tying with a good strong knot.

"Where shall I hide the bread?" Ellen asked him.

"Don't hide it," he told her. "Don't think of hiding it. Just go along swinging this blue bundle as if it were nothing at all. There is only one thing to be careful about, Ellen. Be sure you give the bread to no one but Mr. Shannon."

His eyes grew as hard as they had been earlier that morning, when she surprised him in the kitchen. "No one but Mr. Shannon. He and I might hang if we were caught."

"Hang!" cried Ellen. "You mean on a gallows tree?"

Ellen's hands trembled so that she could hardly button the brass buttons on her jacket. No one had mentioned hanging before. If she had known her grandfather might hang she never would have agreed to do it. It wasn't fair. She gulped and at last the words came out. "I can't do it, Grandfather. I just can't. I'm too scared and I might make a mistake."

"You can do it, Ellen. Better than anyone else. No one in the world will suspect a loaf of bread in the hands of a child. If, perchance, someone found the message in the bread, just act surprised and say you don't know a thing about it!" He smiled at her to encourage her. "Just hang onto the bread good and tight until you see Mr. Shannon. That won't be hard to do, now will it?"

"But don't talk to any strangers, Ellie," Mother pleaded.

"Now, Abby. She has common sense."

"You're sure I won't make a mistake, Grandfather?"

"I can't see where you could go wrong, Ellen. The boatmen are kindly and they take people every day. And at the other end of the trip are my good friends the Shannons."

"Well, then," she said. "I think I am all ready now."

"Good!" cried Grandfather. "When you hand the bread to Mr. Shannon say this to him, 'I have brought you a present for your birthday.' He will understand what it means."

Mother slipped two corncakes into her pocket. "You'll get hungry before you get there, I'm sure." She was trying hard to sound cheerful. "I've always heard about Mistress Shannon's good potpies, and now you can eat one."

Grandfather slipped some coins into her pocket. Then he squeezed her hand until it hurt.

"God bless you, Ellen. I'm proud of you."

Mother pulled the red and white striped cap down around her ears and gave her a pair of mittens as well as a hug that almost smothered her. Then she stepped to the door and opened it. "I think you are a brave girl, Ellen."

Ellen stood at the top of the steps and looked up and down the street. She took a deep breath. Mother had said she was brave and Grandfather had said he was proud of her—well, she hoped they were right.

At first it felt strange to be walking down the same old street, looking like someone else. Ellen was sure people were watching her and wondering why she was dressed as a boy. What should she say if a woman walked up to her and asked, "Why is a girl wearing those clothes? It's not very seemly to show your legs." She'd pretend the woman had mistaken her for someone else.

But after a while, in Ezra's old breeches, her legs free of skirts and petticoats, she found it was fun to stomp along the cobblestones. She forgot what people might say. It was fun to dodge the oxcarts and the wheelbarrows and run against the wind with no cloak to hold her back. No one noticed her at all.

When she came to the pump corner she saw that Dicey and the two Brinkerhoff boys were having a snowball fight.

"That's a fair match," Ellen said to herself. She turned her head so Dicey could not see her. "Let them fight it out."

But she knew Dicey had seen her when she heard her call out, "Stop!" Ellen's heart almost stood still.

"New boy!" Dicey called. "What's your name?"

Why, Dicey didn't know her! It was just like being invisible. Dicey had looked at her and didn't know her.

Ellen peeped over her shoulder just in time to see Aaron Brinkerhoff push Dicey against a tree trunk and hold her there while Arnie gleefully scrubbed her face with handfuls of snow.

"Stop!" screamed Dicey. "Stop! Two against one ain't fair." She kicked and twisted away from them. Then, to Ellen's surprise, Dicey turned and ran away, crying like a bawling calf. Ellen stood and stared at her. For a moment she even felt sorry for her.

"Well, at least she didn't know me," Ellen said to herself. "I feel invisible."

"I'm invisible, I'm invisible," she kept saying as she ran happily down the street. Already she felt better about making the trip.

And then she felt a whack on her back that sent her spinning across the slippery cobblestones. The blue kerchief with her grandfather's loaf of bread flew from her hands.

Swift as hawks after a field mouse the two Brinkerhoff boys swooped down and snatched up her blue bundle.

"Try and get it! Try and get it!" Aaron called out. He held it out to her with an impudent grin on his face. When his brother Arnie grabbed for the bundle, Aaron snatched it away and ran. They played with it as if it were a ball, tossing it back and forth and daring her to chase them.

Ellen stood frozen with fear. What if the bread was torn apart. And the snuffbox fell out. And the British officers learned that Grandfather was a spy! It was too horrible to think of. Grandfather hanging on a gallows tree.

Her hands became fists as she thought how two laughing boys could put them all in such danger.

"Thieves!" she could hear herself shouting. "Stop those thieves!" She surprised herself by shouting those words in a loud strong voice. She surprised herself, too, by racing after the boys, dodging in and out of the crowds, tripping over children and ducking under the noses of dray horses.

"Stop those thieves!" she screamed. "They stole my bread!"

She ran up to two redcoats who stood on the steps of a bakeshop, eating hot little pies while they flirted with a group of kitchen maids.

"Please, sirs!" she gasped, "those thieves have stolen my bread!"

The soldiers shrugged and laughed. "Plenty of bread inside. The baker has just opened his ovens."

Now the boys were playing a game in front of a tailor's shop. They were tossing the blue bundle across his sign and hurling it between the wooden blades of a giant pair of scissors. Around them a crowd formed a circle to watch the fun.

"Give me my bread!" Ellen shouted as she leaped from one side to the other. She felt as nimble as a lamb without her long skirts and petticoats, but she never was quick enough to catch the bread.

Aaron mocked her. "Give the poor child his bread. He's starving!"

"Starving! Starving!" shrieked little Arnie. He held the bread out to her and then snatched it away when she jumped for it.

Two beggars watched with hungry eyes. Their bony fingers reached out to grab the bread. Even the public pig who ate scraps of garbage in the streets raced around them with greedy alert little eyes. The crowd laughed, but no one helped.

A little old woman who swept the steps of the tailor's shop with a broom of corn straw called out sharply. "What ails you Brinkerhoff boys? Always making trouble! Give the boy his loaf of bread!" She stepped down into the street and shook her broom at them. "Can't you see he's thin and hungry?"

Angrily she pushed her way through the crowd. Her back was so bent she was hardly as tall as Ellen, but she seemed to know what to do.

"Here," she said as she thrust her broom handle into Ellen's hands. "Here, trip them up. Bread is precious these days."

Ellen snatched the broomstick from the old woman.
Without a moment's hesitation she raised it up and brought it
down with a whack across Aaron's legs. Her eyes were blazing
as she watched him duck out of her way. It made her feel good
to hear him yell, "Stop," and see him dance away from her.

Arnie snatched the bundle from his brother's hands, and
whirling it about his head, he grinned at her. "Try and get it!"
he shrieked as he turned to push his way through the circle
of people.

Ellen rushed after Arnie and whacked his legs, too. Her
anger was so great she whacked at his legs until he fell sprawling
on the ground.

Quick as a flash she scooped up the bundle, dropped her
broom and looked for a way out of the circle.

"This way!" cried the little old woman gleefully.
She held out her arms and made an opening for Ellen
to get through. "Run like the wind, boy," she cried.
"They'll be after you."

Ellen raced down the street. Her feet seemed to have wings. "Where to go? Where to hide?" she thought desperately as she looked over her shoulder and saw that the boys and the hungry beggars and even that awful public pig were after her.

Two boys might catch a girl who never had run on cobblestones before. But no one could catch a girl who held her grandfather's secret snuffbox in her arms.

"Stop him!" she could hear Arnie Brinkerhoff shout. "Stop the thief!"

The thief! Why, it was her loaf of bread. And why would they want it? It was just a game to them. No more important than a snowball.

She jumped over the low stone wall of a churchyard and raced across the flat gravestones. Looking back, she could see that she must have lost the beggars and the pig. Only the boys were following her. And a church warden who ran after her flapping his arms and shouting, "Be gone! Be gone!"

Over the wall she scrambled and into a street filled with haycarts going to the officers' stables. Under one cart and around another she darted. Farmers shook their pitchforks at her as she whirled past. "Don't alarm the horses!" they cried. But Ellen didn't hear them.

She had no idea where she was now as she raced around corners and down streets filled with rubble. Everywhere there were black walls of houses with roofs that had fallen in.

Gasping for breath she darted through a doorway of a broken-down house and crept into an old fireplace to hide. She was sure she had outrun the boys, but she couldn't stop the shaking of her knees. They jerked up and down like puppets on strings.

She sat down in the old ashes of the fireplace, tucked her arms around her knees and put her head on her arms. Her breath came in great sobs and blew the ashes up around her, covering her breeches with a fine dust.

"This must be the way rabbits feel—when the hounds chase them. If only I were back at home—I could crawl into bed and pull the covers over my head."

Those boys! Those horrible boys! To spoil everything at the beginning. It wasn't to have been such a long walk to Front Street. She had done it before with Grandfather.

"And now I don't know where I am," she wailed.

Grandfather had never brought her to the west side of town where the great fire burned block after block last September. It made him too sad to look at it, he said. Six hundred houses had been burned. And Trinity Church. It was lucky the whole city didn't burn up!

Slowly she began to collect her wits. Grandfather would have to find someone else to carry his message. She'd go home and tell him he had asked too much of her. She couldn't go out on the streets and roister about like a boy. She couldn't go sailing across the Bay to a place where she had never been and find a man she had never seen. That was asking too much of a ten-year-old girl. She'd go home and tell him he must find someone else.

She waited a long time to make sure the boys had not followed her. As she waited she grew calm and a strange happy feeling came over her.

She, Ellen Toliver, had fought two boys in front of a crowd of people. She not only had raced them and beaten them but she had saved her grandfather's message. The bread was here with the snuffbox still inside. She could hardly believe it.

As she sat quietly, a new feeling of confidence came to her. "Perhaps I can try to walk to the docks after all." She took a deep breath. "Perhaps I can go to Jersey after all. Grandfather said it wasn't hard. I can start over again from here, if I can find my way to Front Street."

Very carefully she crept out of the fireplace and looked around. There were tents where people must be living amidst the broken-down walls. But she saw no one around. Only stray cats that slunk away in the rubble.

"It must be getting near ten o'clock," she said to herself. There were no church bells to ring the hour, for the wardens had hidden the bells when the British came. She looked up at the hazy sun that struggled wanly in a gray sky. Grandfather always pointed out directions by the shadows the sun cast. "If the sun is on my left side—that must be the east. And the East River would be that way."

Very carefully she picked her way through the black rubble flecked with white snow. And at last she came to streets lined with fine houses and beech and sycamore trees. These streets looked familiar and the breeze had the salty fish smell of the river.

As she stepped quickly along she had a feeling the trip wouldn't be so bad after all.

from

From Sea to Shining Sea

Paul Revere's Ride

by

Henry Wadsworth Longfellow

illustrations by Anita Lobel

Listen, my children, and you shall hear
Of the midnight ride of Paul Revere,
On the eighteenth of April, in Seventy-five;
Hardly a man is now alive
Who remembers that famous day and year.

He said to his friend, "If the British march
By land or sea from the town tonight,
Hang a lantern aloft in the belfry arch
Of the North Church tower as a signal light,—
One, if by land, and two, if by sea;
And I on the opposite shore will be,
Ready to ride and spread the alarm
Through every Middlesex village and farm,
For the country folk to be up and to arm."

Then he said, "Good night!" and with muffled oar
Silently rowed to the Charlestown shore,
Just as the moon rose over the bay,
Where swinging wide at her moorings lay
The *Somerset*, British man-of-war;
A phantom ship, with each mast and spar
Across the moon like a prison bar,
And a huge black hulk, that was magnified
By its own reflection in the tide.

Meanwhile, his friend, through alley and street,
Wanders and watches with eager ears,
Till in the silence around him he hears
The muster of men at the barrack door,
The sound of arms, and the tramp of feet,
And the measured tread of the grenadiers,
Marching down to their boats on the shore.

Then he climbed the tower of the Old North Church,
By the wooden stairs, with stealthy tread,
To the belfry-chamber overhead,
And startled the pigeons from their perch
On the somber rafters, that 'round him made
Masses and moving shapes of shade,—
By the trembling ladder, steep and tall,
To the highest window in the wall,
Where he paused to listen and look down
A moment on the roofs of the town,
And the moonlight flowing over all.

Beneath, in the churchyard, lay the dead,
In their night-encampment on the hill,
Wrapped in silence so deep and still
That he could hear, like a sentinel's tread,
The watchful night-wind, as it went
Creeping along from tent to tent,
And seeming to whisper, "All is well!"
A moment only he feels the spell
Of the place and the hour, and the secret dread
Of the lonely belfry and the dead;
For suddenly all his thoughts are bent
On a shadowy something far away,
Where the river widens to meet the bay,—
A line of black that bends and floats
On the rising tide, like a bridge of boats.

Meanwhile, impatient to mount and ride,
Booted and spurred, with a heavy stride
On the opposite shore walked Paul Revere.
Now he patted his horse's side,
Now gazed at the landscape far and near,

Then, impetuous, stamped the earth,
And turned and tightened his saddle-girth;
But mostly he watched with eager search
The belfry-tower of the Old North Church,
As it rose above the graves on the hill,
Lonely and spectral and somber and still.
And lo! as he looks, on the belfry's height
A glimmer, and then a gleam of light!
He springs to the saddle, the bridle he turns,
But lingers and gazes, till full on his sight
A second lamp in the belfry burns!

A hurry of hoofs in a village street,
A shape in the moonlight, a bulk in the dark,
And beneath, from the pebbles, in passing, a spark
Struck out by a steed flying fearless and fleet;
That was all! And yet, through the gloom and the light,
The fate of a nation was riding that night;
And the spark struck out by that steed in his flight,
Kindled the land into flame with its heat.
He has left the village and mounted the steep,
And beneath him, tranquil and broad and deep,
Is the Mystic, meeting the ocean tides;
And under the alders, that skirt its edge,
Now soft on the sand, now loud on the ledge,
Is heard the tramp of his steed as he rides.

It was twelve by the village clock
When he crossed the bridge into Medford town,
He heard the crowing of the cock,
And the barking of the farmer's dog,
And felt the damp of the river fog,
That rises after the sun goes down.

It was one by the village clock,
When he galloped into Lexington.
He saw the gilded weathercock
Swim in the moonlight as he passed,
And the meeting-house windows, blank and bare,
Gaze at him with a spectral glare,
As if they already stood aghast
At the bloody work they would look upon.

It was two by the village clock,
When he came to the bridge in Concord town.
He heard the bleating of the flock,
And the twitter of birds among the trees,
And felt the breath of the morning breeze
Blowing over the meadows brown.
And one was safe and asleep in his bed
Who at the bridge would be first to fall,
Who at the bridge would be lying dead,
Pierced by a British musket-ball.

You know the rest. In the books you have read,
How the British Regulars fired and fled,—
How the farmers gave them ball for ball,
From behind each fence and farmyard wall,
Chasing the redcoats down the lane,
Then crossing the fields to emerge again
Under the trees at the turn of the road,
And only pausing to fire and load.

So through the night rode Paul Revere;
And so through the night went his cry of alarm
To every Middlesex village and farm,—
A cry of defiance, and not of fear,
A voice in the darkness, a knock at the door,
And a word that shall echo forevermore!
For, borne on the night-wind of the Past,
Through all our history, to the last,
In the hour of darkness and peril and need,
The people will waken and listen to hear
The hurrying hoofbeats of that steed,
And the midnight message of Paul Revere.

How to Compile a Year in Review

This review covers one academic (school) year, rather than a calendar (January through December) year.

Recording and categorizing historical events helps to ensure that they won't be forgotten. The most important events of each year can be recorded in a Year in Review.

What is a Year in Review? A Year in Review is a review of major events that happened during the year. Often a Year in Review covers several categories, such as sports, entertainment, and politics. At the end of each year, many newspapers, magazines, and television news programs produce Years in Review.

Photos illustrate some of the most dramatic moments discussed in the review.

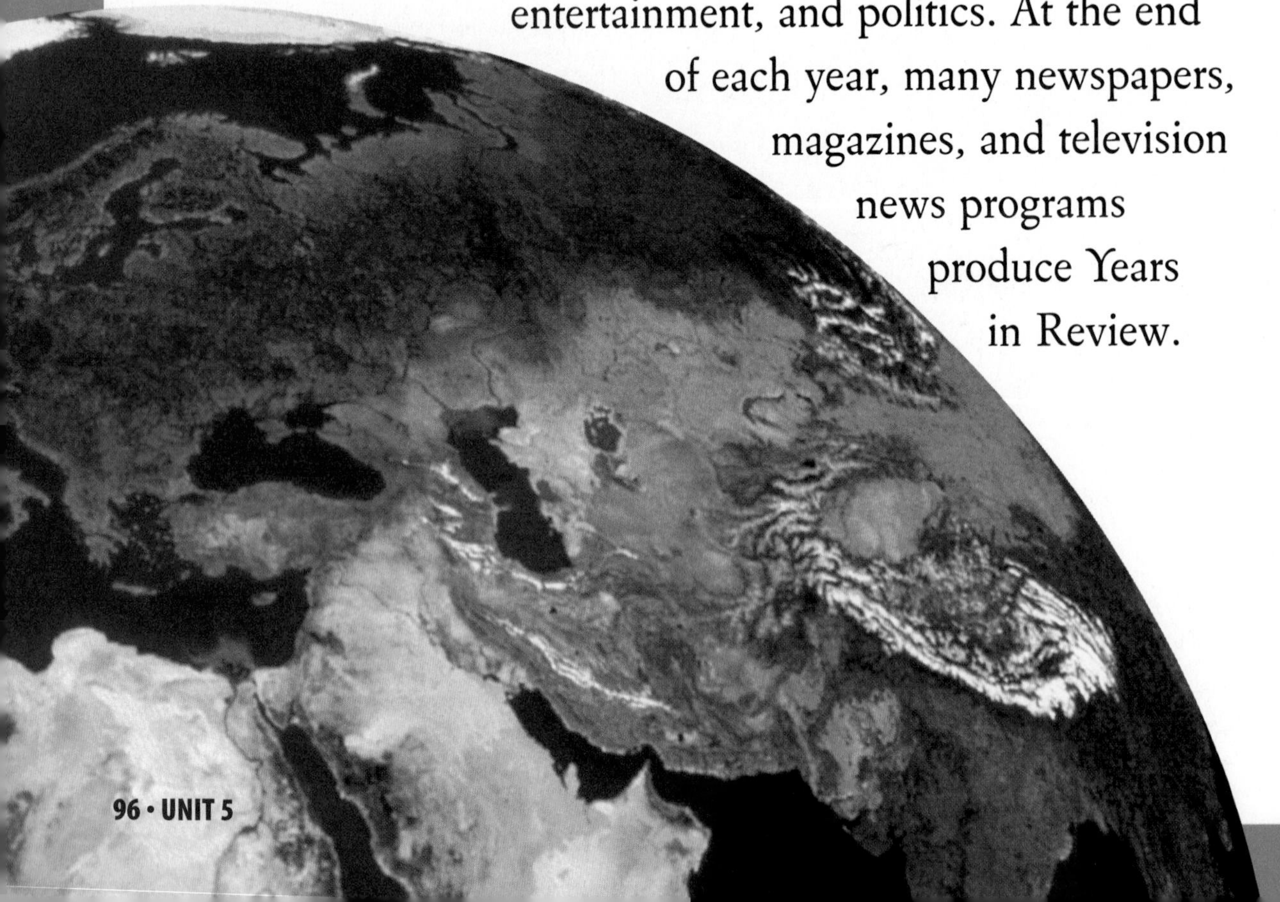

A title tells what type of events the Year in Review will cover.

THE TOP NEWS EVENTS OF 1993–1994

OLYMPICS PROVE GOLDEN

In February, the world was treated to two exciting weeks of sport during the Winter Olympics. The games were held in or near the Norwegian town of Lillehammer. The U.S. Winter Olympic team collected 13 medals, its highest total ever.

UNREST IN RUSSIA

Fears continue that Russia may be in for more upheavals. President Boris Yeltsin's reforms have created many enemies. Rising prices, crime, and other problems have fueled growing dissatisfaction among political opponents as well as the Russian public.

ALL SOUTH AFRICANS VOTE

South Africans cast their votes for a new government. Blacks make up 75 percent of South Africa's people. But it was the first time in the country's history that they were allowed to vote.

MIDDLE EAST PEACE AGREEMENT

For decades, Jews and Arabs in the Middle East have struggled to find some way to live in peace.

In September, the two sides took a big step toward peace. Israeli Prime Minister Yitzhak Rabin and Palestine Liberation Organization (PLO) Chairman Yasir Arafat agreed to a peace plan in Washington, D.C. "Enough of blood and tears. Enough," said Rabin.

DISASTERS ROCK THE U.S.

Relief agencies have been working around the clock to help Americans recover from a string of natural disasters.

1 Plan

Choose a year to review. You may want to examine this year and try to identify the important things that have happened so far. Or, you might choose another year, such as the year you were born. You will need to choose a topic, or several topics, to cover in your Year in Review. Some possibilities include the following:

* sports
* movies
* politics
* school and/or community events

TOOLS

* paper and pencil
* folders
* magazines and newspapers
* art supplies

2 Research

Begin your research by writing down all the important events that you remember from the year you chose. Once you've exhausted your own memory, use the library to continue your search for events. Newspapers, magazines, almanacs, videos, and computerized indexes are all helpful sources of information. Take and file notes on all of the information you've found.

Fashion
"Younger men turned to close-cropped hairstyles..."

Politics
Ronald Reagan becomes President of the United States on November 6, 1984. WIth 525 of a possible 538 votes in the Electoral College, he breaks Franklin Delano Roosevelt's 1936 record.

Sports
(baseball)
Detroit Tigers beat the San Diego Padres 8–4 to win the World Series.

(Olympic Track and Field)
Carl Lewis wins three gold medals at the Summer Olympics in Los Angeles.

Architecture/Historic Preservation
$30 million restora... begun on the Statu... Liberty
* funded by privat... donors; to be fin... in time for a ga... harbor celebrat... July 4, 1986

...ment
...the year:
...ones and
...ple of Doom
...rate Kid
...rek III: The
...ch for Spock

...elevision)
...he Cosby Show makes its debut, paving the way for a new genera- tion of television shows featuring African- American families.

Space
Kathryn Sulli... becomes the ... woman to m... space walk.

Tip Create a separate folder for each category your Year in Review will include. File your notes about each cate- gory in the appropriate folder.

3 Organize

Look through the information you've gathered. Think about how you will organize it in your Year in Review. If you have too much material, decide what's most important and delete the rest.

You may want to use one of the following organizational methods or come up with another on your own:

- Place the information in chronological (date) order.

- Make a top-five list for each category you plan to cover. Choose the five most important events in each category and include only those events.

4 Prepare and Present

Decide how to present your information. You might make a time line and illustrate it with drawings and photos. You could make a collage of clippings from various newspapers and magazines. You might even write a medley of short songs.

When you are finished, present your Year in Review to your classmates. Compare your own Year in Review to theirs. How did they present their information? How did different people cover the same years and events?

If You Are Using a Computer ...

You might want to organize your information using the Newsletter format on your computer. Create a chart or table with columns and headings for each category that you cover.

THINK

What did you learn about what makes an event important or memorable?

Russell Freedman
Historian/Author ▶

VOL. XIV.....NO. 4225.

HANG OUT YOUR BANNERS

UNION
VICTORY!
PEACE!

Surrender of General Lee and His Whole Army.

THE WORK OF PALM SUNDAY.

Final Triumph of the Army of the Potomac.

The Strategy and Diplomacy of Lieut.-Gen. Grant.

Terms and Conditions of the Surrender.

118

Many Voices

Join Toby Hanson, as he learns about the Underground Railroad.

Find out how American history inspired a famous painter.

Meet some very young soldiers who faced a food shortage during the Civil War. Read first-hand accounts of wartime experiences.

PROJECT

Research carefully and think critically as you write a historical account.

HISTORICAL WARMAP.

ASHER & CO.

Entered according to Act of Congress, in the Year 1863, by ASHER, & CO., in the Clerk's Office of the District Court for the State of Indiana.

SCALE OF MILES.

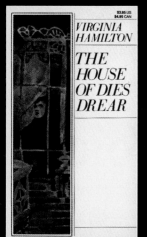

FROM

The House of Dies Drear

By VIRGINIA HAMILTON

Illustrations by KEAF HOLLIDAY

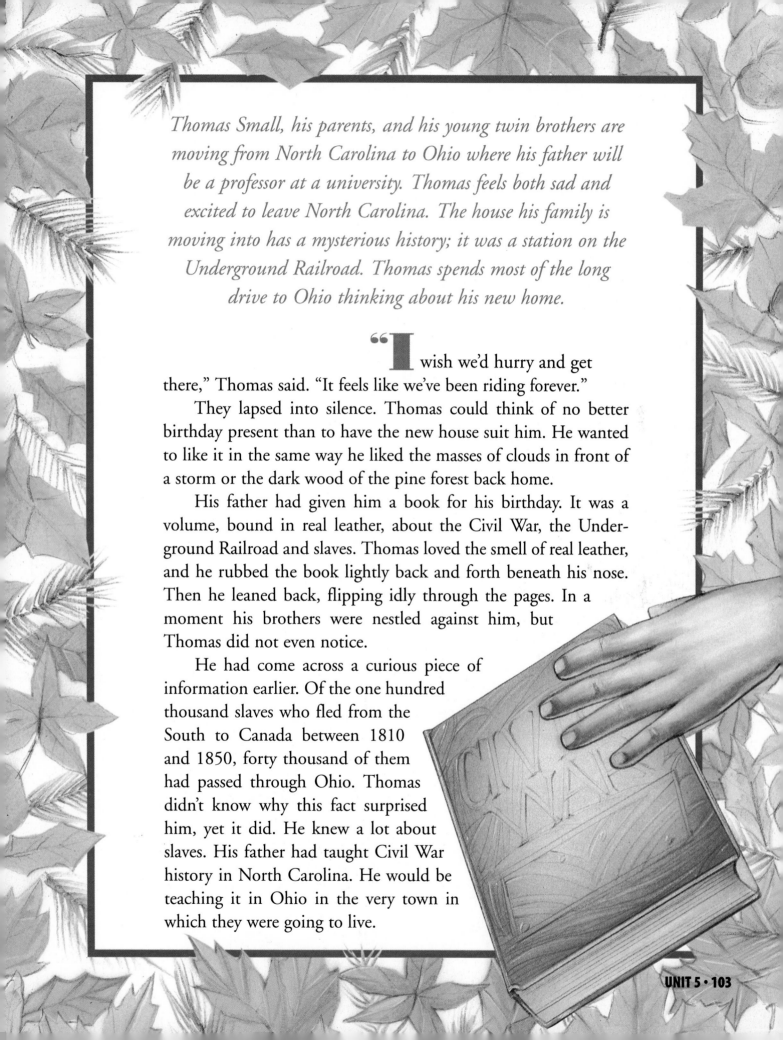

Thomas Small, his parents, and his young twin brothers are moving from North Carolina to Ohio where his father will be a professor at a university. Thomas feels both sad and excited to leave North Carolina. The house his family is moving into has a mysterious history; it was a station on the Underground Railroad. Thomas spends most of the long drive to Ohio thinking about his new home.

"I wish we'd hurry and get there," Thomas said. "It feels like we've been riding forever."

They lapsed into silence. Thomas could think of no better birthday present than to have the new house suit him. He wanted to like it in the same way he liked the masses of clouds in front of a storm or the dark wood of the pine forest back home.

His father had given him a book for his birthday. It was a volume, bound in real leather, about the Civil War, the Underground Railroad and slaves. Thomas loved the smell of real leather, and he rubbed the book lightly back and forth beneath his nose. Then he leaned back, flipping idly through the pages. In a moment his brothers were nestled against him, but Thomas did not even notice.

He had come across a curious piece of information earlier. Of the one hundred thousand slaves who fled from the South to Canada between 1810 and 1850, forty thousand of them had passed through Ohio. Thomas didn't know why this fact surprised him, yet it did. He knew a lot about slaves. His father had taught Civil War history in North Carolina. He would be teaching it in Ohio in the very town in which they were going to live.

He had taught Thomas even more
history than Thomas cared to know.
Thomas knew that Elijah Anderson had been
the "superintendent" of the Underground
Railroad in Ohio and that he had finally died in
prison in Kentucky. He knew that in the space of
seven years, one thousand slaves had died in Kentucky.
But the fact that forty thousand escaping slaves had fled
through Ohio started him thinking.

Ohio will be my new home, he thought. A lot of those
slaves must have stayed in Ohio because Canada was farther
than they could have believed. Or they had liked Elijah
Anderson so much, they'd just stayed with him. Or maybe
once they saw the Ohio River, they thought it was the Jordan
and that the Promised Land lay on the other side.

The idea of exhausted slaves finding the Promised Land on
the banks of the Ohio River pleased Thomas. He'd never seen
the Ohio River, but he could clearly imagine freed slaves riding
horses up and down its slopes. He pictured the slaves living in
great communities as had the Iroquois, and they had brave
leaders like old Elijah Anderson.

"Papa…" Thomas said.

"Yes, Thomas," said Mr. Small.

"Do you ever wonder if any runaway slaves from North
Carolina went to Ohio?"

Mr. Small was startled by the question. He laughed and said,
"You've been reading the book I gave you. I'm glad, it's a good
book. I'm sure some slaves fled from North Carolina. They
escaped from all over the South, and it's likely that half of them
passed through Ohio on their way to Canada."

Thomas sank back into his seat, arranging his sprawling
brothers against him. He smoothed his hand over the book and
had half a mind to read it from cover to cover. He would wake the
twins and read it all to them. They loved for him to read aloud,
even though they couldn't understand very much.

No, thought Thomas. They are tired from being up late last night. They will only cry.

Thomas' brothers were named Billy and Buster and they knew all sorts of things. Once Thomas had taken up a cotton ball just to show them about it. They under-stood right away what it was. They had turned toward Great-grandmother Jeffers' house. She had a patch of cotton in her garden, and they must have seen her chopping it.

They loved pine, as Thomas did, although they couldn't whittle it. Thomas' papa said the boys probably never would be as good at whittling as he was. Thomas had a talent for wood sculpture, so his father said. There were always folks coming from distances offering Thomas money for what he had carved. But Thomas kept most of his carvings for himself. He had a whole box of figures tied up in the trailer attached to the car. He intended placing them on counters and mantles all over the new house.

Thomas could sit in front of his brothers, carving an image out of pine, and they would jump and roll all around him. When the carving was finished, the twin for whom it was made would grab it and crawl off with it. Thomas never need say, and never once were the twins wrong in knowing what carving was for which boy.

They were fine brothers, Thomas knew.

If the new house is haunted, he thought, the twins will tell me!

The sedan headed through the Pisgah National Forest in the Blue Ridge Mountains, and then out of North Carolina.

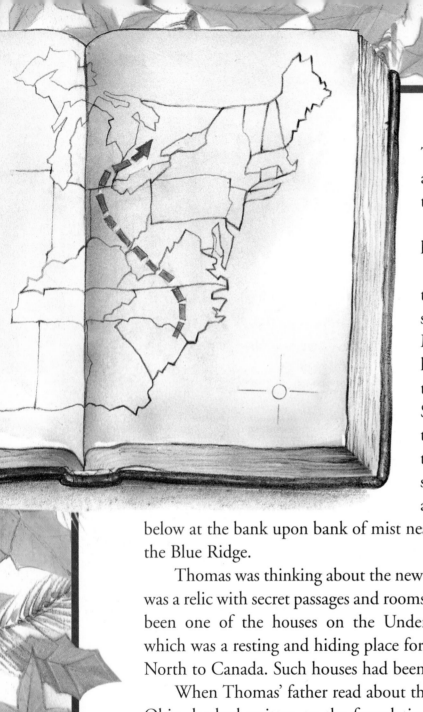

Thomas had seen a sign and knew exactly when they entered Virginia.

"That's done with," he said to himself.

If Mr. Small noticed they had left their home state, he gave no hint. Mrs. Small slept or at least kept her eyes closed. The twins awoke, and Mr. Small told Thomas to give them their lunch. Soon the boys were subdued, staring out the windows and eating, looking far below at the bank upon bank of mist nestled in the deep valleys of the Blue Ridge.

Thomas was thinking about the new house in Ohio. The house was a relic with secret passages and rooms. In Civil War times it had been one of the houses on the Underground Railroad system, which was a resting and hiding place for slaves fleeing through the North to Canada. Such houses had been secretly called "stations."

When Thomas' father read about the station house for rent in Ohio, he had written to the foundation that owned it for a full report. For years he had hoped to explore and possibly live in a house on the Underground Railroad. Now was his chance. But not until he saw the report did he find out how important the Ohio station had been. Those who ran the house in Ohio had an even greater task than the care and concealment of running slaves. They actually encouraged the slaves to let themselves be caught and returned to slavery!

Thomas hadn't believed slaves went willingly back into slavery until his father had explained it to him.

"If you'll recall your history, Thomas, you'll remember that the incredible history of the Underground Railroad actually began in Canada," his father had told him. Slaves who had reached Canada in the very early 1800s and established settlements there returned by the thousands to this country in order to free others. They came back for their families; they became secret "conductors" on the Underground Railroad system. And they returned to bondage hoping to free masses of slaves.

"But slaves continued to flee by whatever means," Mr. Small had said, "with or without help. Upon reaching the Railroad, they might hide in our house in Ohio, where they would rest for as little as a week. Some of them were given rather large sums of money and returned again to slavery."

"What would slaves need with money?" Thomas had wanted to know.

"Even a fleeing slave needs maneuvering money," his father had said. "He would need food and shelter and the best and safest way for him to get it was to buy it from freed Negroes."

"But the slaves connected with the house in Ohio were going back *into* slavery," Thomas had said.

"Yes," said Mr. Small. "And after they were caught and went back, they passed the hidden money on to other slaves, who would attempt to escape."

Still Thomas couldn't believe slaves could successfully hide money on themselves without having it found.

Some slaves did have their money found and taken away, his father said. It was dangerous work they were involved in. But others managed to return to bondage with the money still in their possession.

"Remember," his father had told him, "the slaves we're talking about weren't ordinary folks out for a peaceful stroll. Many had run for their lives for weeks from the Deep South. They had no idea how far they had to travel and they were armed with little more than the knowledge that moss grew only on the northern side of trees. Any who managed to get as far as Ohio and the Underground Railroad line had to be pretty brave and strong, and very clever. Most of them were young, with a wonderful, fierce desire to free themselves as well as others. It was the best of these who volunteered to return to slavery. They were hand-picked by Dies Drear himself, the abolitionist who built our house in Ohio. He alone conceived of the daring plan of returning numbers of slaves to the South with sizable amounts of money hidden on them."

"He must have been something!" Thomas had said.

"He was a New Englander," Mr. Small said, "so independent and eccentric, most Ohio abolitionists thought him crazy. He came from an enormously wealthy family of shipbuilders, and yet his house in Ohio was fairly modest. To give you an idea how odd he was," said Mr. Small, "his house was overflowing with fine antiques, which he neither took any interest in nor sold for profit. All the furniture remained in great piles, with just enough space to get through from room to room, until the house was plundered and Drear was killed.

"But when his plan to send slaves back to slavery worked," said Mr. Small, "there grew among freemen and slaves an enormous respect for him. You know, they never called him by his name, partly because they feared he might be caught, but also because they were in awe of him. They called him Selah. Selah, which is no more than a musical direction to raise the voice. And yet, Selah he was. *Selah*, a desperate, running slave might sigh, and the name— the man—gave him the strength to go on."

Selah. Freedom.

JACOB
LAWRENCE

Harriet Tubman as a baby (detail)

PAINTING

Jacob Lawrence was born in Atlantic City, New Jersey, in 1917. He studied at the Harlem Art Workshop and the American Artists School in New York City. Today, he is one of America's best-known painters.

Lawrence has received many awards and honors during his long career. He served as Commissioner of the National Council of the Arts under President Carter and received the National Medal of Arts from President Bush. His work is represented in the National Gallery of Art, the Metropolitan Museum of Art, the Vatican Museum, and many other public collections.

Runaway slaves asleep in a barn

THE PAST

Harriet Tubman leads runaway slaves across the snows of the North.

The paintings shown on these pages first appeared in a picture-book biography called *Harriet and the Promised Land*. Lawrence wrote and illustrated the book to honor Harriet Tubman and her brave actions as a leader of the Underground Railroad.

Of the book, Lawrence says, "The United States is a great country. It is a great country because of people like John Brown, Frederick Douglass, Abraham Lincoln, Sojourner Truth, and Harriet Tubman.... American history has always been one of my favorite subjects. Given the opportunity to select a subject from American history, I chose to do a number of paintings in tribute to Harriet Tubman, a most remarkable woman...."

Slaves escape in a "chariot" driven by Harriet Tubman.

Harriet Tubman guides a group of escaped slaves through the woods.

SOURCE

THE·BOYS'·WAR

Confederate and Union Soldiers
Talk About the Civil War
by Jim Murphy

Historical
Nonfiction

AWARD
WINNING

Book

A LONG *and* HUNGRY WAR

from

~

The Boys' War

~

~

by

JIM MURPHY

MANY OF THE SOLDIERS WHO FOUGHT IN THE CIVIL WAR WERE BOYS, SIXTEEN YEARS OLD OR YOUNGER. SOME OF THEM WERE AS YOUNG AS ELEVEN OR TWELVE. THEY MANAGED TO JOIN BOTH ARMIES—UNION AND CONFEDERATE— BY A VARIETY OF MEANS, BUT USUALLY BY SIMPLY LYING ABOUT THEIR AGES. IN **THE BOYS' WAR**, AUTHOR JIM MURPHY CHRONICLES THE WAR EXPERIENCES OF THE UNDERAGE SOLDIERS, OFTEN USING FIRST-PERSON ACCOUNTS FROM THEIR LETTERS AND DIARIES. IN THIS EXCERPT, MURPHY DESCRIBES HOW SOME YOUNG SOLDIERS FACED FOOD-SUPPLY SHORTAGES IN THE ARMY CAMPS.

ONCE IT WAS CLEAR TO BOTH SIDES THAT THEY WERE IN A real fight, one that was not simply going to fade away, some important steps had to be taken. First, many more soldiers would be needed. Second, the ragtag amateur soldiers would have to be better trained. And third, somehow, enough supplies and arms had to be found to keep the soldiers in the field.

The first two needs were reasonably easy to address. Before the first year of fighting was over, both the Union and Confederate governments issued calls for massive numbers of enlistments. These would not be ninety-day enlistments; the new soldiers would be signing on for three years! An estimated 2,898,304 would serve in the Union army during the war, while the Confederate side would see almost 1,500,000 join.

Creating good soldiers began with the officers. Many men had become officers through political favoritism or because they had been able to sign up enough recruits to make a regiment. Others were elected by the soldiers themselves, usually because they were popular, easygoing fellows. Such officers did not know how to handle groups of men during battle and never earned their respect, either.

The Union moved quickly to weed out these weak officers. Military boards were set up to examine officers, and over the next few months hundreds of officers were discharged or resigned. This did not put a complete end to the practice of appointing or electing officers, but it did establish some minimum standards for competence.

The South seemed to have gotten a better crop of officers from the start. Why did this happen? One reason is that of the eight military schools the country had in 1860, seven were located in the South. Generally, officers remained loyal to the regions where they were trained. Of the 1,900 men who had attended Virginia Military Academy, over 1,750 would serve for the South. This does not mean that every officer in the Confederate army was a seasoned veteran. One very young officer wrote, "While here at Taylorsville we have daily evening battalion drills, of which I know nothing in the world. In vain do I take Harder's Tactics in hand and try to study out the maneuvers."

It was not at all unusual to see large formations of soldiers being drilled by an officer with his manual of instructions firmly in hand. But as the officers learned their duties, so did the soldiers.

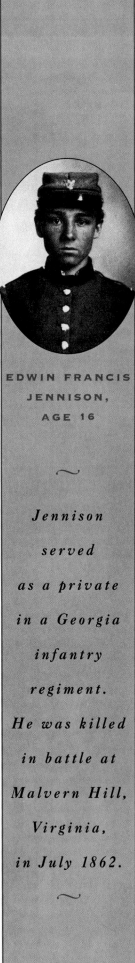

EDWIN FRANCIS JENNISON, AGE 16

~

Jennison served as a private in a Georgia infantry regiment. He was killed in battle at Malvern Hill, Virginia, in July 1862.

~

THE COOKS AT AN ARMY CAMP PREPARE TO SERVE A HOT MEAL.

The one problem neither side quite solved was how to supply their troops with enough food. A few statistics will show the immense size of the problem faced by each side. An army of 100,000 soldiers required 2,500 supply wagons and at least 35,000 horses and mules (for use by the cavalry and to haul the wagons and artillery). Men and horses consumed 600 tons of supplies *every day*!

Food had to be gathered from various growing regions and then shipped hundreds of miles by train to supply bases. Then it had to be loaded into wagons and brought to the troops in the field. As these full wagons were moving in, empty wagons had to be on the way back to the supply depots to load up the next day's supplies. All of this movement had to be timed and

BECAUSE SUPPLIES WERE GENERALLY SCARCE, A REGIMENT WAS ALLOWED A SPECIFIC AMOUNT OF EACH ITEM. HERE LOAVES OF BREAD ARE WEIGHED BEFORE DISTRIBUTION TO THE TROOPS.

carried out with precision if soldiers were going to be fed on time.

After a fumbling first year, both the Union and Confederate armies managed to organize and coordinate their supply efforts. And they worked reasonably well for the most part. Young Thomas Galway seemed pleased with his rations: "The food issued to the soldiers is very good and in ample quantity. It consists of salt pork or fresh beef; soft bread baked in field ovens, and hardtack on the march and in campaign; coffee and sugar; for vegetables, desiccated potatoes; mixed desiccated vegetables for soup; and beans, rice, and onions. Besides these, we can buy from the sutler all sorts of delicacies such as oysters, canned fruit, cheese, (and) raisins.…"

But the food-supply system was a delicate ballet of movement that could be disrupted by any one of a number of things. Spring rains might turn the dirt roads into a quagmire of mud that could delay wagons for several days. A sudden movement of troops might put them in an area without adequate roads, cutting them off from supplies for days or weeks. One sixteen-year-old soldier from New York, Charles Nott, tells about his regiment's troubles during a particularly cold winter: "Again we sat down beside [the campfire] for supper. It consisted of hard pilot-bread, raw pork and coffee. The coffee you probably would not recognize in New York. Boiled in an open kettle, and about the color of a brownstone front, it was nevertheless…the only warm thing we had. The pork was frozen, and the water in the canteens solid ice, so we had to hold them over the fire when we wanted a drink. No one had plates or spoons, knives or forks, cups or saucers. We cut off the frozen pork with our pocket knives, and one tin cup from which each took a drink in turn, served the coffee."

WILLIAM
BLACK,
AGE 12

~

Black

was the

youngest

known soldier

to be wounded

in the

Civil War.

~

Another common complaint among soldiers was that the food they did get was almost always the same—a never-ending diet of salt pork, dried beef, beans, potatoes, turnips, and corn. After eating army food for nearly three years, Frank Carruth wrote to his sister: "I want Pa to be certain and buy wheat enough to do us plentifully—for if the war closes and I get to come home I never intend to chew any more cornbread."

Luxuries such as eggs, milk, butter, wheat flour, and sugar were scarce at the best of times and often absent for months. No wonder that one boy, R.O.B. Morrow, could write with such enthusiasm about this meal: "We are now permitted to get something to eat. I ran into a store, got hold of a tin wash pan, drew it full of molasses, got a box of good Yankee crackers, sat down on the ground in a vacant lot, dipped the crackers into the molasses, and ate the best meal I ever had."

Stores weren't always handy, especially in the wilderness areas. At these times, soldiers could buy things from sutlers. Sutlers were not an official part of the military, but they were permitted to trail after troops and sell things like food, razor blades, paper, and thread. Sutlers acquired these hard-to-come-by items directly from the manufacturers or through European sources. Often, they bought stolen goods and then charged soldiers two or three times the original purchase price. At one point in the war, eggs were selling for six dollars a dozen and bacon cost fifteen dollars a pound!

Sutlers not only charged high prices, sometimes they would refuse to sell food to soldiers they did not know or did not like. Whenever this happened, the young soldiers would find other ways to get a meal. Elisha Stockwell took great delight in outwitting one greedy sutler: "[Ed] saw him put a big sweet potato in one of the wagons, and on the way back he got that potato. It was so long he couldn't hide it in his haversack, so he put the haversack on under his coat, and in camp asked me if I could hide it. I said yes, made a hole in the middle of the fire and covered it with ashes and coals, and we waited till all had laid down [to go to sleep]. We dug it out, it was baked fine and we had all we could eat that night and the next morning." How did Stockwell feel about eating stolen food? Apparently not bad at all. "That was the best as well as the biggest potato I ever saw."

Whether it was in a letter home or a journal, food was probably the most written-about topic. Soldiers were constantly waiting for food supplies to show up or commenting unhappily about the quality, quantity, and variety when they did arrive. At times like this, soldiers often resorted to foraging to supplement their disappointing meals.

SOLDIERS LINE UP TO BUY SUPPLIES FROM A SUTLER.

FORAGING SIMPLY MEANT LIVING OFF THE LAND AROUND THEM. At times, they might hunt deer or bear in the nearby forest, or gather nuts and berries. But these activities took a great deal of time, something a marching soldier did not have. Instead, soldiers had to take a more direct approach to finding a meal— they walked up to a farmer's home and offered to buy whatever food was available. If their request was refused, they would take what they wanted, sometimes at gunpoint.

Both armies had strict rules against foraging, and those caught could find themselves in jail for anywhere from a week to a month. But threats of going to jail did not put a halt to foraging. In fact, when guards were set out at night, they were there to keep soldiers *in* camp as much as to watch for an enemy attack. Still, a hungry boy could always find a way through even the tightest security, as John Delhaney makes clear: "Another nightly occupation is to rob bee hives; and not infrequently when the chorus of [religious] hymns is ascending, parties return from a thieving expedition with hats filled with honey comb."

Finding food was a constant challenge for boys in the Civil War even when safely in camp. Imagine what Charles Nott must have felt after his company became lost in enemy territory and ran out of food. After they had wandered aimlessly for several days and barely escaped capture twice, their luck changed. They stumbled across a house in the woods: "No smoke rises from the chimney. We halt; the sergeant enters the open door; comes back and reports it is just what we want—a deserted house."

After finding corn for the horses, Nott did a quick survey of their newly found bounty. In the yard, he saw chickens, cows, sheep, and pigs. Inside the house, they discovered a jar of molasses, a bag of dried peaches, a haunch of smoked venison, and a barrel of black walnuts, as well as coffee beans and cornmeal.

The food was gathered up, and after the horses had eaten, Nott and his friends continued their search for their army. That night they pitched camp and prepared a truly luxurious meal for themselves. He picks up his story: "Pluck the chickens, and cut them up; mix some meal and water, and make corn dodgers, as the Tennessians do. There are the plates to bake on, and we can try baking it in the ashes. But the coffee—everybody looks forward to it—no matter if it is poor and weak. It is always the tired soldier's great restorative, his particular comfort. The chickens must be stewed in pans and roasted on sticks."

Food for the Civil War soldier was always simple, if not downright plain. Few soldiers were skilled cooks, and even those who did know how to prepare food found themselves hampered by a lack of herbs, spices, and other ingredients. A little salt and pepper might be the only things available to put on a meal. Even so, most boys seem to have found great comfort in any meal, no matter how humble. They were able to escape, even if only for an hour or so, from the fighting and death that surrounded them. A meal was a frail link to their recollections of home and family and a better time.

Charles Nott closes his recollections of foraging with these thoughts: "In the course of half an hour we have good coffee. Chicken and corn dodgers come along more slowly, but after a while we sit around the fire to eat them; and everybody declares that he has had enough, and that it is very good."

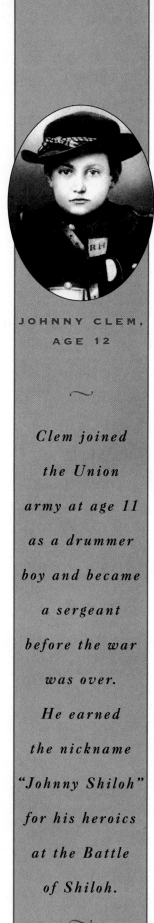

JOHNNY CLEM, AGE 12

~

Clem joined the Union army at age 11 as a drummer boy and became a sergeant before the war was over. He earned the nickname "Johnny Shiloh" for his heroics at the Battle of Shiloh.

~

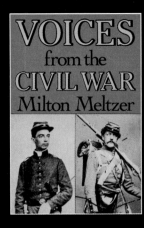

FROM

Voices from the Civil War

AWARD WINNING Book

A Documentary History of the Great American Conflict

Edited by

Milton Meltzer

In the South, the Women's Relief Society was formed to collect funds and provide aid for sick and wounded soldiers. Susan Lee Blackford, a Virginian, was one of the thousands of Southern women who volunteered for nursing duty. She tells of her experience nursing wounded Confederates at Lynchburg in this letter of May 12, 1864:

May 12th

My writing desk has been open all day, yet I have just found time to write to you. Mrs. Spence came after me just as I was about to begin this morning and said she had just heard that the Taliaferro's factory was full of soldiers in a deplorable condition. I went down there with a bucket of rice milk, a basin, towel, soap, etc. to see what I could do. I found the house filled with wounded men and not one thing provided for them. They were lying about the floor on a little straw. Some had been there since Tuesday and had not seen a surgeon. I washed and dressed the wounds of about fifty and poured water over the wounds of many more. The town is crowded with the poor creatures, and there is really no preparations for such a number. If it had not been for the ladies many of them would have starved to death. The poor creatures are very grateful, and it is a great pleasure to us to help them in any way. I have been hard at work ever since the wounded commenced coming. I went to the depot twice to see what I could do. I have had the cutting and distribution of twelve hundred yards of cotton cloth for bandages, and sent over three bushels of rolls of bandages, and as many more yesterday. I have never worked so hard in all my life and I would rather do that than anything else in the world. I hope no more wounded are sent here as I really do not think they could be sheltered.

A Civil War nurse performs her duties.

Evidence of women's work for the war was gathered by Mary Livermore, a social reformer who volunteered for the Sanitary Commission in the Midwest. As she moved about collecting vast amounts of fruits and vegetables to help the Union army overcome the disease called scurvy, she saw what women could do:

Mary Livermore

In the early summer of 1863, frequent calls of business took me through the extensive farming districts of Wisconsin, and Eastern Iowa, when the farmers were the busiest, gathering the wheat harvest. As we dashed along the railway, let our course lead in whatever direction it might, it took us through what seemed a continuous wheat field. The yellow grain was waving everywhere; and two-horse reapers were cutting it down in a wholesale fashion that would have astonished Eastern farmers. Hundreds of reapers could be counted in a ride of half a dozen hours....

Women were in the field everywhere, driving the reapers, binding and shocking, and loading grain, until then an unusual sight. At first, it displeased me, and I turned away in aversion. By and by, I observed how skillfully they drove the horses around and around the wheat field, diminishing more and more its periphery at every circuit, the glittering blades of the reaper cutting wide swaths with a rapid, clicking sound that was pleasant to hear. Then I saw that when they followed the reapers, binding and shocking, although they did not keep up with the men, their work was done with more precision and nicety, and their sheaves had an artistic finish that those lacked made by the men. So I said to myself, "They are worthy women, and deserve praise: their husbands are probably too poor to hire help, and, like the 'helpmeets' God designed them to be, they have girt themselves to this work—and they are doing it superbly. Good wives! Good women!"

One day my route took me off the railway, some twenty miles across the country. But we drove through the same golden fields of grain, and between great stretches of green waving corn. Now a river shimmered like silver through the gold of the wheat and oats, and now a growth of young timber made a dark green background for the harvest fields. Here, as everywhere, women were busy at the harvesting....

I stepped over where the girls were binding the fallen grain. They were fine, well-built lasses, with the honest eyes and firm mouth of the mother, brown like her, and clad in the same sensible costume.

"Well, you are like your mother, not afraid to lend a hand at the harvesting, it seems!" was my opening remark.

"No, we're willing to help outdoors in these times. Harvesting isn't any harder, if it's as hard as cooking, washing, and ironing, over a red-hot stove in July and August—only we have to do both now. My three brothers went into the army, all my cousins, most of the young men about here, and the men we used to hire. So there's no help to be got but women, and the crops must be got in all the same, you know."

A farm woman at work in the fields during the Civil War.

How to
Prepare a Historical Account

Use multiple *resources* to **interpret** *your* favorite piece of *history!*

A historical account is a document that contains detailed information about an event, a time period, or the achievements of an important person. When historians prepare accounts, they include plenty of well-researched facts from a variety of sources. But that's not all they must do. To prepare truly interesting accounts, historians must offer their own inter-pretations of history. Preparing a historical account is a good way to bring history to life!

JOHN GLENN – ASTRONAUT

FIRST TO ORBIT THE EARTH

Research a Topic

How can you learn more about a past event? You can research it, of course! Choose a topic to research. The topic might be any historical event or era that interests you. It might even be a famous person who lived long ago!

TOOLS

- paper and pencil
- note cards
- folder
- research materials

Begin your research by gathering basic information about the topic you chose. Go to the library and look for books, encyclopedias, almanacs, and magazines that tell about your topic. Check out your local video store— maybe there's a video you can use. Be sure to compare different accounts of the same event. Find as many different sources as possible. As you locate information, take notes and file them in a folder.

Tip Keep track of each source of information you use. Jot down the name of the source at the top of each note card or sheet of paper.

2 Personalize Your Research

Once you have acquired adequate knowledge of your topic, think about ways to make your account unusual and exciting. For instance, eyewitnesses are great sources of information. Is there someone you can interview who has firsthand knowledge of your topic? If your event took place a long time ago, you might search for a collection of letters, journal entries, or oral histories from people who were alive at that time. Look for magazine photos or create visual aids to illustrate

your account. Perhaps you could even visit a site related to your topic and get more information there.

3 Make an Outline

Many historical accounts are organized chronologically—in the order that events happened. Then the reader can understand how history unfolded. Start your outline with a heading that tells what happened first and when it happened. Beneath the heading, note the important details you've collected about that particular incident. Continue with the next major item and keep going until your outline is complete. The last item on your outline should be the most recent. Remember that an outline is a way to organize your information in note form—you need not write out all your information as you will in your account.

How Am I Doing?

Before you prepare your historical account, take a minute to ask yourself these questions:

- Do I have all the information I need to write my account?

- Have I used many different sources of information?

- Have I located some unusual details?

- Have I outlined my account so that I know what to write?

4 Write Your Account

Now it's time to write your account. Try to make your topic sound exciting and fresh. Use your outline to help you write. Keep in mind that your account should be clear and interesting to read.

You might need to write several drafts before you are satisfied. Ask a classmate to read your first draft and make notes of anything he or she doesn't understand or wants to know more about. When you revise the draft, respond to your classmate's comments.

When you write your final draft, remember to leave spaces for any visual aids you plan to include. Put your historical account together in booklet form.

If You Are Using a Computer...

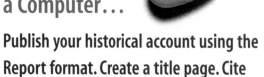

Publish your historical account using the Report format. Create a title page. Cite references using the Bibliography Maker.

5 Present Your Account

Have a History Day. Present your historical account to your classmates and share theirs. The accounts might be presented according to time period, starting with the earliest event and working up to the most recent. Look for ways that the accounts relate to one another. Did other students write about the same topic you chose? How are their accounts different from or similar to yours?

CONGRATULATIONS

You've discovered how to manage information about the past and bring a slice of history to life!

Russell Freedman
Historian/Author ▶

Glossary

ab·o·li·tion·ist
(ab′ə lish′ə nist) *noun*
A person who worked to end slavery in the United States.

ar·til·ler·y
(är til′ə rē) *noun*
Large guns mounted on wheels or on vehicles such as Jeeps.

bat·tal·ion
(bə tal′yən) *noun*
A large group of soldiers, made up of smaller companies or divisions.

bond·age
(bon′dij) *noun*
Slavery.

bri·dle (brīd′l) *noun*
The part of a horse's harness that goes over the horse's head. It is used to control or guide the horse.

bron·co
(brong′kō) *noun*
An untamed horse.

cav·al·ry
(kav′əl rē) *noun*
A group of soldiers who fight on horseback.

chap·ar·ral
(shap′ə ral′) *noun*
An area thick with shrubs and thorny bushes.

Civil War
(siv′əl wôr′) *noun*
The war between the North and the South in the United States, 1861–1865. During the *Civil War*, the United States was divided by issues such as slavery.

bronco

con•duc•tor
(kən dukʹtər) *noun*
A leader of the
Underground Railroad.

con•fi•dence
(konʹfi dəns) *noun*
A powerful belief or trust
in oneself or someone else.
Getting an A on her
science test built Zoe's
confidence in herself.

cun•ning (kunʹing) *noun*
Clever or sly ways of
getting what one wants or
of escaping one's enemies.
The mouse used *cunning*
to get the cheese.

dank (dank) *adjective*
Unpleasantly damp or
humid.

de•ter•mi•na•tion
(di tûrʹmə nāʹshən) *noun*
Persistence; the ability to
work steadily toward a goal
until it is achieved. Jackie's
determination helped her
finish the marathon.

droves (drōvzʹ) *noun*
Groups of animals, such as
cows or sheep, that are
herded together from place
to place. ▲ **drove**

Thesaurus

droves
flocks
herds
packs
swarms

em•i•grants
(emʹi grənts) *noun*
People who leave one
country to settle in another.
▲ **emigrant**

en•list•ments
(en listʹmənts) *noun*
The lengths of time for
which people have joined
the military. ▲ **enlistment**

eth•nic
(ethʹnik) *adjective*
Of or relating to a group of
people who have the same
national origins, language,
and culture.

fear•less
(fērʹlis) *adjective*
Brave; unafraid.

im•mi•grants
(imʹi grənts) *noun*
People who come to a
new country to live.
▲ **immigrant**

Word History

Immigrant is based on
the word *migrate*, which
comes from a Latin word
meaning "to move from
one place to another."

a	add	o͝o	took	ə =
ā	ace	o͞o	pool	a in *above*
â	care	u	up	e in *sicken*
ä	palm	û	burn	i in *possible*
e	end	yo͞o	fuse	o in *melon*
ē	equal	oi	oil	u in *circus*
i	it	ou	pout	
ī	ice	ng	ring	
o	odd	th	thin	
ō	open	ŧh	this	
ô	order	zh	vision	

Glossary

in•fan•try
(in′fən trē) *noun*
A group of soldiers who have been trained to fight mainly on foot.

in•tent•ly
(in tent′lē) *adverb*
With sharply focused attention. John gazed *intently* at the questions on his history test.

lar•i•at (lar′ē ət) *noun*
A long, light rope with a sliding hoop at one end, used to catch horses and cattle; a lasso.

Word History

Lariat came from the Spanish *la reata*, which means "the rope."

make•shift
(māk′shift) *adjective*
Used as a temporary replacement for the usual item. The kitchen table served as a *makeshift* ironing board.

Pa•tri•ot
(pā′trē ət) *noun*
One who loves and supports his or her country.

pi•o•neer
(pī′ə nēr′) *noun*
A person who is among the first to enter or settle a region.

range (rānj) *noun*
A large area of land on which cattle and sheep graze.

re•cruits
(ri krōōts′) *noun*
People who have recently joined an organization or group such as the military.
▲ **recruit**

rick•e•ty
(rik′i tē) *adjective*
Weak and shaky.

sage•brush
(sāj′brush′) *noun*
A grayish-green bush or shrub with white or yellow flowers that grows on the dry plains in the western United States and smells like the herb sage.

sagebrush

sta•tion (sta′shən) *noun*
A regular stopping place along a route.

stir•rups (stûr′əps) *noun*
The metal or leather loops that hang from a saddle and hold a rider's feet.
▲ **stirrup**

stirrup

stock (stok) *noun*
All of the animals raised on a farm; livestock. Because of the storm, the *stock* had to be herded into the barn.

su•per•in•tend•ent
(sōōp′ər in ten′dənt)
noun
The person who is in charge of a building, organization, or project. The *superintendent* manages our apartment building.

ten·e·ment
(ten′ə mənt) *noun*
A run-down and crowded apartment building in a poor section of a city.

un·bear·a·ble
(un bâr′ə bəl) *adjective*
Intolerable; too unpleasant or distasteful to tolerate.

Un·der·ground Rail·road
(un′dər ground′ rāl′rōd′) *noun*
A system set up before the Civil War to help run-away slaves escape to the northern United States, to Canada, and to other places of safety.

va·que·ros
(vä kâr′ōz) *noun*
Latin American cowboys who worked in Mexico and the southwestern United States. ▲ **vaquero**

Word History

Vaquero comes from the Spanish word *vaca*, which means "cow."

veteran
(vet′ər ən) *noun*
A person who has served in the armed forces.

winch·es
(winch′iz) *noun*
Machines that use a chain or rope to pull or lift things. It took two *winches* to tow the car out of the mud. ▲ **winch**

winch

yoke (yōk) *noun*
A curved piece of wood that fits over a work animal's neck and is used to hitch the animal to a cart.

yoke

a	add	o͝o	took	ə =
ā	ace	o͞o	pool	a in *above*
â	care	u	up	e in *sicken*
ä	palm	û	burn	i in *possible*
e	end	yo͞o	fuse	o in *melon*
ē	equal	oi	oil	u in *circus*
i	it	ou	pout	
ī	ice	ng	ring	
o	odd	th	thin	
ō	open	ŧh	this	
ô	order	zh	vision	

Authors & Illustrators

Esther Wood Brady *pages 72–89*
Writing historical fiction was a natural choice for this award-winning author. She grew up listening to her grandparents tell stories about her ancestors, who were early colonists. Brady began writing in 1936 and wrote many historical novels over the next four decades. She died in 1987.

Virginia Hamilton *pages 102–109*
This Newbery Medal-winning author has written many books based on her childhood in Yellow Springs, Ohio. Her grandfather, Grandpaw Levi Perry, was an escaped slave who found safety at an Underground Railroad station much like the one in *The House of Dies Drear*.

Henry Wadsworth Longfellow *pages 90–95*
This nineteenth-century poet was one of the most popular writers of his day. His poems celebrate nature, family, and American history. Few Americans of Longfellow's era knew who Paul Revere was until they read "Paul Revere's Ride."

Michael McCurdy *pages 10–29*

Writer and artist Michael McCurdy lives in Massachusetts, where he runs his own publishing company. He has written and illustrated numerous picture books, as well as illustrating classic works by authors such as Isaac Asimov, Charles Dickens, and Louisa May Alcott. His art has been shown at museums and libraries around the country.

Jim Murphy *pages 116–125*

This author says that he likes doing nonfiction projects because they allow him to investigate topics that really interest him. In researching *The Boys' War,* Jim Murphy read through hundreds of journals and letters. He went on to complete *The Long Road to Gettysburg,* another award-winning book about the Civil War.

Chief Satanta *pages 32–33*

Satanta, chief of the Kiowa tribe, was not an easy man to forget. The white settlers who came to Kiowa territory in the 1860s knew him as a powerful leader. Satanta was an eloquent speaker and often used the power of words to make peace with the settlers. But words were not enough, and Satanta led his people into war. He was sent to prison for his actions and died there in 1878.

Books &

Author Study

More by Russell Freedman

Buffalo Hunt
In this book, Freedman uses beautiful historical paintings to help tell the story of the buffalo and its importance in the lives of some Native Americans.

Lincoln: A Photobiography
This Newbery-winning biography brings to life one of America's greatest presidents.

Abraham Lincoln

The Wright Brothers: How They Invented the Airplane
The story of how these inventors fulfilled their life-long dream is told through words and pictures in this book.

Fiction

Kate's Book
by Mary Francis Shura
Kate and her family encounter danger and adventure when they go west in a covered wagon to start a new life in the Oregon Territory.

The Sign of the Beaver
by Elizabeth George Speare
It's 1768. Twelve-year-old Matt has been rescued from disaster by a Penobscot chief and his grandson. Now the tribe is moving on, and Matt must decide if he should go with them.

The Secret of Gumbo Grove
by Eleanora Tate
Raisen loves hearing about the past from Miss Effie, the oldest resident of Gumbo Grove. But when one of Miss Effie's stories leads Raisen to a mystery, she won't give up until she finds out whether African-American heroes once lived in her town.

Nonfiction

And Then What Happened, Paul Revere?
by Jean Fritz
The personality and accomplishments of the Revolutionary War hero are amusingly presented in this book.

The Secret Soldier: The True Story of Deborah Sampson
by Ann McGovern
Deborah Sampson disguised herself as a man to fight in the American Revolution. Her story is detailed here.

Spanish Pioneers of the Southwest
by Joan Anderson
photographs by George Ancona
This photo essay describes life in the New Mexico territory.

Undying Glory
by Clinton Cox
During the Civil War, the 54th Regiment of Massachusetts became famous for the courage of its African-American soldiers. Here is their story.

xMedia

Software

The Oregon Trail
MECC
(Apple II, IBM, Mac)
As you follow in the footsteps of the pioneers you will face all the hurdles the settlers did. With some clever thinking and luck, you can make it.

Time Riders in American History
***The Learning Company
(IBM)***
Explore history by interviewing people from the past in this exciting game.

Videos

As the Wind Rocks the Cradle
APL Educational Video
Using diaries, journals, and memoirs, this video dramatically re-creates the experiences of five pioneer women who traveled the Oregon Trail. (60 minutes)

Forever Free (The Civil War, volume 3)
PBS/Pacific Arts
This episode of the award-winning series tells the story of the Battle of Antietam, one of the most tragic episodes in American history. (60 minutes)

Magazines

Cobblestone
Cobblestone Publishing
Each issue of this magazine focuses on a specific event or person in American history. Articles, photos, folklore, games, and more bring the topic to life.

Monkeyshines on America
North Carolina Learning Institute for Fitness & Education
This playful magazine stresses state history, geography, and folklore.

A Place to Write

**Association on American Indian Affairs
245 Fifth Avenue
New York, NY 10016**

Include a large, self-addressed stamped envelope when you write to request an information packet about Native American history.

CITYSCAPES

Visit an Urban Planner's Office

Cities depend on the strengths and skills of the people who live and work there.

Touring America's Cities

The people and places of a city give it an identity.

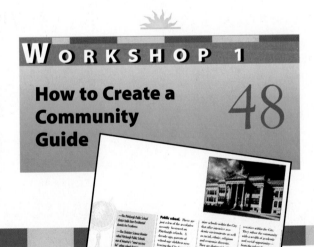

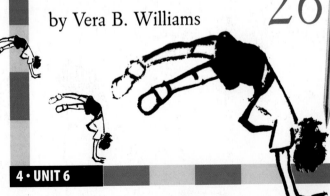

City Challenges

Cities face many complex challenges.

Reaching Out

City dwellers can work together to improve their quality of life.

Trade Books

The following books accompany this *Cityscapes* SourceBook.

Cities

by Fiona
MacDonald

Fiction

A Jar of
Dreams

by Yoshiko
Uchida

AWARD
WINNING

Book

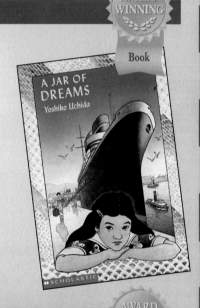

Fiction

Tails of the Bronx

by Jill
Pinkwater

AWARD
WINNING

Author

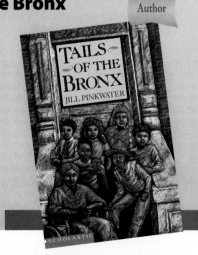

Photo Essay

Where the River Runs

by Nancy
Price Graff
photographs by
Richard Howard

AWARD
WINNING

Book

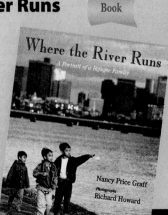

The City By The Golden Gate
© Wooster Scott

The people and places of a city give it an identity.

Touring America's Cities

Explore San Francisco and discover what makes it special. Search for facts in a chart about other cities around the country.

Read about Elana Rose Rosen, who's just moved into a city apartment building. Look at cities from a poet's point of view, and examine a painting by a famous city artist.

WORKSHOP 1

Create a guide to the biggest and best things about a place you know.

SOURCE

The City by the Bay
A MAGICAL JOURNEY AROUND SAN FRANCISCO
Illustrated by ELISA KLEVEN Written by TRICIA BROWN
and THE JUNIOR LEAGUE OF SAN FRANCISCO

Travel Book

FROM

The City by the Bay

A MAGICAL JOURNEY AROUND SAN FRANCISCO

By **TRICIA BROWN**
and **THE JUNIOR LEAGUE OF SAN FRANCISCO**
Illustrated by **ELISA KLEVEN**

AWARD WINNING

Book

For centuries, perhaps millennia, San
Francisco and its Bay were known
only by native peoples who lived in
small communities throughout Central
California. Typically, each community had
its own distinct language. As a result,
there was never a common name used
for the population as a whole.

When the Spanish arrived, they called the
natives *costeros,* or "coast people." Later,
the English-speaking settlers referred to
them as *Costanoans.* Today, descendants
of the early natives generally call
themselves *Ohlones.*

In the late 16th century, explorers from
around the globe began sailing the waters
surrounding the San Francisco peninsula.
Since that time, San Francisco's
population has been made up of an
ever-changing mosaic of cultures.

Chinatown

Gung Hay Fat Choy! That means "Happy New Year!" in Chinese. New Year's is a special time in this neighborhood, the largest Chinese community in the western hemisphere. People wish one another good luck and happiness, and children receive *lai-see*—small red envelopes filled with money.

The holiday is celebrated in January or February, depending on the cycle of the moon. Each year is named after one of the twelve animals in the Chinese zodiac. There are many parades and ceremonies. Lots of firecrackers are set off to scare away evil spirits and bring good fortune.

Chinatown is colorful all year round. Walk down Grant Avenue, with its street lights that look like lanterns and street signs written in Chinese. Look at the fresh vegetables and fruits overflowing out to the sidewalk from the grocery stores. Smell the aromas coming from all the different restaurants. Is it time for *dim sum*, a Chinese lunch?

The Cable Cars and Lombard Street

Before 1922, the famous crooked block of Lombard Street was straight, and so steep that it could not be traveled by carts or wagons. The only way for people to get up and down the hill was on foot. After the invention of the automobile, the city added eight turns so that cars would be able to travel the street as well. Today, tourists wait in line to drive down this twisting street.

Visitors can also view Lombard Street from the cable car that runs along Hyde Street. Andrew Hallidie introduced the cable car to San Francisco in 1873 because he felt sorry for the horses pulling wagons up the steep hills. People laughed at his idea at first, but he didn't give up. Today, San Francisco's cable cars are a National Historic Landmark.

The Golden Gate Bridge

Looking from the Marin Headlands to San Francisco on clear evenings, you can watch the twinkling lights of the city, the Golden Gate Bridge, and the San Francisco–Oakland Bay Bridge. On other nights, when the fog rolls in, you can hear the foghorns, and feel the cool fog as it wraps around the Golden Gate Bridge like a blanket.

Although the name of this bridge is the Golden Gate, the paint used to cover it is actually "International Orange." The bridge is named after the strait at the bay's entrance—the Golden Gate.

Some people believed that a bridge could never be built across the Golden Gate, but a group of determined engineers found a way. Built in 1937, the bridge spans a length of 6,450 feet—that's longer than twenty football fields! The tallest tower is 746 feet high—as tall as a 70-story building. The amount of wire used for the main cable is enough to wrap three times around the earth.

The Palace of Fine Arts

Although it was originally intended as a temporary exhibit for the 1915 Panama-Pacific Exhibition, the Palace of Fine Arts was so well-loved that it was later rebuilt to become a permanent part of San Francisco's skyline. The beauty of this graceful palace is reflected in a natural lagoon, which is bordered by lawns and trees. The sight is especially stunning at night when the palace is spectacularly lighted. It's a wonderful place to take a stroll, to have a picnic, or to feed the swans and ducks.

The palace is a majestic domed rotunda, with six supporting columns, that is as tall as an eighteen-story building. The angel sculptures inside the rotunda are twenty feet tall. If you want to get an idea of how big that is, you can go into the neighboring Exploratorium and stand next to one of the original angels from the 1915 exhibition!

Lighthouses, foghorns, and buoys guide ships as they navigate San Francisco Bay. Mariners identify the different foghorns by the length and frequency of their "blasts" and the length of the pauses between blasts.

There are eleven islands within San Francisco's city limits: Angel Island, Yerba Buena, Alcatraz, Treasure Island, and the Farallones (a group of seven islands outside the Golden Gate).

The Bay Bridge's deepest pier drops 242 feet into the water. Its tallest tower (from bedrock, below the Bay, to the very top) measures nearly 550 feet, making it taller than the largest of the Egyptian pyramids.

San Francisco Bay is not really a bay at all—it's an estuary. (A bay is filled with ocean water. An estuary is filled with a combination of salt water and fresh water.) It is the largest estuary on the west coast of the United States, and has one of the most diverse populations of marine life in the world.

Sutro Tower, San Francisco's tallest structure, transmits television and radio signals from the top of Mt. Sutro.

In 1850, when sourdough bread was delivered to San Franciscans, loaves were placed on spikes outside the doors so that animals could not reach them. Sourdough bread is unique to San Francisco—the wild yeast that is used to make it rise won't grow anywhere else!

San Francisco has more than 3,000 restaurants.

The Bay Bridge is actually made up of four bridges: two suspension bridges on the San Francisco side, and a cantilever bridge and a truss bridge on the Oakland side. The two pairs of bridges are connected by a tunnel through Yerba Buena Island.

City by the Bay...

"BART" stands for Bay Area Rapid Transit, the computer-operated, electric-rail train system that connects San Francisco with the East Bay and the Peninsula.

• • • • • • • • • • • • • • • •

BART's Transbay Tube is 3.6 miles long and rests on the Bay floor, 135 feet beneath the surface of the water. It is made up of 57 giant steel and concrete sections.

• • • • • • • • • • • • • • • •

Chocolate was not the first product to be manufactured at Ghirardelli Square—it was originally the site of the Pioneer Woolen Mill, which produced uniforms and blankets for the Union Army during the Civil War.

The San Francisco Ballet is the oldest ballet company in America. Founded in 1933, it was the first American ballet company to perform "Nutcracker" and "Swan Lake."

• • • • • • • • • • • • • • • •

Cable cars are pulled along by underground cables that are constantly moving. A gripman pulls a lever that grips the cable through a slot in the street. When the gripman lets go, a brakeman stops the cable car with wheel and track brakes. The gripman and brakeman ring bells to tell each other when to brake (stop) or grip (go).

San Francisco's firefighters locate emergency water reserves by looking for circles on the streets. 151 intersections have large circles of bricks set into the pavement—each marks a reserve tank holding about 75,000 gallons of water.

• • • • • • • • • • • • • • • •

Abandoned sailing ships from the Gold Rush days lie buried beneath the streets of San Francisco. The ships were covered by landfill during the city's early days of expansion.

Cities at a Glance

According to the 1990 census, over half the U.S. population lives in cities. Cities around the country have to make sure they can accommodate the growing number of new citizens. This chart shows how the two largest cities from each region of the country meet the needs of their residents.

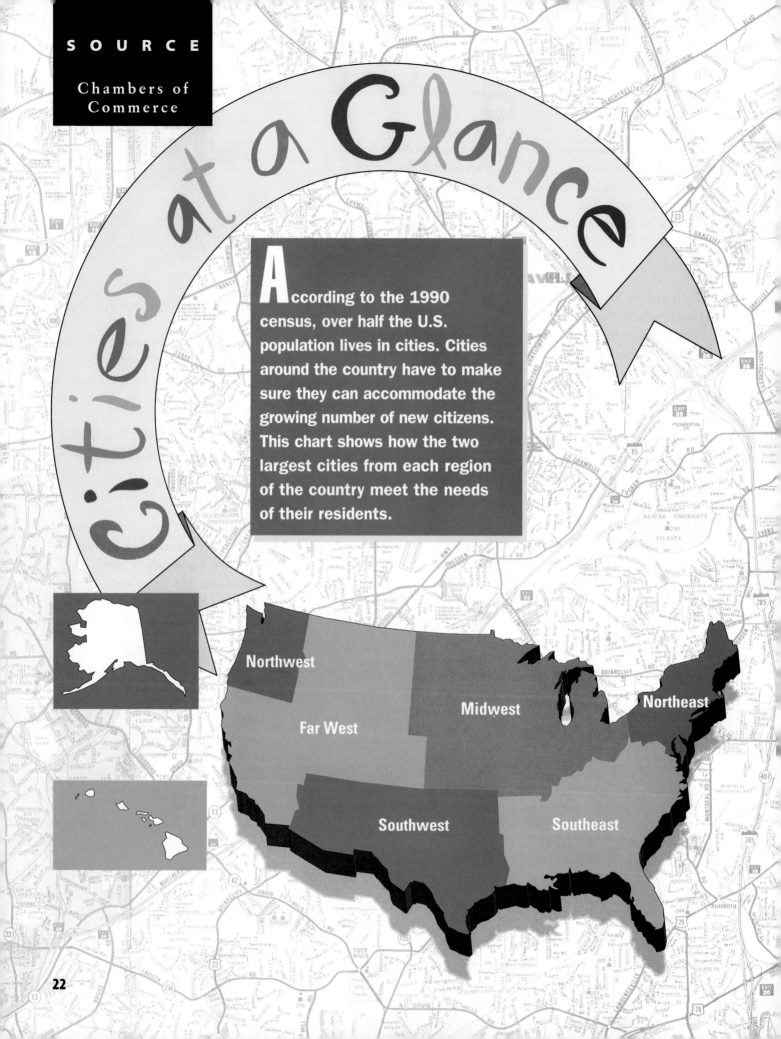

Northwest

Far West

Midwest

Northeast

Southwest

Southeast

	NORTHEAST		SOUTHEAST	
	NEW YORK	**PHILADELPHIA**	**JACKSONVILLE**	**MEMPHIS**
POPULATION	7,323,000	1,600,000	672,971	610,000
GETTING AROUND	Three subway systems run 230 miles in the city.	Trains connect the city to its suburbs.	Mass transit takes a back seat to cars here.	The city bus and the Main Street Trolley
FAVORITE SPORTS TEAM	Basketball's Knicks and baseball's Yankees	Baseball's Phillies	The Jacksonville Jaguars football team	The Memphis State University Tigers basketball team
MOST RECOGNIZABLE FEATURE	The Statue of Liberty	The Liberty Bell	Jacksonville Landing, a horseshoe-shaped marketplace	The Pyramid, a multipurpose arena that seats 22,500 spectators
LARGEST NEWSPAPER	*The New York Times:* circulation 1,141,366	*The Philadelphia Inquirer:* circulation 486,000	*The Florida Times-Union:* circulation 181,593	*The Commercial Appeal:* circulation 218,000
CITY HELPERS	Teenagers in the City Volunteer Corps help with city events and services.	Action AIDS helps people with the HIV virus.	Volunteer Jacksonville serves the city's many needs.	The Metropolitan Inter-Faith Association uses 3,000 volunteers.
WHERE TO VISIT	The Empire State Building	The Liberty Bell	Twenty miles of white, sandy beaches	Graceland, the home of Elvis Presley
MAJOR INDUSTRIES	Manufacturing, trade, and finance	Banking, insurance, healthcare, and education	Banking and insurance	Education, transportation, and communication
WHERE IT IS	New York	Pennsylvania	Florida	Tennessee

	MIDWEST		NORTHWEST	
	CHICAGO	**DETROIT**	**SEATTLE**	**PORTLAND**
POPULATION	2,783,726	1,028,000	516,000	437,319
GETTING AROUND	Bus and rail systems make 1.8 million trips daily.	A car is a must in the motor city.	The Washington State Ferry System is the largest in the U.S.A.	The MAX (Metropolitan Area Express) — a light-rail system
FAVORITE SPORTS TEAM	The Bulls basketball team, baseball's Cubs, and football's Bears	Baseball's Tigers and Hockey's Detroit Red Wings	Basketball's Supersonics and football's Seahawks	Basketball's Portland Trail Blazers
MOST RECOGNIZABLE FEATURE	The Sears Tower, the tallest building in the world	The Renaissance Center, the tallest hotel in North America	The Space Needle, a tower with a revolving restaurant on top	The beautiful snow-capped peaks of Mt. Hood
LARGEST NEWSPAPER	*The Chicago Tribune:* circulation 697,349	*The Detroit Free Press:* circulation 556,116	*The Seattle Times:* circulation 238,600	*The Oregonian:* circulation 348,000
CITY HELPERS	The Children's Home and Aid Society of Illinois helps children and teenagers.	The Detroit Grand Prix Association volunteers at the huge annual auto race.	Patrons of Northwest Civic Cultural and Charitable Organizations raise money for the arts.	The Royal Rosarians pitch in for Portland's famous annual Rose Festival.
WHERE TO VISIT	The Lincoln Park Zoo	The Motown Museum	Pike Place Market, where merchants throw fish to customers	The Oregon Museum of Science and Industry
MAJOR INDUSTRIES	The service industry (workers who do things for others)	Automobile manufacturing and related industries	Aerospace	Timber and manufacturing
WHERE IT IS	Illinois	Michigan	Washington	Oregon

	SOUTHWEST		FAR WEST	
	HOUSTON	**DALLAS**	**LOS ANGELES**	**SAN FRANCISCO**
POPULATION	1,600,000	1,006,877	3,485,398	724,000
GETTING AROUND	Because Houston is spread out over many miles, the most popular form of transit is the car.	DART— Dallas Area Rapid Transit	The new metro system provides a new way to get around LA.	Cable cars provide a picturesque way to get from here to there.
FAVORITE SPORTS TEAM	Basketball's Rockets and football's Oilers	Football's Dallas Cowboys	Basketball's Lakers and baseball's Dodgers compete for fans.	Football's Forty-Niners
MOST RECOGNIZABLE FEATURE	The Astrodome, the first domed stadium ever built	Reunion Tower, a tall, skinny building with a big ball on top	The Hollywood sign sits high in the Hollywood Hills.	The Golden Gate Bridge
LARGEST NEWSPAPER	*The Houston Chronicle*: circulation 417,459	*The Dallas Morning News*: circulation 527,387	*Los Angeles Times*: circulation 1,090,000	*The San Francisco Chronicle*: circulation 526,824
CITY HELPERS	The Green Houston organization supplies fresh produce for soup kitchens.	Big Brothers/Big Sisters pairs adults with kids from single-parent families.	The Tree People plant and maintain city trees.	The St. Anthony Foundation serves San Francisco's inner city.
WHERE TO VISIT	Astroworld amusement park and Galveston Island	The School Book Depository, from which Lee Harvey Oswald shot President Kennedy	Beverly Hills and Universal Studios	Oceanfront Fisherman's Wharf and Pier 39
MAJOR INDUSTRIES	Oil and gas	Financial services — banks, investing, etc.	Entertainment, finance, and tourism	Tourism. This is the most popular destination in the world.
WHERE IT IS	Texas	Texas	California	California

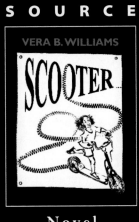

From

SCOOTER

By

VERA B. WILLIAMS

When Elana Rose Rosen first moved to 514 Melon Hill, Apartment 8E, the first thing she unpacked was her scooter. For the first few days she leaned on her scooter and looked out the window of her new apartment at the people in the city below. One day, her mom pushed Elana and her scooter out the apartment door, into the elevator, through the lobby, and out the front door and said, "See you at supper time."

SCOOTER
CAN'T YOU
OPEN THE DOOR ?
OPEN THAT FRONT DOOR !
TAKE
ELANA OUT....
RIDE AND RIDE

I pushed on into the courtyard. It was bright and blurry. Sun bounced off the chrome of my scooter.

Outside our building, 514, and between the other Melon Hill buildings, there's a long sidewalk. It's great to ride on. The very first day my mom brought me here, when the trailer was being unloaded, I watched the other kids riding bikes there. There's a really smooth cement ramp. It has wide, flat steps that make a drop just right to jump the scooter.

I was practicing jumping my scooter. I could already even it up fast on the straightaway so there was no wobble. Then I started practicing my double heel click. That's a very special trick I invented. You have to have good balance to try it. And you have to have lots of room, so don't try it on a

short runway. Get going fast. Then lean with all your might on the handlebars. Let your legs go way up in back and knock them together fast as you can. Then knock them together again. Simple? It's truly a beautiful trick. I've since even learned to do a triple heel click. But I bet nobody can do a quadruple.

Of course, you do have to have a good scooter. Mine has great balance on account of it has such tremendous wheels. It's beautiful, too. The wheels have a wide silver line all around and a skinny blue stripe like a ribbon around the silver.

Mostly then I was practicing jumps. They were spectacular. After supper my mom came down to watch. It stayed light late then. High up between the buildings you could see a piece of sky turning a special blue. I got my mother to sit so she could see me driving right toward her.

I got a quick start, and I was going fast. Then suddenly there was a big loose thing like a whole piece of sidewalk sticking up in front of me. I just didn't see it soon enough. I couldn't jump that fast.

I landed smash on my face. I think my mom screamed. I think she shook me. She grabbed me and ran out to the street with me. Someone helped us get one of those yellow taxis and told the driver the name of the hospital to take me to.

In the cab I held on to my mother. I was scared of all the blood. I was excited, too. I hoped the taxi would go fast like an ambulance. I wished it had a siren.

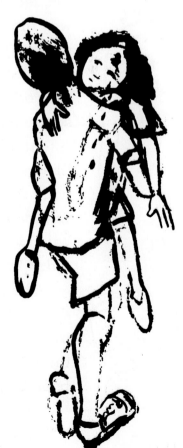

The taxi bounced a lot. My mother held her arm tight around me. She talked and cried. She said at least I didn't lose any of my beautiful teeth. She said I was too wild for my own good. She said she was definitely sending the scooter back to Grandma and Grandpa. That made me cry. I said I would go with it if she sent it back. She said I mustn't cry, it made my chin bleed more. She held more tissues to my chin.

The taxi driver started to talk. He told us how he cut his head real bad falling out of a tree when he was a kid. He said to look at the scar on the back of his head. That man was so kind he wouldn't even let my mom pay. He ran into the emergency room with us to show us the way.

The nurse looked at my head and my chin and said the doctor would take care of me soon. Then I had to wait and wait. The arrow with the word E M E R G E N C Y was made of red, red light that kept moving up the arrow. It looked the way the blood pounding in my head felt. The bottom part of my face was getting stiff and couldn't feel.

There was a man with a bandage on his foot bigger than a basketball, even. My mom said not to stare. You see scary things in the hospital. It smells weird, too.

At last the doctor could sew up my cuts. It hurt, and I felt like I was going to be sick. I held so tight to my mother's hand that her hand got numb. My mother told the doctor I wouldn't have had this accident if I wasn't always such a wild kid on my scooter. She told the doctor I was so wild she didn't know what to do with me.

The doctor told my mother not to worry. It wasn't really such a bad accident for a stunt rider. She said I mustn't fall on my head again, though. She bandaged my chin extra thick. When she showed me my face in the mirror, the bandage looked tremendous. I loved the doctor.

I wanted to ride home in a taxi. I liked that taxi driver. My mom said we'd never get the same taxi again. And the bus came right then. I was so sleepy riding home in the bus that the red and green and yellow lights swam together. People's heads swam together. I can't even remember how I got into my bed. I still ask my mother, "But how did I get all the way up in the elevator and undressed and everything, and I didn't even know?"

Way later I woke up. It was in the middle of the middle of the night. I couldn't see. I couldn't tell . . . was I in my grandpa and grandma's house? Was I in our old house with my father before he moved away? Were we still staying at my cousin Nanette's apartment, so full of my cousins' beds you could hardly walk? But on my cousins' street the streetcar went by all night long. How come I couldn't hear the streetcar? Why was there a big lumpy thing on my chin and on my head? And where was my scooter? <u>Where was my scooter?</u>

My mother says she just flew to me when she heard me yelling for my scooter.

She switched on the lights. On the wall between the windows, the funny little light made to look like a candle came on. There was my scooter right in the place I had made for it by the window. I stood on it and looked way down into the streets below. It was raining and the streets were black and wet. I thought I could see the bump that had tripped up my scooter.

"How did my scooter get back up here?" I asked my mother. She told me I was pretty lucky for such a reckless kid. One of our new neighbors, a little boy, Petey, had picked it up and set it by our door. There was just some mud on the wheels and stuff.

"What did he say?" I asked.

"Nothing," my mom said. "He just brought it and stood there...wouldn't say a word. Then he went away."

My mom made us cocoa. I had to drink it in little sips. I tried a cookie, but the bandage made it hard to chew. We sat wrapped up in blankets in the kitchen. Our bathrobes seemed to have disappeared when we moved. My mom says if we have to keep moving finally everything will get lost. Boxes from our dishes were still around us. You never saw so many boxes as when you move. My mom just couldn't wait till she got enough time to get rid of all the boxes. But I liked it. It felt as if we were camping.

Our big blue pot with speckles and our frying pan and our toaster were sitting around the legs of my chair. I told my mom that the big blue pot was asking the frying pan and the toaster how they liked their new kitchen.

My mom said she thought the big blue pot was saying how glad it was that I was okay, and the toaster was saying how it hoped I would be able to eat toast real soon. I laughed, but that hurt my chin, too. Then I took my cocoa to my bed.

But I didn't even get back in my bed. I found a rag so I could clean every bit of mud off my scooter. I looked through the boxes and found the one marked FIX . I got the little squirt can of oil out. I oiled the wheels. Then I polished and I polished the silver stripe with the blue stripe like a ribbon around it till I made those stripes so bright you could even see them in the dark.

**FRIENDS
REALLY ARE
IMPORTANT,
ESPECIALLY
NICE FRIENDS.
DIFFICULT FRIENDS
SOMETIMES ARE GREAT TOO.**

The day after the day after my accident I had to wait in the elevator a long time on seven. A lady was holding the door for her friend, who had run back to her apartment to unplug her iron even though <u>everybody</u> thought it wasn't fair to hold the elevator that long. I was telling Cecelia from right next door about my ride to the hospital. Then this kid ran into the elevator, saw it wasn't going anywhere and ran out, ducked back in, and pulled me out down the hall with him.

"You know me, I'm Jimmy Beck right under you in 7E. Listen, I'll show you how we get down fast in this building." He pushed open the heavy door to the fire stairs.

"I guess you know everything," I said, to be sarcastic. It's the meanest way I know to be, since I can't stand when people make sarcastic remarks to me. But it didn't bother him. He was leaping the steps from the seventh floor to the sixth in bunches. When I caught up with him on the landing, he was writing hard into the skin of his arm with a ballpoint: J.B. KNOWS EVERYTHING.

"Jimmy Beck knows everything," he sang, running down the stairs to five. I love to run and jump down stairs fast, too, and I wanted to see this back part of our building and where we'd come out. Only I couldn't run now. It made my head hurt. So Jimmy got to all the landings first. He jumped the last half of each flight and ran back up so he wouldn't ever have to stop talking.

From the fifth to the fourth, he told me Eduard with the skateboard lived in 4K and the scooter tricks he saw me doing were almost as good as Eduard's skateboard stuff. For a girl, that is, he added.

From the fourth to the third, he explained that he didn't get a skateboard because he got a fifteen-speed instead, and did I know a kid named Vinh on the third floor?

From the third to the second, he told me he knew day before yesterday I was going to wreck up on that piece of broken pavement, and he had yelled at me to watch out, but I was too stuck-up to listen.

On the second, he stood still (sort of) to tell me he had once had an accident standing on a swing going over the top, and blood ran out his nose and his mouth and his ears and his eyes just like the Mississippi. Running again, he pointed down the hall and said a dumb little kid named Petey lived there. He made a sign with his finger that Petey was crazy.

On the first floor, he said Adrienne lived down the hall and her parents owned the variety store only they charged way too much for everything.

We finally pushed open the fire door to the outside. "C'mon," Jimmy called, racing for the courtyard. But I had

had enough of Jimmy Beck, so I took my time. I wanted to explore every bit of Melon Hill Houses. There were two playgrounds and tables for games, I knew, but I had the feeling there was lots more to find than I had noticed right off.

I met a lot of kids that day and the next. And it was partly thanks to Jimmy Beck's big mouth, I have to admit. Kids had heard about my accident, about lots of blood (<u>much</u> more than there was) and about a scooter that had huge silver and blue wheels and maybe you could get rides on.

I'm not at all sure Jimmy Beck can be what I call a friend. But Vinh or Eduard or Adrienne will be. All three of us might do a lot of things together. They're all in the same class in the school where I'll be going. I'll be in their class, too, after the summer when we start school.

Siobhan and Beryl are in other classes. Beryl wears lipstick already, and she likes to act sexy. And Adrienne from the first floor, her mother is going to have a baby real soon. Eduard's like me with my scooter. Only he's much more of a single-minded person than I am about wheels. He <u>never</u> goes out without his skateboard. He even rides it in the halls. We're not allowed to ride in the halls. But you should see how he can come right up to the elevator door, then stop in one little inch!

Then there's Petey. I've heard the kids say things about Petey. He's the little kid who brought home my scooter after my accident. I haven't met him yet, but I know he lives in my building and I know where. I bet it won't be long, either, till I know every kid in this building. But I am especially curious about Petey.

LOOK
UP, LOOK DOWN, LOOK ALL AROUND
CAN'T EVER
KNOW FOR SURE
YOUR LUCKY DAY!

A few days after my accident Adrienne rang our bell. She wanted to see the bandage on my head. She was never even in an apartment on the eighth floor before. She said she liked standing up on the scooter and looking out the window.

"I'd be so scared to live here, Lanny," she said. "You're almost to the roof." She didn't really like it. She's used to the first floor. Only she got excited when she found Thieu's Variety Store. That's her parents' store. Then she saw our school. "You can see pretty much from up here," she said.

She asked me where I slept, so I showed her my couch. Anyone can tell it's mine because mine is on my side of our big room right by my scooter. It has the cover with the rosy flowers. My mom's has the cover with brown and blue flowers, and the rug is in between. And mine has my old bear and my lion on it. I wanted my own room so bad, but my mom said it would be quite awhile before she could afford that. When I suggested she ask my father for money for more rent, she said, like she usually does, "Put <u>that</u> out of your mind, honey!" (But I never <u>really</u> do.)

Adrienne said I needed to get a screen like she has to separate her bed from her little brother's bed. She said their apartment has two rooms besides the kitchen, but her mom and dad had one whole room and she and her brother shared the little room. Then her uncle made a screen for her and that was much better. She took me down to show her mother my bandage.

Her mother said she was so sad that my head was hurt. She said my hair was very pretty and it would grow back nice where they had to cut it for the bandage. Then she said I shouldn't ride that scooter anymore and how my mother should know what a bad toy that scooter is for a young girl. She was really upset about that and went on talking about it to herself and shaking her head. Adrienne showed me her own bed with the screen around it. It was almost better than a real door. It made it look private and secret and cozy. I decided I was going to have a screen like that around my bed, too.

We kneeled on Adrienne's bed and leaned on her windowsill. You can actually talk to people and see everything just like you're down in the street. We could see our super, Benny Portelli, helping the man who drives the special big white truck. The truck only comes on Fridays to take away old furniture no one wants anymore.

And then my special thing happened to me. Suddenly I got lucky again! My mother says the fairies must have come when I was born, just like in the story, to bring me their special gifts. She says one of them must have brought me good luck, because over and over anyone can see that I'm one really lucky kid.

And I am, too. At that very minute Mr. Portelli was handing a screen to the garbageman in the back of the truck. It looked a lot like Adrienne's screen, with wood all around like a picture frame and red cloth.

"Wait . . . Wait, Benny . . . Mr. Portelli! Wait!" I yelled.

"Excuse me!" I yelled to Mrs. Thieu. I had to really race through their kitchen.

"Your head!" Mrs. Thieu called after me. "Your head!"

I could feel my bandage sliding down over my eyes, but I ran right over to Benny.

"Mr. Portelli!" I remembered my mom said I should say "Mr. Portelli." "Don't throw away that screen. Please. Please, I need it."

"You want it?" He held it out to me. "It's yours. Just don't let me find it out here tomorrow."

Adrienne came down to help me take it up to my house. It was not an old thing at all. There was nothing broken or

torn. It was very dusty, and the wooden frame was scrappy looking. Adrienne helped me clean it all up. I set it around my bed. Adrienne said I was an amazingly lucky person.

When my mother came in, she agreed it was the perfect thing. She kept hitting her head and saying she didn't know how come she never even thought of a screen for me.

I told her how I saved it from the garbage truck just in time.

"Because you're lucky," she said. She hugged me. She started to cry. She fussed getting my bandage straight. "You were lucky you didn't break your head," she said, "Elana Rose Rosen."

On Saturday, she took all the cloth off the screen, and I scrubbed it. Then we could see how pretty and bright it really was. She tacked it all back on the frame tight with special new brass upholstery tacks. She sent me to see if Mr. Portelli had a little upholsterer's hammer we could use, and I helped her hammer in the tacks. Then I made my sign.

EVERY DAY SHE RIDES HER SCOOTER

LOVES TO DANCE AND LOVES MUSIC

ADMITS SHE ACTS STUPID AND STUCK UP SOMETIMES

NOW SHE HAS FRIENDS AT MELON HILL HOUSES

AND NANETTE IS COMING

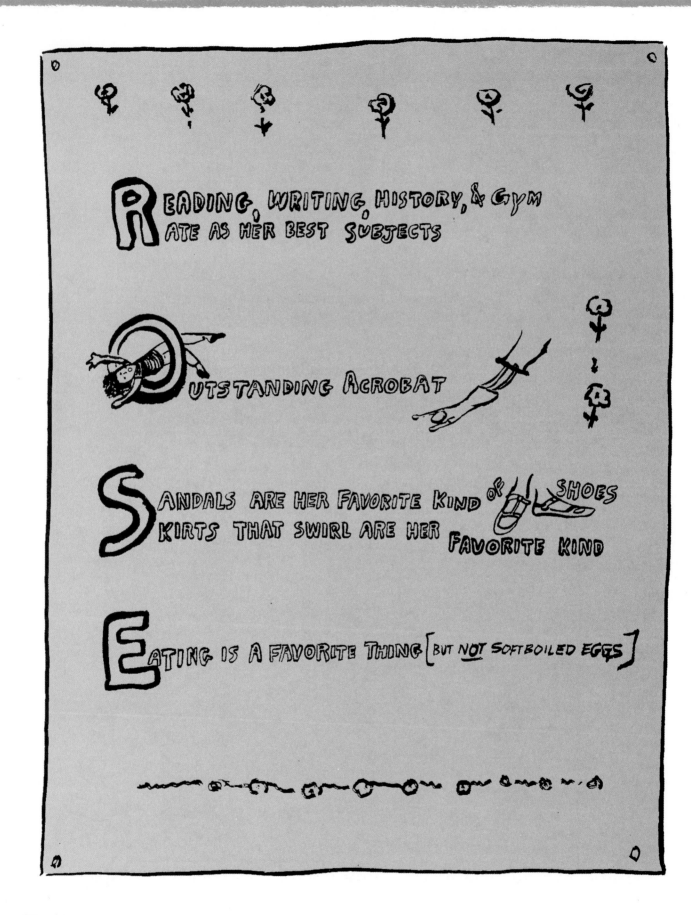

READING, WRITING, HISTORY, & GYM RATE AS HER BEST SUBJECTS

OUTSTANDING ACROBAT

SANDALS ARE HER FAVORITE KIND of SHOES SKIRTS THAT SWIRL ARE HER FAVORITE KIND

EATING IS A FAVORITE THING [BUT <u>NOT</u> SOFTBOILED EGGS]

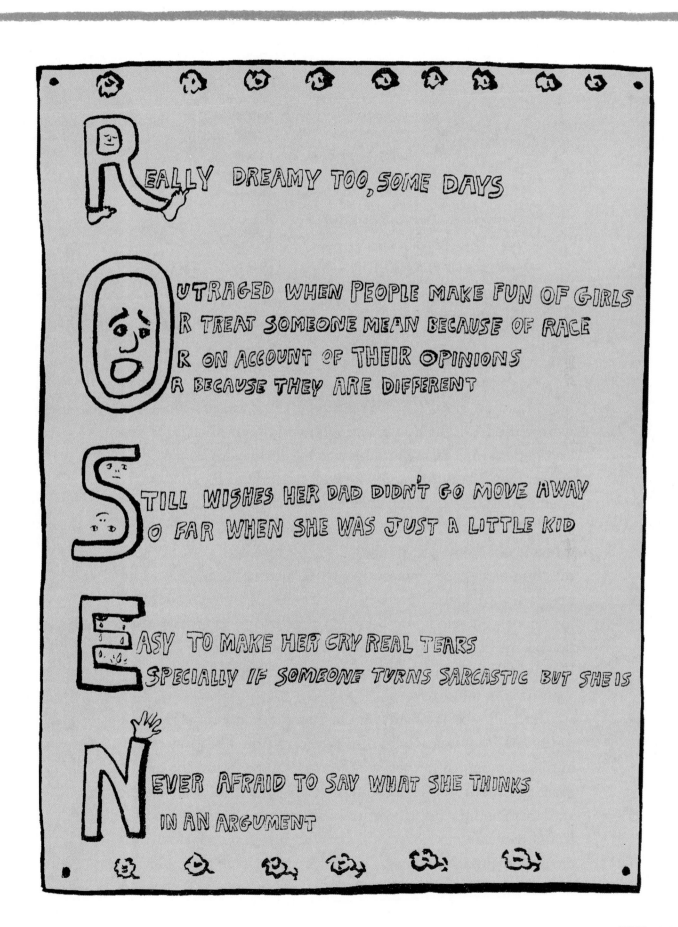

REALLY DREAMY TOO, SOME DAYS

OUTRAGED WHEN PEOPLE MAKE FUN OF GIRLS
R TREAT SOMEONE MEAN BECAUSE OF RACE
R ON ACCOUNT OF THEIR OPINIONS
R BECAUSE THEY ARE DIFFERENT

STILL WISHES HER DAD DIDN'T GO MOVE AWAY
O FAR WHEN SHE WAS JUST A LITTLE KID

EASY TO MAKE HER CRY REAL TEARS
SPECIALLY IF SOMEONE TURNS SARCASTIC BUT SHE IS

NEVER AFRAID TO SAY WHAT SHE THINKS
IN AN ARGUMENT

PETEY is my shadow!
EVERYWHERE I GO HE GOES TOO.
TALKS NOT AT ALL!
ESPECIALLY FUN TO PLAY WITH.
YOU COULD LOVE HIM LOTS!
YOU COULD GET MAD AT HIM TOO!

A week after my accident, I met Petey for real.

When the elevator door opened to let me out on eight, he was standing there. He followed me to our door. His shoelaces were untied, and he had to stop and wiggle his shoe back on. I waited for him. I was sure he was the little kid who saved my scooter. I thought maybe he was five or four like my twin cousins. But they can tie shoes.

"Can't you tie your shoes?" I asked him. He wouldn't answer. "What's your name?" I asked him. He wouldn't tell me that, either, but he nodded when I said "Petey?" And he nodded again when I asked was he the Petey who saved my scooter. While I was bending over trying to unlock our door, I could feel him touching the bandage on my head. It's just a small bandage now, and the doctor will take out the stitches tomorrow.

He followed me right in. On Tuesdays, my mom doesn't get home from her school and her job till just before supper. I was glad Petey was there. We went and looked at my bandage in the bathroom mirror. I took him in to see the scooter. The handlebars were high for him, but he stood on it just like he was riding it. I showed him the great features of this particular scooter. I held it up a little so he could spin the wheels and watch the silver and blue stripes blur. I let him help me polish them.

He never even said anything the whole time. I asked him if he could talk. He polished very hard but he didn't answer.

Petey came next door to Cecelia's with me. Cecelia is how come we found this apartment. She was a friend of my mom's a long time ago, even before my mom got married. (She even knew my father.) Cecelia works at the supermarket, but only part-time. When my mom gets home late, Cecelia is usually home. I go there, and she gives me a snack. We do puzzles and play Scrabble. She has fish and a big parrot that talks, and she has plants in cans all over the windowsill and hanging up. I am teaching the parrot new words. But Petey was scared of the parrot. Very scared. He stood in the corner and never moved his eyes from that big bird. And he never said anything.

Cecelia told me in the kitchen that as far as she was informed he never did say a word. But she couldn't say for sure if he could or not. She gave us both glasses of cranberry juice and told me where to take Petey back to his baby-sitter, Mrs. Greiner, down at the other stairs on nine. That's how I first met Mrs. Greiner and got a job.

I help Mrs. Greiner take care of Petey. Because he runs and runs, and she complains she's much too slow and much too fat for that. She wears special furry slippers. They don't do much for her because feet such as hers are beyond help, she says. But she finds Petey real smart and quick. "Turn around and he's gone! Turn around again and he's back!" Mrs. Greiner just loves Petey. She's crazy about him. She'd be sad if she couldn't be Petey's baby-sitter. So I do the running after, and she does the looking after. I listen to her complaining. I do errands for her. Besides baby-sitting, she strings beads for people when their necklaces break. And I'm the delivery girl.

Don't think it is an easy thing to restring beads the way they were. It isn't. You have to make a knot between each bead, and each knot has to be in the exact right spot.

Mrs. Greiner tried to teach me, but my knots never came out in the right place. So then she told me she could see that I was meant to be a messenger, not a knitter or a knotter or any of those things.

But she can do all of those things very fast: knit and crochet and embroider and fix broken cups and earrings and carve teeny animals from wood.

And you can't always tell about Mrs. Greiner. When she's busy she won't stop for anything. But when she feels like it she tells long stories about when she was a child. And she has a lot to say about Melon Hill Houses, and the borough and the city and the whole world . . . . But she has a lot of things that hurt her besides her feet, I think. She says when it's hot out she can hardly move and when it's cold her bones can feel it bad. And wind gets to her. And rain. And when the news is bad it puts her off her food.

But she doesn't make good things to eat. Petey doesn't like to eat at Mrs. Greiner's, and neither do I. Petey likes to eat at my house. One time after she had been talking at me the whole morning about Melon Hill Houses not being kept up nice anymore and about things she read out of the newspaper about people who have nowhere to live and about how much fake pearls and those necklace clasps cost . . . I decided I better just go home. She has a special sad voice when she says all those things. It makes me feel I, Elana Rose Rosen, better do something right away about the mayor and the price of beads . . . and housing . . . whatever . . . immediately!

The next time I walked up the stairs to her apartment, I made up a nickname to call her.

REALLY LOVES HER
ELANA RUSE ROSEN
NO WONDER THAT
IS AN UNUSUAL LADY
HAS NO T.V. IN HER HOUSE
WINS AT SCRABBLE MOST TIMES

EVERY SHAPE AND EVERY COLOR
HAS THOUSANDS OF BEADS
TELLS THE GREATEST STORIES

RUMBLES IN HER STOMACH AND WE LAUGH
EATS THINGS SHE SAYS AREN'T GOOD FOR HER
NEVER GIVES UP WHEN HER WOOL TANGLES
IS ALWAYS TALKING POLITICS TO EVERYBODY
ESPECIALLY ADORES PETEY
RAINY DAYS MAKE HER FEET HURT
GUESSES RIDDLES AND GUESSES WHAT'S BOTHERING YOU

SHE CAN JUST FORGET I'M A KID AND NOT A GROWN-UP
REALLY NICE TO ME BUT A LITTLE UNPREDICTABLE TOO
MAKES LUMPY SOUP, BURNED TOAST AND RUNNY EGGS

THE GREATEST CITY

Poet

by Walt Whitman

What do you think endures?
Do you think the greatest city endures?
Or a teeming manufacturing state? or
    a prepared constitution? or the best
    built steamships?
Or hotels of granite and iron? or any
    chef-d'oeuvres of engineering,
    forts, armaments?
Away! These are not to be cherished
    for themselves,
They fill their hour, the dancers dance,
    the musicians play for them,
The show passes, all does well enough
    of course,
All does very well till one flash of defiance.

The greatest city is that which has the
    greatest men and women,
If it be a few ragged huts, it is still the
    greatest city in the whole world.

Study for Grand Central, 1993
Red Grooms
Watercolor on paper, 22½ X 30"
Courtesy, Marlborough Gallery

46

How to
Create a Community Guide

In many cities and towns, municipal organizations publish guides that describe their communities. People who are interested in living or working in a particular place might consult a community guide to learn more about it.

What is a community guide? A community guide helps answer important questions such as: Where will I live? How will I get to work? Where are community schools and hospitals located? A community guide also tells about the special features that make a city or town unique—community events, things to do for fun, and natural resources like beaches or mountains.

Recent awards and honors received by the local public schools

—The Pittsburgh Public School district holds four Presidential Awards for Excellence.

—*The Christian Science Monitor* called Pittsburgh Public Schools one of America's "most successful" urban school districts.

—Pittsburgh Public Schools was ranked in the Top Six "progressive" U.S. urban school districts in a major Rand Corporation report.

—*Town and Country* named Pittsburgh's Allderdice High School among the Top Seven Urban High Schools nationwide.

—The U.S. Department of Education cited Schenley High School as a "School of Excellence."

—In 1990, the Clarissa Hug Award recognizing the International Teacher of the Year in Special Education went to a Pioneer School teacher in the Pittsburgh school district.

—*Newsweek* cited the district's Arts Propel program as the best arts education program in the world.

—In recent years, four Pittsburgh Public School teachers have been honored as Pennsylvania Teacher of the Year.

Additional information of interest to local professionals

Names of the community's nine colleges and universities

Public school. These are just a few of the accolades recently bestowed on Pittsburgh schools. A decade ago, parents of school-age children were leaving the City for wealthier suburban schools. Today, suburban residents are moving back because of the quality and diversity of the City's schools. For students K-12, Pittsburgh offers comprehensive programs in such subjects as creative and performing arts, international studies, geographic and life sciences, polytechnics, computer science, high technology, law and public service, and teaching as well as general academic programs at neighborhood schools. They also provide early childhood programs, day care, after school care, Head Start, a handicapped preschool and both half-day and full-day kindergartens. Innovative programs such as these have increased Pittsburgh's enrollment ... so much so that Pittsburgh Public Schools is one of the few school districts in Allegheny County that is reopening elementary schools.

Private school. Pittsburgh's private schools are highly regarded. The Independent Schools of Greater Pittsburgh include nine schools within the City that offer intensive academic environments as well as racial, ethnic, religious and economic diversity. They are distinguished by small class sizes, which promote one-on-one teacher/student relationships conducive to learning. Financial assistance is available to help with tuition, which ranges from $6,000 to $10,000 per year, depending on the school. In addition, the Catholic Diocese operates 29 elementary and middle schools, and four secondary schools within Pittsburgh. They emphasize the religious principles of the Catholic tradition in addition to a progressive academic curriculum. Subsidized by parishioners, the cost of Catholic schooling in Pittsburgh is in the $2,000-a-year range.

Higher education. Pittsburghers derive enormous benefits through access to the nine colleges and universities within the City. They infuse the community with a wealth of academic and social opportunity— from the talent they recruit, to the resident students who volunteer in the community ... from the theatre, concerts, lectures and symposiums featuring universally known speakers and artists that they sponsor, to the credit and non-credit courses they teach. Pittsburgh's array of postsecondary technical schools, such as the Pittsburgh Art Institute and the Pittsburgh Culinary Institute, also offer unique educational opportunities. Whether you're interested in an M.B.A. or a Ph.D., an elective course in speech writing or skydiving, sending your second grader to college computer camp, or becoming a world class chef, one of Pittsburgh's institutions of higher learning will meet your need.

PHOTO BY HERB FERGUSON COURTESY OF THE UNIVERSITY OF PITTSBURGH

Pittsburgh Colleges & Universities

Carlow College

Carnegie Mellon University

Chatham College

Community College of Allegheny County

Duquesne University

Pittsburgh Theological Seminary

Point Park College

Robert Morris College

University of Pittsburgh

PHOTO COURTESY OF PITTSBURGH HISTORY & LANDMARKS FOUNDATION

Fortune has rated Pittsburgh the Eighth Best City for Business and the Fifth Largest Corporate Headquarters City. *Savvy* has named it the Third Most Livable City for Women; *Working Mother* has called it the Second Best City for Working Mothers. All told, Pittsburgh is a good place to grow professionally— for men and women.

Corporate diversity. Pittsburgh is headquarters to 12 *Fortune* 500 industrial companies, including *Fortune* 100 giants like Westinghouse Electric, H.J. Heinz, USX, Alcoa and PPG, and four *Fortune* 500 service firms. The skyline reflects this corporate prestige— seven skyrise office complexes have opened Downtown since 1980. Pittsburgh's economy is fueled today by health care, education, finance, light manufacturing and service businesses. High technology businesses are also flourishing— Pennsylvania ranks third in the U.S. behind California and Massachusetts in the number of high technology businesses, and the Pittsburgh region is home to 35 percent of the state's high tech companies. There are nearly 80 companies and 65,000 employees in advanced technology in the Pittsburgh area. More than 170 research centers are located in Pittsburgh, which has one of the highest concentrations of engineers, scientists and technicians in the nation.

Media. Pittsburgh ranks among the Top 20 media markets in the U.S. with eight television stations (including the country's first public television station, WQED-TV) and 33 radio stations (including the nation's first, KDKA-AM). Both a morning and evening daily newspaper as well as an assortment of well-read weekly and monthly publications catering to the business, cultural and multi-ethnic communities keep Pittsburgh professionals informed.

Networking. Two hundred chapters of national professional organizations, from Toastmasters to the National

Pittsburgh
PIT
Before je
the vans
for airpor

Information about the community's schools

Types of companies found in the community

1 Brainstorm

First, choose the community you'd like to create a guide for—either your own or a neighboring city or town. You might also choose a community where you've lived in the past, or a city that you've often visited. Then, brainstorm a list of things about that community that you think people who are moving there would want to know about. It might help to think of different subjects you want to cover in your guide, such as weather, transportation, schools, museums, businesses, neighborhoods, people, things to do, or any other subjects you think are important or interesting.

TOOLS

• paper and pencil

• colored pencils, crayons, or markers

• resource materials

Tip You don't have to stick to information you get from books and pamphlets when you plan your guide. Do you have a favorite place to play ball or ride your skateboard? Or a person in your community you really admire? Including personal information can help others enjoy your city.

2 Research

Review the list of subjects you'd like to include in your guide. Then, decide what kind of information you want to present about each subject. For example, if you'd like to include museums in your guide, you could find out how many museums are in your community, their opening and closing times, what famous things are on display there, and how many people visit them each year. To find the information you need, you might want to check some or all of these sources: a history book about the community, a brochure from the Chamber of Commerce, a map of the city, an almanac or encyclopedia, or a clerk at City Hall.

3 Write Guide Entries

Now that you've researched the subjects, it's time to write your guide. You might want to write a short paragraph describing each entry. Or, you could put the information you've found in list or chart form. Before putting together the final version of your guide, review your entries to make sure you've included all of the information you found. Revise the entries if necessary.

4 Assemble Your Guide

You might want to organize your guide into sections, with such labels as "Places to Go," "Things to Do," and "How to Get Around." Draw pictures or use photos and maps to illustrate the entries in your guide. If you found any quotes about your community, you can include them, too. Create a cover for your guide, using photos of life in your community. When you're finished, share your guide with the class.

If You Are Using a Computer

Use the Newsletter format to write your guide. You can write headlines for each section, then type the entries. Print out and assemble your guide, adding photos, maps, and drawings.

THINK
An urban planner must know a lot about her city. What did you learn about your community that you didn't know before?

Karen Heit
Urban Planner ▶

Cities face many complex challenges.

City Challenges

Read a fantastic story about a city whose streets are overrun by giant trucks.

Meet urban planner Karen Heit, who keeps Los Angeles on the move.

Discover where cities stash growing piles of trash. Learn about a group of kids who work hard to keep their city streets clean.

WORKSHOP 2

Conduct a needs assessment to find out what your community needs most.

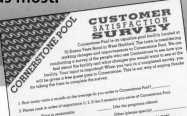
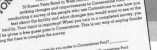

CORNERSTONE POOL

CUSTOMER SATISFACTION SURVEY

Cornerstone Pool is an aquatics pool facility located at 55 Buena Vista Road in West Hartford. The town is considering making changes and improvements to Cornerstone Pool. We are conducting a survey of the people who use Cornerstone to see how you feel about the facility and what changes you would want to see at the facility. Your input is important! When you turn in a completed survey, you will be given a free guest pass to Cornerstone. This is our way of saying thanks for taking the time to complete the survey.

1. How many visits a month on the average do you make to Cornerstone Pool?___

2. Please rank in order of importance (1, 2, 3) the 3 reasons you swim at Cornerstone Pool.
___ Price is reasonable   ___ Like the programs offered
___ Convenient location   ___ Other (please specify)

___ Frequency (1, 2, 3) the three programs you participate in most:
___ instructional lessons

53

From

THE PUSHCART WAR

By Jean Merrill
Illustrated by Beata Szpura

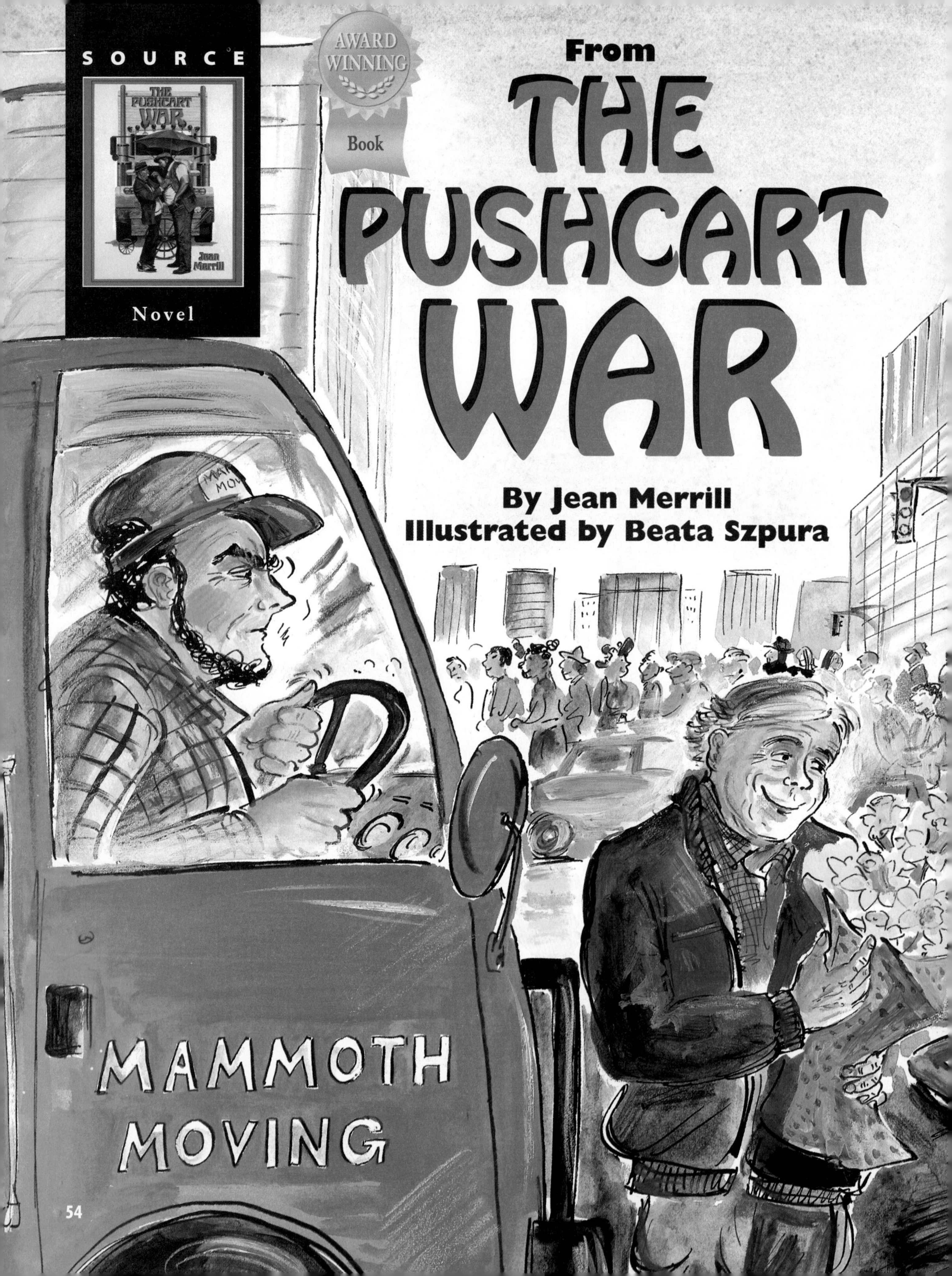

MAMMOTH
MOVING

How It Began: The Daffodil Massacre

The Pushcart War started on the afternoon of March 15, 1998, when a truck ran down a pushcart belonging to a flower peddler. Daffodils were scattered all over the street. The pushcart was flattened, and the owner of the pushcart was pitched headfirst into a pickle barrel.

The owner of the cart was Morris the Florist. The driver of the truck was Mack, who at the time was employed by Mammoth Moving. Mack's full name was Albert P. Mack, but in most accounts of the Pushcart War, he is referred to simply as Mack.

It was near the corner of Sixth Avenue and 17th Street in New York City that the trouble occurred. Mack was trying to park his truck. He had a load of piano stools to deliver, and the space in which he was hoping to park was not quite big enough.

When Mack saw that he could not get his truck into the space by the curb, he yelled at Morris the Florist to move his pushcart. Morris' cart was parked just ahead of Mack.

Morris had been parked in this spot for half an hour, and he was doing a good business. So he paid no attention to Mack.

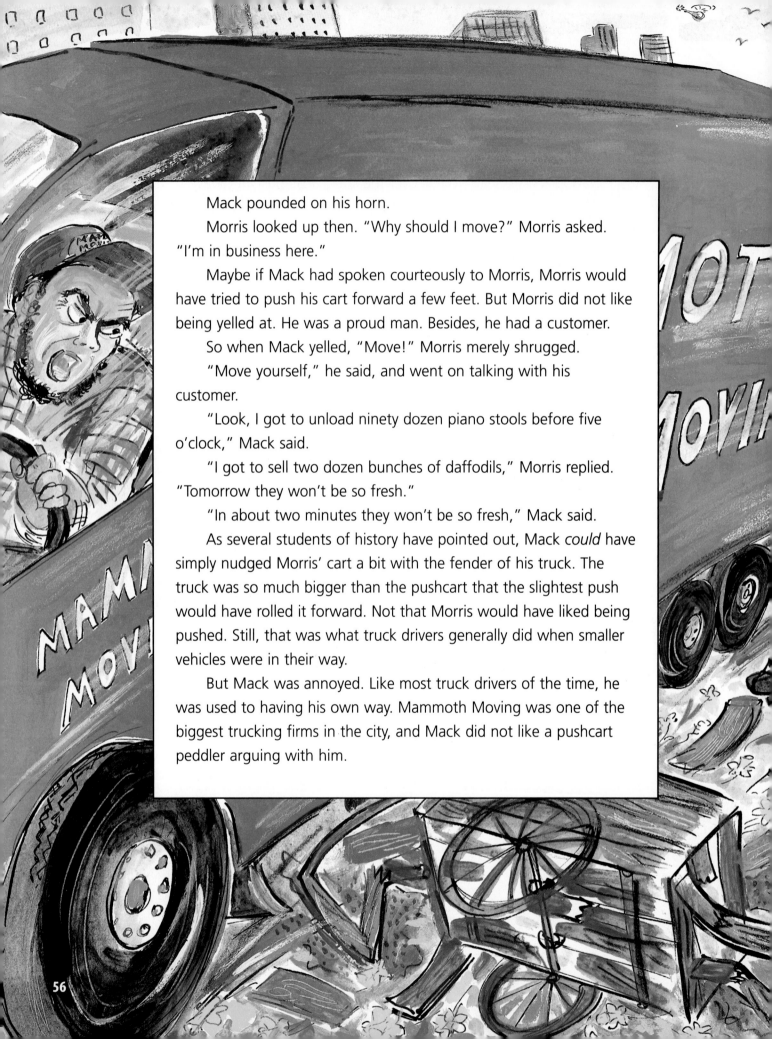

Mack pounded on his horn.

Morris looked up then. "Why should I move?" Morris asked. "I'm in business here."

Maybe if Mack had spoken courteously to Morris, Morris would have tried to push his cart forward a few feet. But Morris did not like being yelled at. He was a proud man. Besides, he had a customer.

So when Mack yelled, "Move!" Morris merely shrugged.

"Move yourself," he said, and went on talking with his customer.

"Look, I got to unload ninety dozen piano stools before five o'clock," Mack said.

"I got to sell two dozen bunches of daffodils," Morris replied. "Tomorrow they won't be so fresh."

"In about two minutes they won't be so fresh," Mack said.

As several students of history have pointed out, Mack *could* have simply nudged Morris' cart a bit with the fender of his truck. The truck was so much bigger than the pushcart that the slightest push would have rolled it forward. Not that Morris would have liked being pushed. Still, that was what truck drivers generally did when smaller vehicles were in their way.

But Mack was annoyed. Like most truck drivers of the time, he was used to having his own way. Mammoth Moving was one of the biggest trucking firms in the city, and Mack did not like a pushcart peddler arguing with him.

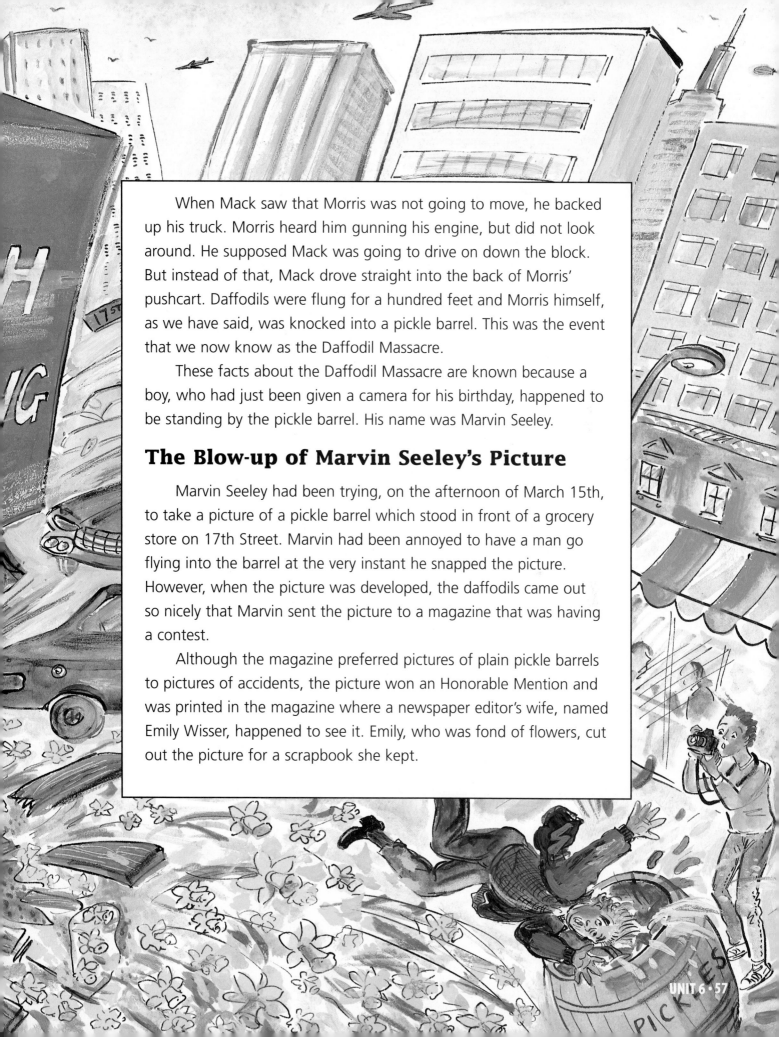

When Mack saw that Morris was not going to move, he backed up his truck. Morris heard him gunning his engine, but did not look around. He supposed Mack was going to drive on down the block. But instead of that, Mack drove straight into the back of Morris' pushcart. Daffodils were flung for a hundred feet and Morris himself, as we have said, was knocked into a pickle barrel. This was the event that we now know as the Daffodil Massacre.

These facts about the Daffodil Massacre are known because a boy, who had just been given a camera for his birthday, happened to be standing by the pickle barrel. His name was Marvin Seeley.

The Blow-up of Marvin Seeley's Picture

Marvin Seeley had been trying, on the afternoon of March 15th, to take a picture of a pickle barrel which stood in front of a grocery store on 17th Street. Marvin had been annoyed to have a man go flying into the barrel at the very instant he snapped the picture. However, when the picture was developed, the daffodils came out so nicely that Marvin sent the picture to a magazine that was having a contest.

Although the magazine preferred pictures of plain pickle barrels to pictures of accidents, the picture won an Honorable Mention and was printed in the magazine where a newspaper editor's wife, named Emily Wisser, happened to see it. Emily, who was fond of flowers, cut out the picture for a scrapbook she kept.

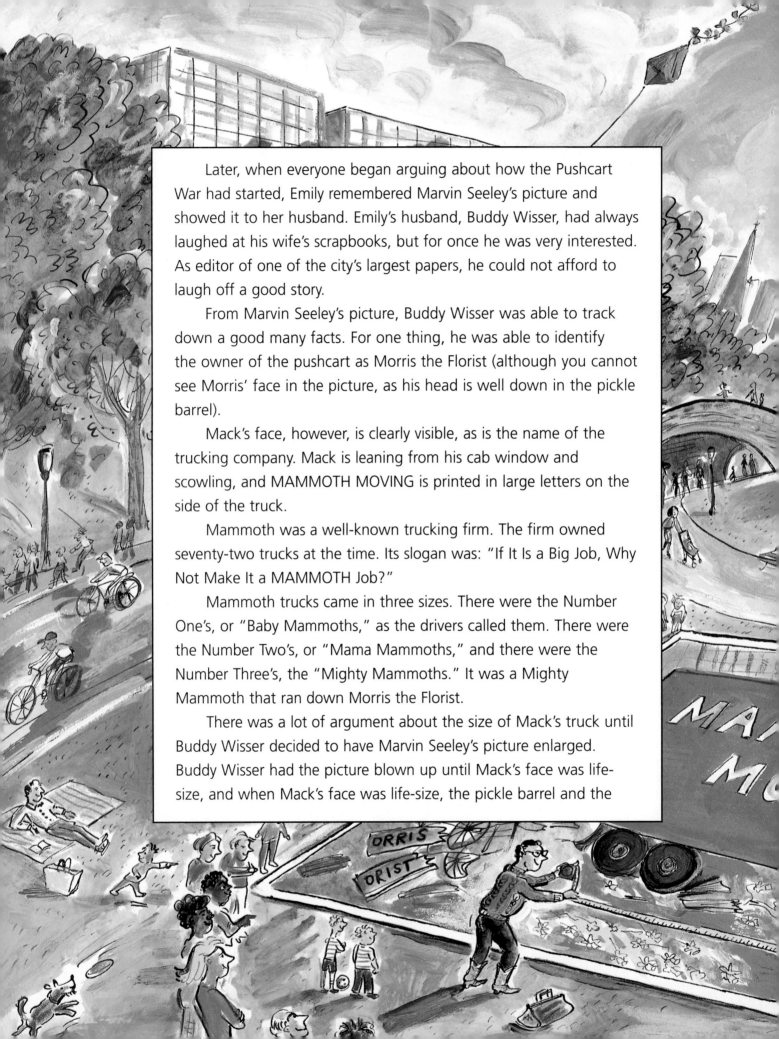

Later, when everyone began arguing about how the Pushcart War had started, Emily remembered Marvin Seeley's picture and showed it to her husband. Emily's husband, Buddy Wisser, had always laughed at his wife's scrapbooks, but for once he was very interested. As editor of one of the city's largest papers, he could not afford to laugh off a good story.

From Marvin Seeley's picture, Buddy Wisser was able to track down a good many facts. For one thing, he was able to identify the owner of the pushcart as Morris the Florist (although you cannot see Morris' face in the picture, as his head is well down in the pickle barrel).

Mack's face, however, is clearly visible, as is the name of the trucking company. Mack is leaning from his cab window and scowling, and MAMMOTH MOVING is printed in large letters on the side of the truck.

Mammoth was a well-known trucking firm. The firm owned seventy-two trucks at the time. Its slogan was: "If It Is a Big Job, Why Not Make It a MAMMOTH Job?"

Mammoth trucks came in three sizes. There were the Number One's, or "Baby Mammoths," as the drivers called them. There were the Number Two's, or "Mama Mammoths," and there were the Number Three's, the "Mighty Mammoths." It was a Mighty Mammoth that ran down Morris the Florist.

There was a lot of argument about the size of Mack's truck until Buddy Wisser decided to have Marvin Seeley's picture enlarged. Buddy Wisser had the picture blown up until Mack's face was life-size, and when Mack's face was life-size, the pickle barrel and the

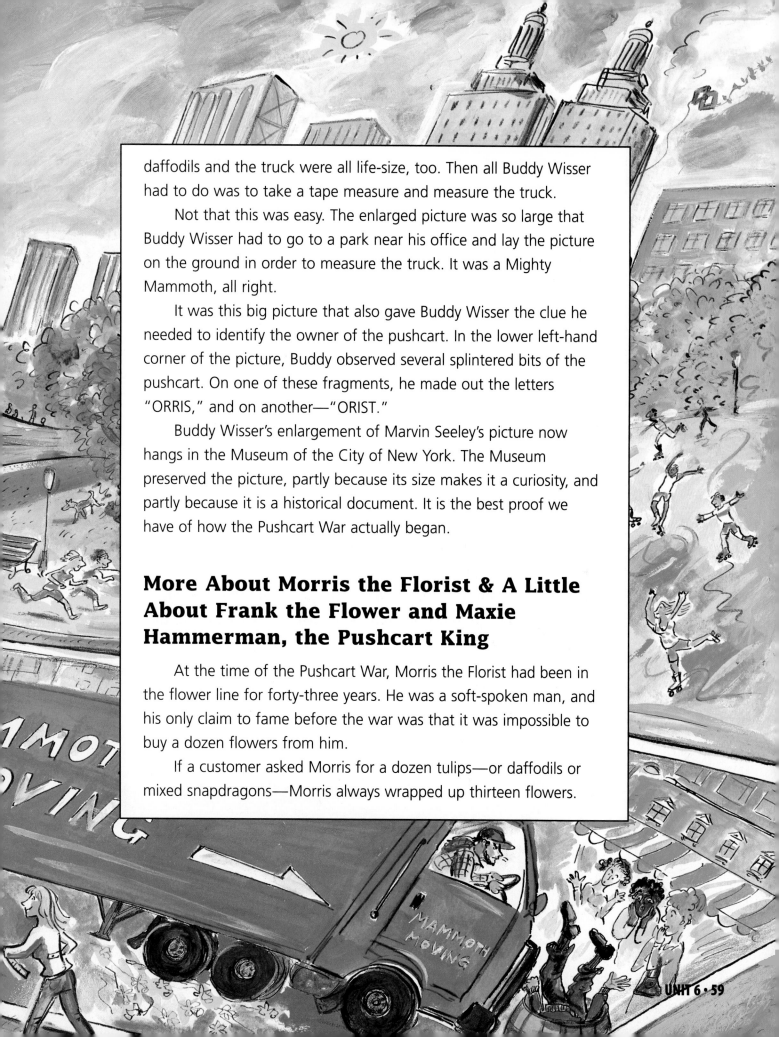

daffodils and the truck were all life-size, too. Then all Buddy Wisser had to do was to take a tape measure and measure the truck.

Not that this was easy. The enlarged picture was so large that Buddy Wisser had to go to a park near his office and lay the picture on the ground in order to measure the truck. It was a Mighty Mammoth, all right.

It was this big picture that also gave Buddy Wisser the clue he needed to identify the owner of the pushcart. In the lower left-hand corner of the picture, Buddy observed several splintered bits of the pushcart. On one of these fragments, he made out the letters "ORRIS," and on another—"ORIST."

Buddy Wisser's enlargement of Marvin Seeley's picture now hangs in the Museum of the City of New York. The Museum preserved the picture, partly because its size makes it a curiosity, and partly because it is a historical document. It is the best proof we have of how the Pushcart War actually began.

More About Morris the Florist & A Little About Frank the Flower and Maxie Hammerman, the Pushcart King

At the time of the Pushcart War, Morris the Florist had been in the flower line for forty-three years. He was a soft-spoken man, and his only claim to fame before the war was that it was impossible to buy a dozen flowers from him.

If a customer asked Morris for a dozen tulips—or daffodils or mixed snapdragons—Morris always wrapped up thirteen flowers.

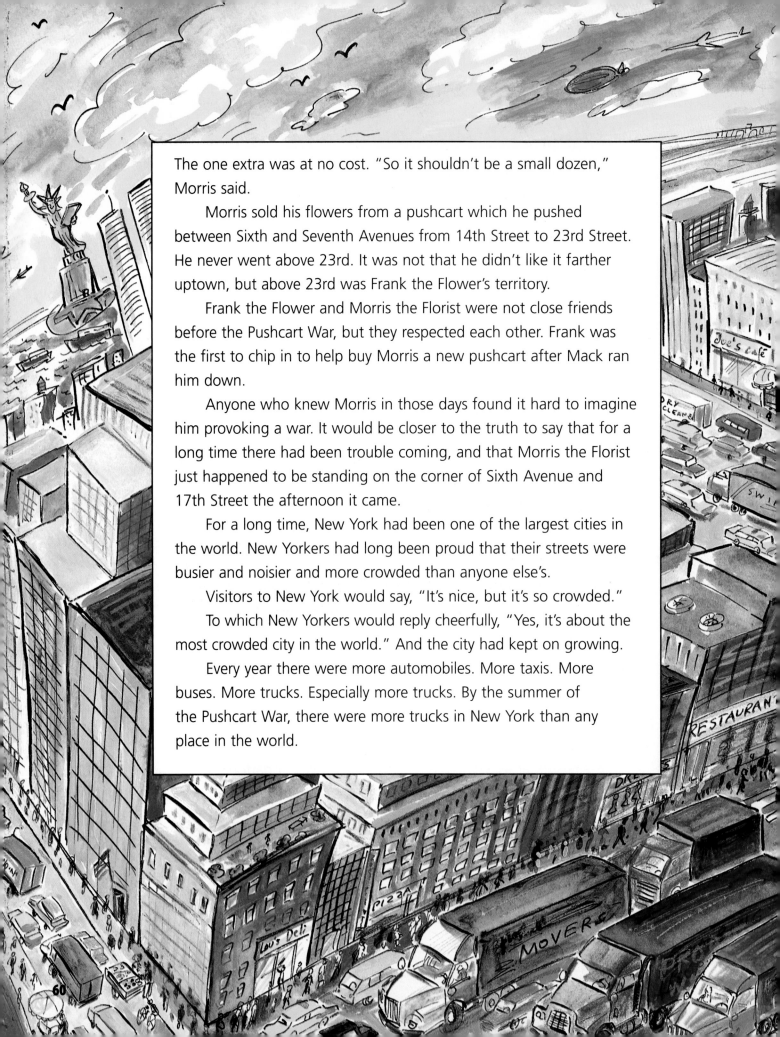

The one extra was at no cost. "So it shouldn't be a small dozen," Morris said.

Morris sold his flowers from a pushcart which he pushed between Sixth and Seventh Avenues from 14th Street to 23rd Street. He never went above 23rd. It was not that he didn't like it farther uptown, but above 23rd was Frank the Flower's territory.

Frank the Flower and Morris the Florist were not close friends before the Pushcart War, but they respected each other. Frank was the first to chip in to help buy Morris a new pushcart after Mack ran him down.

Anyone who knew Morris in those days found it hard to imagine him provoking a war. It would be closer to the truth to say that for a long time there had been trouble coming, and that Morris the Florist just happened to be standing on the corner of Sixth Avenue and 17th Street the afternoon it came.

For a long time, New York had been one of the largest cities in the world. New Yorkers had long been proud that their streets were busier and noisier and more crowded than anyone else's.

Visitors to New York would say, "It's nice, but it's so crowded."

To which New Yorkers would reply cheerfully, "Yes, it's about the most crowded city in the world." And the city had kept on growing.

Every year there were more automobiles. More taxis. More buses. More trucks. Especially more trucks. By the summer of the Pushcart War, there were more trucks in New York than any place in the world.

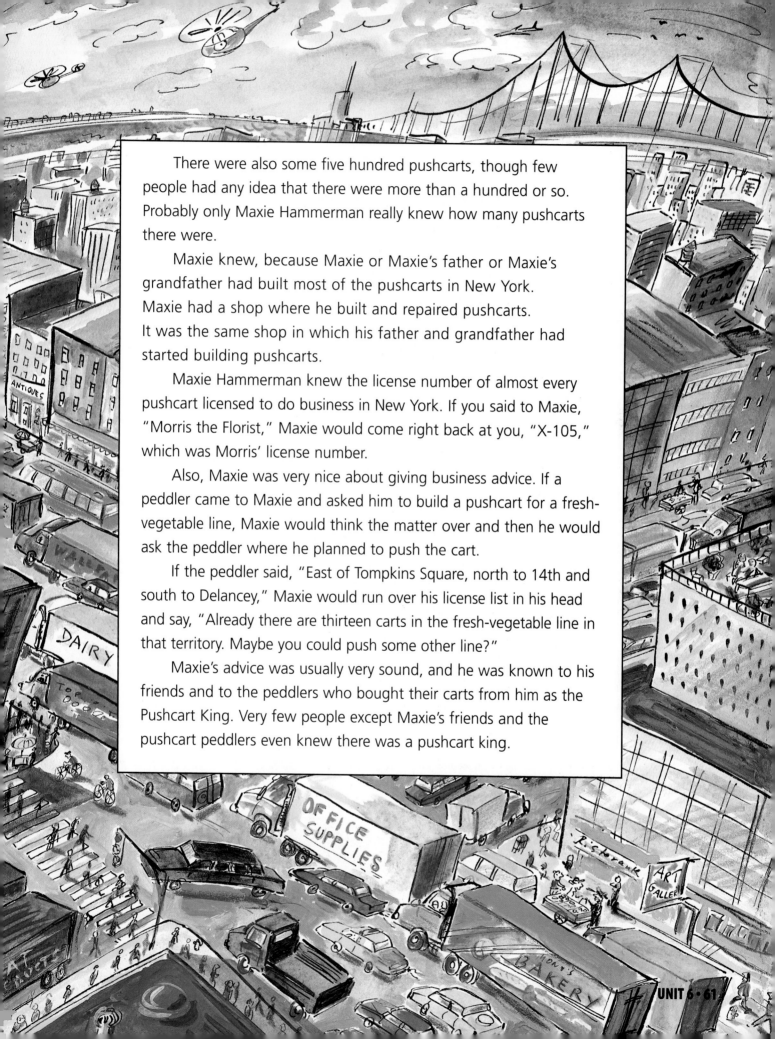

There were also some five hundred pushcarts, though few people had any idea that there were more than a hundred or so. Probably only Maxie Hammerman really knew how many pushcarts there were.

Maxie knew, because Maxie or Maxie's father or Maxie's grandfather had built most of the pushcarts in New York. Maxie had a shop where he built and repaired pushcarts. It was the same shop in which his father and grandfather had started building pushcarts.

Maxie Hammerman knew the license number of almost every pushcart licensed to do business in New York. If you said to Maxie, "Morris the Florist," Maxie would come right back at you, "X-105," which was Morris' license number.

Also, Maxie was very nice about giving business advice. If a peddler came to Maxie and asked him to build a pushcart for a fresh-vegetable line, Maxie would think the matter over and then he would ask the peddler where he planned to push the cart.

If the peddler said, "East of Tompkins Square, north to 14th and south to Delancey," Maxie would run over his license list in his head and say, "Already there are thirteen carts in the fresh-vegetable line in that territory. Maybe you could push some other line?"

Maxie's advice was usually very sound, and he was known to his friends and to the peddlers who bought their carts from him as the Pushcart King. Very few people except Maxie's friends and the pushcart peddlers even knew there was a pushcart king.

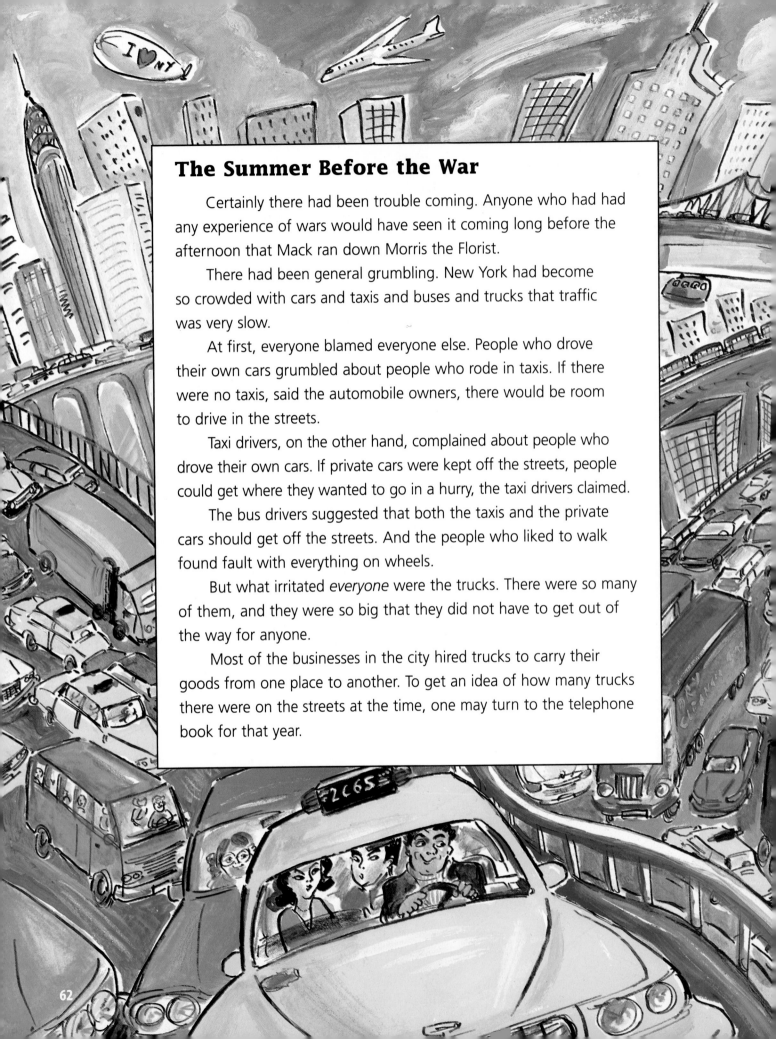

The Summer Before the War

Certainly there had been trouble coming. Anyone who had had any experience of wars would have seen it coming long before the afternoon that Mack ran down Morris the Florist.

There had been general grumbling. New York had become so crowded with cars and taxis and buses and trucks that traffic was very slow.

At first, everyone blamed everyone else. People who drove their own cars grumbled about people who rode in taxis. If there were no taxis, said the automobile owners, there would be room to drive in the streets.

Taxi drivers, on the other hand, complained about people who drove their own cars. If private cars were kept off the streets, people could get where they wanted to go in a hurry, the taxi drivers claimed.

The bus drivers suggested that both the taxis and the private cars should get off the streets. And the people who liked to walk found fault with everything on wheels.

But what irritated *everyone* were the trucks. There were so many of them, and they were so big that they did not have to get out of the way for anyone.

Most of the businesses in the city hired trucks to carry their goods from one place to another. To get an idea of how many trucks there were on the streets at the time, one may turn to the telephone book for that year.

In the classified section, for instance, if one opens to the "P" listings, a few of the products one will find advertised there are:

Package Handles
Paint
Pajama Trimmings
Pancake Mixes
Pants
Paper Plates
Parachutes
Park Benches
Parking Meters
Parquet Floors
Party Favors
Paste
Patent Medicines
Patterns
Paving Brick
Pawn Tickets
Peas
Peanut Butter
Pearls
Pecans
Pencils
Pen Knives
Penicillin
Pennants
Pens
Pepper
Perambulators
Percales
Perfumes
Periodicals
Permanent Wave Machines
Pet Shop Supplies
Petroleum
Pewter
Pharmaceuticals
Phonographs
Photographic Supplies
Piano Stools
Piccolos
Pickle Barrels
Picnic Tables

Picture Frames
Picture Post Cards
Picture Windows
Pies
Pigskins
Pile Drivers
Pillows
Pins
Pipe
Pipe Organs
Pistol Belts
Piston Rings
Pizza Pie Supplies
Place Cards
Planetariums
Plant Foods
Plaques
Plaster of Paris
Plastics
Plate Glass
Platforms
Platinum
Playground Equipment
Playing Cards
Playsuits
Playthings
Pleating Machine Part
Plexiglass
Pliers
Plows
Plugs
Plumbago
Plushes
Plywood
Pocketbooks
Podiums
Poker Chips
Poisons
Poles
Police Badges
Polish

Polo Mallets
Pompoms
Ponchos
Pony Carts
Pool Tables
Popcorn Machines
Porch Furniture
Postage Stamp Affixers
Posters
Potatoes
Potato Peelers
Pot Holders
Potted Plants
Pottery
Poultry
Powder Puffs
Precious Stones
Precision Castings
Premium Goods
Preserves
Pressing Machines
Pressure Cookers
Pretzels
Price Tags
Printing Presses
Propellers
Projectors
Prunes
Public Address Systems
Publications
Pulleys
Pulpits
Pumice
Pumps
Punch Bowls
Puppets
Purses
Pushcart Parts
Putty
Puzzles

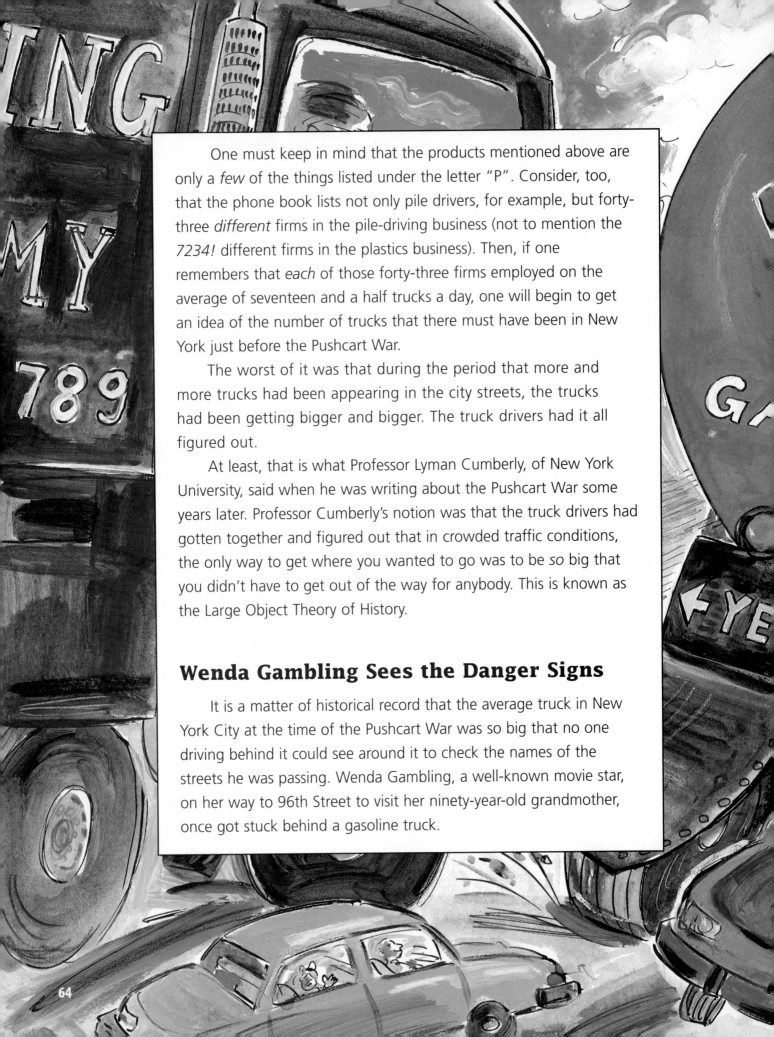

One must keep in mind that the products mentioned above are only a *few* of the things listed under the letter "P". Consider, too, that the phone book lists not only pile drivers, for example, but forty-three *different* firms in the pile-driving business (not to mention the *7234!* different firms in the plastics business). Then, if one remembers that *each* of those forty-three firms employed on the average of seventeen and a half trucks a day, one will begin to get an idea of the number of trucks that there must have been in New York just before the Pushcart War.

The worst of it was that during the period that more and more trucks had been appearing in the city streets, the trucks had been getting bigger and bigger. The truck drivers had it all figured out.

At least, that is what Professor Lyman Cumberly, of New York University, said when he was writing about the Pushcart War some years later. Professor Cumberly's notion was that the truck drivers had gotten together and figured out that in crowded traffic conditions, the only way to get where you wanted to go was to be *so* big that you didn't have to get out of the way for anybody. This is known as the Large Object Theory of History.

Wenda Gambling Sees the Danger Signs

It is a matter of historical record that the average truck in New York City at the time of the Pushcart War was so big that no one driving behind it could see around it to check the names of the streets he was passing. Wenda Gambling, a well-known movie star, on her way to 96th Street to visit her ninety-year-old grandmother, once got stuck behind a gasoline truck.

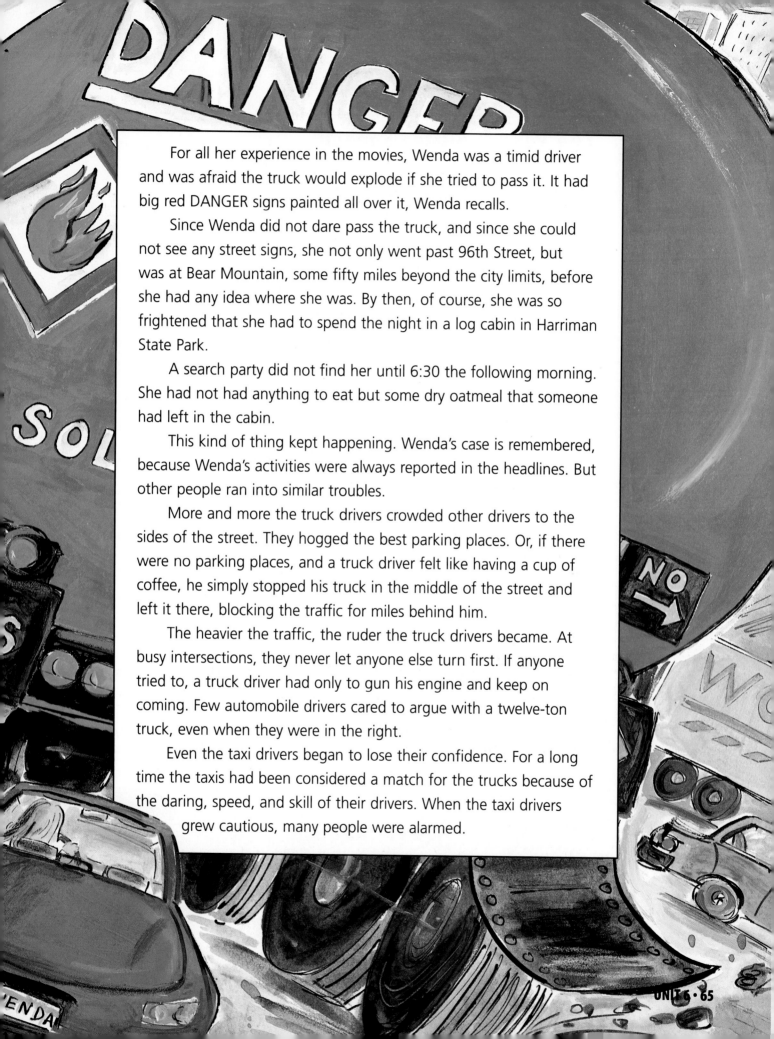

For all her experience in the movies, Wenda was a timid driver and was afraid the truck would explode if she tried to pass it. It had big red DANGER signs painted all over it, Wenda recalls.

Since Wenda did not dare pass the truck, and since she could not see any street signs, she not only went past 96th Street, but was at Bear Mountain, some fifty miles beyond the city limits, before she had any idea where she was. By then, of course, she was so frightened that she had to spend the night in a log cabin in Harriman State Park.

A search party did not find her until 6:30 the following morning. She had not had anything to eat but some dry oatmeal that someone had left in the cabin.

This kind of thing kept happening. Wenda's case is remembered, because Wenda's activities were always reported in the headlines. But other people ran into similar troubles.

More and more the truck drivers crowded other drivers to the sides of the street. They hogged the best parking places. Or, if there were no parking places, and a truck driver felt like having a cup of coffee, he simply stopped his truck in the middle of the street and left it there, blocking the traffic for miles behind him.

The heavier the traffic, the ruder the truck drivers became. At busy intersections, they never let anyone else turn first. If anyone tried to, a truck driver had only to gun his engine and keep on coming. Few automobile drivers cared to argue with a twelve-ton truck, even when they were in the right.

Even the taxi drivers began to lose their confidence. For a long time the taxis had been considered a match for the trucks because of the daring, speed, and skill of their drivers. When the taxi drivers grew cautious, many people were alarmed.

The Peanut Butter Speech

One of the first people to speak out against the growing danger was a man named Archie Love. Archie Love was running for Mayor at the time, and he promised to reduce the number of trucks in the streets.

It looked briefly as if Archie Love might be elected on the strength of this promise alone. But that was before Archie's opponent, Emmett P. Cudd (who was already Mayor and did not want to lose his job), made his famous "Peanut Butter Speech" in Union Square.

Mayor Cudd repeated the Peanut Butter Speech ninety times in one week. It went more or less as follows:

"Friends and New Yorkers: New York is one of the biggest cities in the U.S.A. We are proud of that fact.

"What makes a city big? Big business, naturally.

"And what is the difference between big business and small business? It is this: If you order fourteen cartons of peanut butter, you are running a small business. If you order four hundred cartons of peanut butter, you are running a big business.

"Fourteen cartons of peanut butter, you can get delivered in a station wagon. But for four hundred cartons of peanut butter, you need a truck. And you need a *big* truck. Big trucks mean progress.

"My opponent, Archie Love, is against trucks. He is, therefore, against progress. Maybe he is even against peanut butter."

Naturally, all the truck drivers voted to re-elect Mayor Cudd, and so did a lot of other people. Very few people wanted to be against progress. No one wanted to be against peanut butter. And *everyone* wanted to be proud of their city, because they always had been. Thus, Archie Love did not get elected, and the trucks kept getting bigger.

As the trucks increased in size, traffic—as Archie Love had predicted—grew steadily worse until, in the spring before the Pushcart War, the city was one big traffic jam most of the time. One day it took a taxi four hours to drive five blocks.

The passenger in the taxi was Professor Lyman Cumberly, who did not complain because he was working on his Large Object Theory of History and found the situation interesting from a scientific point of view. During this ride, Professor Cumberly fell into conversation with an impatient young man from Seattle who was trapped in an adjoining taxi.

The young man was shocked that so many New Yorkers accepted the terrible conditions in their streets without protest, and Professor Cumberly recalls that the visitor had very definite ideas what should be done about the trucks. In fact, encouraged by Professor Cumberly's interest, the young man flew back to Seattle and wrote a book.

The book, called *The Enemy in the Streets*, was a fearless attack on the trucks. However, as the author was unknown, the book did not receive much notice at the time it was published. It is remembered today largely because the author is now President of the United States.

The Words That Triggered the War
(Wenda Gambling's Innocent Remark)

What finally brought matters to a head was a television program called "The Day the Traffic Stopped." The day before the program, the traffic *had* stopped entirely, and one of the television stations had hurriedly called in a panel of experts to explain why.

The members of the panel were:

Robert Alexander Wrightson—Traffic Commissioner of New York

Alexander P. Wolfson—head of Wolfson & Wolfson, specialists in traffic coordination

Dr. Wolfe Alexander—a traffic psychologist

Wenda Gambling—a well-known movie star

Wenda Gambling was hardly an expert on traffic. But as the three other panel members were elderly men (one stout, one bald, and one near-sighted), the moderator of the program felt that the panel would be more interesting to the audience if Wenda were at the table.

In introducing Wenda, the moderator of the program said, "As we all know, Miss Gambling's new movie, *The Streets of New York*, is being shot on the streets of New York, and as the streets of New York are the subject of our discussion tonight, it is very appropriate that she should be here."

Wenda tactfully left most of the talking to the experts. Each of the three men had a different theory as to why the traffic had stopped.

Robert Alexander Wrightson said that there was no cause for alarm, that the whole thing was a simple matter of what he liked to call "the density of moving objects."

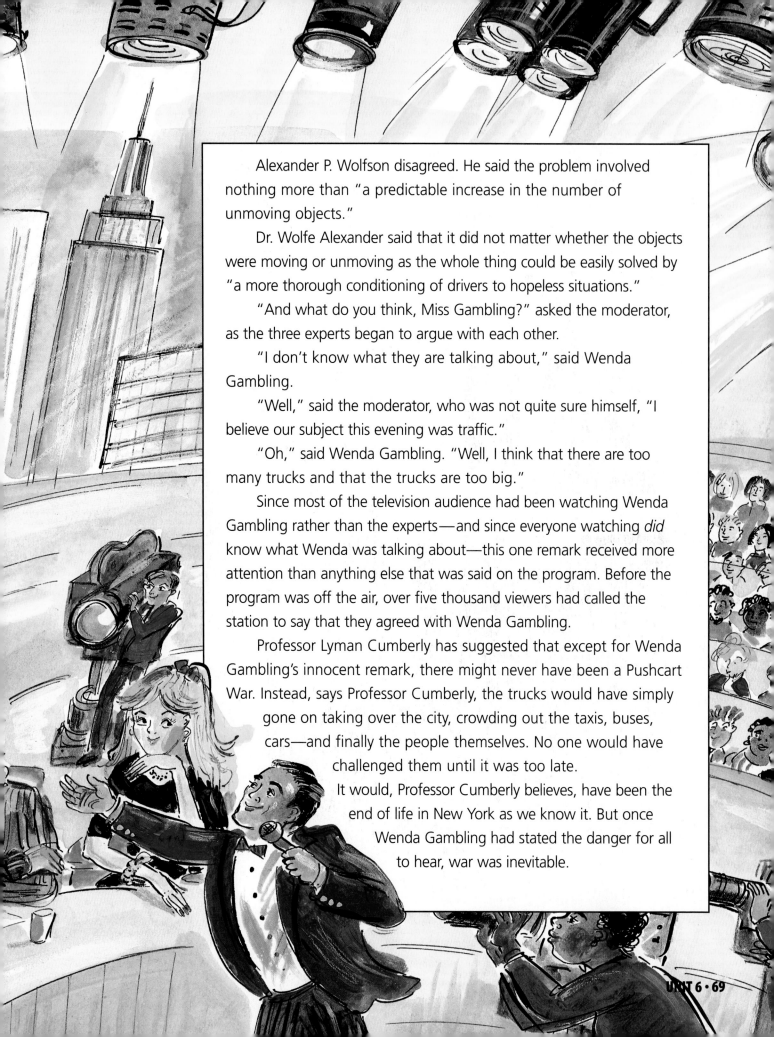

Alexander P. Wolfson disagreed. He said the problem involved nothing more than "a predictable increase in the number of unmoving objects."

Dr. Wolfe Alexander said that it did not matter whether the objects were moving or unmoving as the whole thing could be easily solved by "a more thorough conditioning of drivers to hopeless situations."

"And what do you think, Miss Gambling?" asked the moderator, as the three experts began to argue with each other.

"I don't know what they are talking about," said Wenda Gambling.

"Well," said the moderator, who was not quite sure himself, "I believe our subject this evening was traffic."

"Oh," said Wenda Gambling. "Well, I think that there are too many trucks and that the trucks are too big."

Since most of the television audience had been watching Wenda Gambling rather than the experts—and since everyone watching *did* know what Wenda was talking about—this one remark received more attention than anything else that was said on the program. Before the program was off the air, over five thousand viewers had called the station to say that they agreed with Wenda Gambling.

Professor Lyman Cumberly has suggested that except for Wenda Gambling's innocent remark, there might never have been a Pushcart War. Instead, says Professor Cumberly, the trucks would have simply gone on taking over the city, crowding out the taxis, buses, cars—and finally the people themselves. No one would have challenged them until it was too late.

It would, Professor Cumberly believes, have been the end of life in New York as we know it. But once Wenda Gambling had stated the danger for all to hear, war was inevitable.

MENTOR

Karen Heit

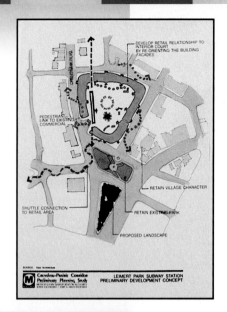

LEIMERT PARK SUBWAY STATION
PRELIMINARY DEVELOPMENT CONCEPT

Urban Planner

Urban planners *plot* the future of our cities.

The job of any urban planner is to think of ways to improve a city's future. In Los Angeles a better transportation system is needed. Each day millions of cars jam the city's freeways and pollute its air. The residents of Los Angeles hope to see an improved traffic situation in their future. That's where Karen Heit comes in. She's an urban planner specializing in transportation.

PROFILE

Name: Karen Heit

Occupation: urban planner for the Los Angeles County Transportation Authority

Job title: Director, South Bay Area Team

Pets: two dogs, two turtles, a tadpole, and a tarantula

Favorite place to go in L.A.: the beach

Favorite way to get around L.A.: walking—until the subway system is completed!

Long Beach

71

UESTIONS
for Karen Heit

Here's how *urban planner* Karen Heit gets L.A. moving.

 What kind of transportation problems does Los Angeles have?

 For 20 years, L.A. has been known for having one of the worst traffic situations in the country. During an event like an L.A. Lakers basketball game, the highways become one big parking lot.

 So what's the solution?

 It lies in expanding the rail system. We've got two lines running now, but we need to build many more.

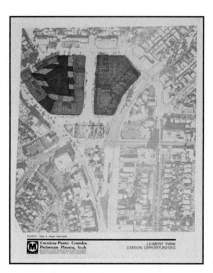

 How do you plan the rail lines?

 First, my staff and I determine the best place to run the lines. We conduct surveys and talk with community members to come up with possible locations.

 What happens next?

 I plot out routes for the lines on maps. It can take 12 to 13 years to complete a rail line! When the lines are up and

Q In your opinion, what quality helps an urban planner most?

A The number-one resource for urban planning is imagination. We have to be able to visualize a community springing back to life, then make it happen.

running, we continue to deal with the concerns of the people who live near them. We hold community meetings on a regular basis to get input from residents.

Q Will the rail lines help the community in other ways besides easing traffic?

A Absolutely. Our latest line will be built in a high-unemployment area. The line should attract new businesses and services, making the area a better place to live.

Karen Heit's
Tips for Assessing and Responding

1 Survey community residents to find out what sorts of improvements they would most like to see in their community.

2 Interview local business owners and service persons to learn about the commercial needs of the area.

3 Meet with community members to get their feedback about changes in the community.

From Garbage!

Where It Comes From, Where It Goes

AWARD WINNING Book

by Evan and Janet Hadingham

Imagine walking in New York City on a hot summer day. Sweaty pedestrians packed on the pavements, taxi horns, police sirens, sticky air, and traffic fumes can all make your walk pretty unpleasant. But that's nothing compared to what it was like about a hundred years ago.

Back then, there were no regular city-wide collections of garbage. You tossed your trash in wooden barrels lined up on the pavement. In between the barrels were big piles of coal or wood ash on which you dumped the ashes from your fireplace each morning. And you probably didn't think twice about throwing food or even toilet waste directly into the gutter.

But when you ventured out for a walk, you could scarcely ignore the filthy streets of New York. If you were a woman, you were wearing long skirts and had to lift them frequently to avoid the messes on the sidewalk. On some street corners you could scarcely breathe because of the fumes from breweries, slaughterhouses, and factories, combined with the stink from the gutter.

◀

Putting out the garbage on Ludlow Street, New York City, in 1881. The sidewalks were littered with heaps of ashes emptied from fireplaces and furnaces.

▲

Since 1900, New York's garbage trucks have improved, but the job they do has stayed much the same. At a city waterfront, trucks tip trash onto barges in 1980 (top) and around 1900 (bottom).

Boxes, Boxes Everywhere

In just one day, Americans toss out 150,000 tons (136,000 metric tons) of packaging material. This amount would fill about 10,000 tractor trailers. If all the trucks were lined up end-to-end, they would stretch for 120 miles (190 km).

Get Nosey About Your Garbage

Be a garbage detective. Figure out what goes into your garbage pail: Is it mostly food scraps or packaging? Do some research. For one week, instead of tossing packaging material into your regular garbage pail, collect it in a separate cardboard box.

Then try to identify the different materials (plastic, paper, aluminum, etc.). Notice the many different types of plastic— some are stiff, others light and supple; can you tell why that particular type of plastic was chosen for each package?

Can you figure out the main purpose of each packaging item? Was it to keep the food fresh? To protect it from damage during shipping? Do you think any of the items are examples of *overpackaging*— packaging that's there simply to make the item bigger and more eye-catching?

Continue your detective work next time you're at the grocery store. Which are the most overpackaged brands? If you or your parents avoid buying them, you'll be helping to solve the garbage problem.

And even though today's car fumes can make New York unpleasant and unhealthy, "exhaust" from horses presented quite a problem in the days before the automobile. A century ago, Brooklyn's horses produced 200 tons (180 metric tons) of manure a day (enough to fill eight railroad freight cars). In springtime, farmers visited the city with wagons and removed some of the horse manure to spread on their fields as fertilizer. But by summer, much of it ended up ground into the mud in the city's unpaved back alleys.

Many of New York's poor neighborhoods were so filthy and overcrowded that serious diseases such as typhoid and cholera spread easily. One such outbreak in 1892 helped shake up citizens and officials, who finally realized that garbage had become a serious problem. But how could they solve it?

The first solution was to dump it at sea. Around 1900, most of New York's trash was loaded on barges, towed out of the harbor for about ten miles (16 km), then heaved into the Atlantic. Bathers at New Jersey's crowded beaches were sometimes startled when they swam up against objects such as floating mattresses and dead dogs. In fact, the problem became so bad that New Jersey's state officials forced New York City to stop ocean dumping in 1933.

But even today, many east coast beaches are forced to close down for days or weeks during the summer. The reason? Washed-up trash, sewage, sometimes even waste from hospitals that may carry germs or viruses. Some of the garbage is spilled accidentally or blown from landfills close to the ocean, like New York's giant trash mound at Fresh Kills on Staten Island. But much of it is dumped illegally. While New York and other coastal cities were forced to give up ocean dumping long ago, the pollution continues.

Some people with a garbage problem on their hands are still prepared to break the law and use the ocean as a dump.

▶

Around 1900, most of New York City's trash was carried out to the harbor in barges, where it was shoveled into the sea.

▶

Trash dumped in New York's harbor would often drift down to New Jersey beaches to surprise bathers.

A Day in the Life of New York's Garbage

Every day, 1,000 garbage trucks crawl through the streets of New York City, each operated by a two-person crew. After picking up a full load, the crew drives its truck to one of thirteen different piers on the city's waterfront. There they put the truck into reverse and back it up to the edge of the pier, dumping their load into a barge waiting in the water below. Each

Today, New York's eight million residents throw out enough garbage every month to fill up the Empire State Building. After curbside collection, most of it ends up on barges that are towed past the skyscrapers of Manhattan and out into the harbor.

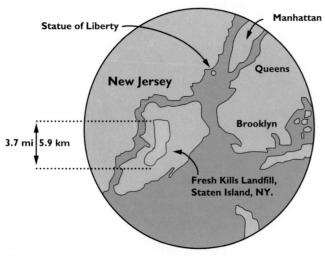

Statue of Liberty

Manhattan

New Jersey

Queens

Brooklyn

3.7 mi / 5.9 km

Fresh Kills Landfill, Staten Island, NY.

barge can hold 6,000 tons of trash. Tugboats then pull the barges across the harbor to their destination: the world's largest dump, Fresh Kills, on Staten Island. ("Kills" comes from the original Dutch settlers' word for "channel.") This dump covers an area of 3,000 acres (1,215 ha), equal to 16,000 baseball diamonds.

Once the barges arrive, giant cranes shift the trash into wagons, which are then pulled by tractors up onto the summit of Fresh Kills. Bulldozers help spread the trash and cover it with dirt. In summer, water containing insecticide is sprayed everywhere to keep down the clouds of dust and flies.

After ocean dumping was banned in 1933, New York's garbage had nowhere to go except to dumps like Fresh Kills and to a few *incinerators* (garbage-burning plants). For a while, dump sites were plentiful. But as the city grew and more and more New Yorkers objected to living near the dumps, one by one they were shut down.

The barges finally arrive at Fresh Kills on Staten Island, where a giant crane unloads the trash and bulldozers push it around, creating a human-made mountain.

Fresh Kills is now one of only two dumps remaining in operation. The vast majority of the city's rubbish ends up here—some 22,000 tons (20,000 metric tons) of it a day. By the year 2000 or even earlier, Fresh Kills will be full and the city will have to come up with another garbage solution. By that time, the mound will be over five hundred feet (150m) high—about the height of the Washington Monument. It will be the highest spot on the eastern seaboard south of Maine.

The Packaging Explosion

Back when your great-grandparents were children, a trip to a grocery store was very different from what it is today. There was much less packaging and instead of picking up new bags from the store, you always took your own basket or canvas bag for carrying groceries home.

Many items were stored out of reach behind the counter. If you had a large family you probably bought big bags of flour and sugar. (And when the cotton sacks were empty, you didn't throw them away. Instead, you bleached and sewed them into children's underwear.)

Every Day Americans Throw Out:

an average of about 4 pounds (1.8 kg) of garbage each. If you piled everyone's daily trash together in a single giant heap, it would weigh more than 438,000 tons (398,000 metric tons). Or if you managed to load it all into garbage trucks, you would need 63,000 of them. Lined up end to end, these 63,000 trucks would stretch for nearly 370 miles (600 km), about the distance from San Francisco to Los Angeles.

A few food items were sold in metal cans, but these were expensive. Besides, like most people, you probably did your own canning in glass jars that you used again year after year. If you did buy canned food, you kept the cans to store household objects like nails or buttons.

In 1879, a businessman named Frank Woolworth opened the first five-and-ten store in upstate New York. (It was called five-and-ten because back then many items cost a dime or less.) Woolworth was the first to pioneer the idea of displaying store goods on open shelves so that customers could see and touch the items themselves.

In the Days Before Plastic

Ask the oldest person you know what it was like to go shopping when he or she was a child. Were there grocery carts? How many kinds of breakfast cereal were available? What came in cans? How were groceries brought home from the store? Was any packaging material saved and reused? What happened to food scraps? How was life different without the convenience foods we have today?

This meant there had to be a lot more packaging of individual items, partly to catch the customer's eye and partly to make it a little harder for anyone to slip the items into a pocket and steal them from the store.

Packaging also keeps food fresh longer, and that helped to make the whole idea of convenience foods possible. But the popularity of such items as ready-made soups, cake mixes, and frozen dinners has led to an explosion in the amount of disposable plastic, paper, and aluminum we take into our homes at the end of every shopping trip.

So many items crowd the supermarket shelves that food companies compete with each other to make their packages brighter, shinier, more appealing. That means a lot of overpackaging— far more than is necessary to keep food from spoiling. And it costs us all money: One out of every ten dollars you spend on groceries pays for the cost of packaging them.

What's in our trash: This diagram gives a rough idea of the different percentages of materials typically thrown out by Americans.

36% Paper and cardboard

20% Yard wastes

9% Food wastes

9% Metals

8% Glass
7% Plastics
6% Textiles & wood
3% Rubber & leather
2% Miscellaneous

Throwaway World

In 1955, *Life* magazine reported on a popular trend—"throwaway living." The 1950s were a boom time for middle-class Americans. They had been through years of restrictions and shortages during the Second World War, when they had to save every little scrap. Now they rushed out to buy disposable plates, knives, forks, frying pans, diapers—anything that promised to cut down on tedious chores. In this article, *Life* also reported on bizarre items such as disposable curtains, disposable duck-hunting decoys, and a 79-cent barbeque grill that you used once and tossed out.

While many items never caught on, a lot of products today are still designed to be used only once or twice. For instance, think of plastic shaving razors, mini-

Throwaway Living in the 1990s

Each year, Americans get rid of 350 million disposable plastic cigarette lighters, 1½ billion ballpoint pens, and 2 billion plastic shaving razors.

flashlights that you throw out once the bulb burns out, disposable cameras good for only one roll of film...all bound for the garbage, sooner rather than later.

Some brands of VCRs, hair dryers, telephones, and other appliances are built so cheaply that they only last a year or two. When they break, it often costs less to buy a new one than to have the old one repaired. And so it ends up in the trash, too.

SOURCE

Ranger Rick

Magazine

50
CAN-DO
KIDS

By Kathy Love

Photos by
Paul Childress

AWARD
WINNING

Magazine

In 1987, a man named Neil Andre decided to start a new environmental group. "Great!" his friends said. Then he told them he was going to start it with inner-city kids (kids who live in the poorest part of the city). "You're crazy!" they told him.

"Everyone said that kids can't do anything about the environment," Neil remembers, "and that inner-city kids have too many other problems to worry about besides the Earth."

Oh, yeah?

Meet the Dolphin Defenders—a church group of 50 kids in fifth and sixth grade from St. Louis, Missouri. (We'll tell you later why they're called Dolphin Defenders.) Since this group got started, they've won 60 national awards for their work for the environment.

The Dolphin Defenders pile up 48,000 aluminum cans they collected on their city streets.

Think Globally, Act Locally

The kids raise money for environmental projects in the United States and around the world. But mostly, the Defenders work for the environment close to home. They've helped their neighborhood in lots of ways:

- *The kids hold Trash Bashes, Glass Passes, and Can Scans to clean up their neighborhood.*

- *They hunt through dumpsters for good junk. Then they reuse the items by turning them into things such as furniture or game pieces. Or they sell them to raise money.*

- *The Defenders have recycled 15,000 pounds (6750 kg) of glass and over 193,000 aluminum cans. Now they've started recycling used tires.*

- *They've created four wildlife habitats under a program run by the National Wildlife Federation (the group that publishes* Ranger Rick*). The habitats are now home to many plants and animals. "We have bird feeders and birdbaths in our wildlife habitats, where we can watch cardinals, chickadees, blue jays—lots of different birds," says Dolphin Defender Lela Ford. The areas have even attracted raccoons, opossums, and a red fox family!*

Number One Problem: Drugs

For the Defenders, cleaning up their city neighborhood is no easy thing. Gangs and drug dealers roam through the area, taking over the local park and some of the streets. The kids have learned to clean up the park in the morning. That way, they're out of there before the drug dealers arrive in the afternoon.

The Defenders try to teach their neighbors about the environment. For example, they talked to local people about a plan to turn part of a city park into a parking lot. The people then voted to save the park.

The Defenders also ask people not to litter. But it doesn't always

Dolphin Defenders are totally into trash bashing. They roam the streets looking for stuff to recycle (left).

work. "Some people don't care about cleaning up the environment," says Defender Dianna Hogan. "They just want to drive around in big cars, play loud music, and throw their trash everywhere. If you tell them not to, they get mad."

Some people do worse things than litter. The Defenders spent 85 hard-earned dollars to buy a top-of-the-line bird feeder for one of their habitats. But some people from the neighborhood destroyed it.

"The Defenders live with violence every day," says their leader. "Some of them have had family members killed by gangs. But the amazing thing about them is that they're able to look beyond their own problems and focus on the problems of planet Earth."

So why do they work for the environment? The Defenders say it makes them feel good. "If you really like what you're doing, it doesn't seem like work," says Dianna Hogan.

Neil thinks another reason is that the kids

believe they need to defend the Earth. Their belief shows in their name —Dolphin Defenders.

When dolphins are attacked, Neil says, they cooperate with each other to defend against the attack. "So the kids try to defend the Earth the same way dolphins defend each other," Neil explains. "That's why they call themselves the Dolphin Defenders."

Defending the Earth turns out to be something these kids are really good at. "See?" says Neil. "An environmental group with inner-city kids *wasn't* such a crazy idea!"

How to Write a Needs Assessment

An introduction tells the purpose of the survey.

Questions in surveys are numbered. Space is provided for the person's answers.

Rating systems allow the respondents to tell what's most important to them.

Questions that have a quick yes or no answer help determine whether people agree.

Nobody knows the needs of a community or neighborhood better than the people who live and work there. Before any changes or improvements are made in the community, its residents and businesspeople should be consulted. Conducting a needs assessment is one way to find out what community members think.

What is a needs assessment? Often, a needs assessment takes the form of a survey. People who write a needs-assessment survey have identified a problem they want to solve or an area they want to improve. The survey takers turn to community members to find out whether they agree.

CORNERSTONE POOL

CUSTOMER SATISFACTION SURVEY

Cornerstone Pool is an aquatics pool facility located at 55 Buena Vista Road in West Hartford. The town is considering making changes and improvements to Cornerstone Pool. We are conducting a survey of the people who use Cornerstone to see how you feel about the facility and what changes you would want to see at the facility. Your input is important! When you turn in a completed survey, you will be given a free guest pass to Cornerstone. This is our way of saying thanks for taking the time to complete the survey.

1. How many visits a month on the average do you make to Cornerstone Pool?_____

2. Please rank in order of importance (1, 2, 3) the 3 reasons you swim at Cornerstone Pool.

_____ Price is reasonable

_____ Convenient location

_____ Like the programs offered

_____ Other (please specify) _____

3. Please rank in order of frequency (1, 2, 3) the three programs you participate in most:

_____ Early Bird swim

_____ 11 AM - 1 PM adult swim

_____ 8 - 9 lap swim

_____ Youth instructional lessons

_____ Adult instructional lessons

_____ Weekend lap swim

4. Do you find the pool staff members to be friendly and courteous?

☐ Yes   ☐ No   ☐ Varies

5. Overall, do you feel that the pool itself is:

Clean   ☐ Yes   ☐ No
Safe   ☐ Yes   ☐ No
In good condition ☐ Yes   ☐ No
Overcrowded   ☐ Yes   ☐ No

6. What are the three things you like most about Cornerstone?
_____

7. What are the three things you like least about Cornerstone?
_____
_____

● Open-ended questions require longer answers in order to get detailed ideas and input.

1 Choose a Topic

What should your survey be about? Start by brainstorming things that you think your community needs. Perhaps your community needs more movie theaters, better bike paths, a larger library or a public swimming pool.

Choose something from your list that interests you and that you know something about. Use a needs assessment survey to find out whether others feel the same way.

TOOLS

• paper and pencil

2 Plan Your Survey

Start by making a list of issues that your survey should cover. For example, if you think your community needs better bike paths, your survey should be designed to find out whether better bike paths really are a concern of people who live there. You might ask if people own bicycles, how often they ride, and their opinions about the safety of the road. Review your list to make sure you have covered all the issues that are important for your topic.

3 Write Your Survey

Once you've decided what to cover in your survey, you need to write questions. Decide which type of question is best for each issue you want to cover. Some issues can be covered by simple yes-or-no questions. Sometimes people find it easier to answer questions if you supply them with a number of answers to choose from. Open-ended questions let people give thorough answers. Try to write at least six questions. When you are finished, think of a title for your needs assessment survey. Make sure that the questions are easy to read and that there is enough space for people to answer them.

Tip As you review the completed surveys, record all the answers on one blank survey. Then add up the results.

4 Take Your Survey

Make at least ten copies of your survey. Decide to whom you will distribute it. Think about people who might care about your issue. Your friends or neighbors might be good choices. After you've collected your surveys, look at how people answered them. How many people are satisfied with the way things are? How many want to change things? What did most people want to change? Tally the results of your surveys and report your results to your class.

If You Are Using a Computer...

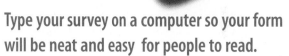

Type your survey on a computer so your form will be neat and easy for people to read.

THINK

How did your survey change or reinforce your ideas about what your community needs?

Karen Heit
Urban Planner ▶

City dwellers can work together to improve their quality of life.

Reaching Out

Find out how two make-believe gangs try to settle their differences. Meet real-life kids who work together to make their city beautiful.

Read a story about a homeless boy called Maniac Magee, who finds a special place with a new family.

PROJECT

Create an action plan to improve your community.

93

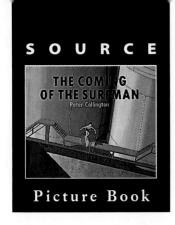
THE COMING OF THE SURFMAN

BY
Peter Collington

There are two gangs in my neighborhood: the Hammers and the Nails. They are sworn enemies.

I was skateboarding home one day when the Hammer gang grabbed me. Their leader, Hammerhead, lifted me off the ground by my collar, pushed his face close to mine, and showed me his fist.

"You're joining us," he said. It wasn't an invitation. It was a statement of fact. As I might want to smile again sometime—and it would be essential I had some teeth to do it with—I nodded.

"A wise decision," Hammerhead said, putting me down. "Now wear this." He handed me a red bandanna, the Hammers' color. As I walked away, struggling to put it around my head, I noticed the Nail gang up ahead. I quickly stuffed the bandanna into my pocket. Nailhead, the gang leader, looked me over. My foot tapped nervously on my skateboard. Nailhead's eyes lowered to my board.

"You wanna grow up. Skateboards are for kids." As I *was* a kid, it was quite logical that I should have a skateboard, but something made me keep quiet. It was my teeth again. Nailhead handed me a blue bandanna. "Wear this," he said. "You're one of us."

So I belong to two gangs, and if either of them finds out, I'm done for.

That night, I was lying awake thinking about my predicament when I heard a motor running. I looked out of my bedroom window and saw a van parked opposite, outside the boarded-up store. A man wearing beachwear stepped out. He looked around, the streetlight flashing on his sunglasses, and walked over to the store's front door. He jiggled with some keys and went in. He began unloading long cardboard cartons from his van.

After a while, I must have dropped off to sleep, but I was woken by the sound of an electric sander moaning and whining. The man had taken down the boards from the store window and was now working on the peeling paint.

The old store had closed down long ago because the owner was fed up with vandals breaking his windows and with neighborhood gangs harassing his customers. So a new store would be welcome.

The man had now opened some paint cans and was brightening up the woodwork. I couldn't wait until morning to find out what kind of a store it was going to be. A pizza place, a video rental shop—even a new food store would be fine. We wouldn't have to lug groceries from eight blocks away anymore.

Then my heart sank. I remembered the gangs and what they might do to me tomorrow.

When I got up and went outside, the two gangs were waiting for me. At least that's what I thought at first, but then I noticed they weren't looking at me but at the new store. The gangs stood well apart and were pointing to the window display.

Both Hammerhead and Nailhead took turns laughing and their respective gangs imitated them. The name of the store, emblazoned in bright neon lights, was SURFING SUPPLIES. In the store window were surfboards and different types of surfing wear.

I began to laugh myself, partly out of relief that the gangs had forgotten about me and partly because I shared their amusement. It was quite simple. There was nowhere around here to surf. The beach was a two-day drive away.

Who would open a store selling surfing stuff in a run-down neighborhood like this? Only someone who was two bread rolls short of a picnic. Someone who was seriously weird. The gangs laughed, and I laughed with them.

The SURFING SUPPLIES store opened regularly at nine o'clock every morning and closed at five-thirty on the dot. No one went into the store to buy anything, and no one came out.

The store owner became known as the Surfman, and people hooted and laughed whenever his name was mentioned. I didn't know what to think, but I was glad about one thing. Since he had come, the Hammers and Nails had forgotten entirely about me and hardly fought each other anymore. The blank, angry stares were gone; expression was leaking into their faces. I had seen that look before—especially in cats. It was a look of obsessive curiosity. Their brains were straining to figure out why the Surfman was here. Anyone weird could also be dangerous. So both gangs set up around-the-clock surveillance.

A pattern of behavior was emerging. Every Monday morning the Surfman cleaned his windows and swept the sidewalk. Once a month he took stock, even though he had sold nothing.

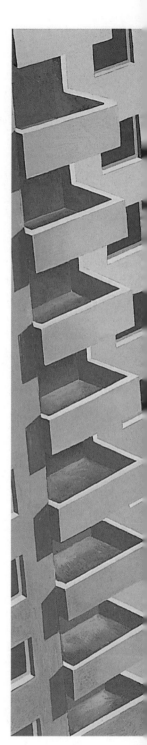

High-intensity binoculars revealed that he ate a mixed salad and yogurt for lunch and ran 200 miles a week on his exercise machine. He *had* to be training for something—but what?

Then one night I spotted him. He came out of his store about eleven o'clock and walked over to the abandoned factory across the way. He took out a large piece of paper and studied it by flashlight. He looked up at the factory and then down at the sheet of paper. He walked around the factory for a while and then went back to the store.

After this, the Surfman started appearing regularly at night, carrying a tool kit. He had more in common with the gangs than I had at first thought: he was very good at wrecking things. He was systematically demolishing the factory. It was crazy. Each night there was hammering and banging for hours on end. But as the weeks went by, there seemed to be some method in his madness.

With the help of the old factory crane, the Surfman ripped off the factory roof and sent the metal sheets crashing down onto the floor below. Then he began bolting the sheets onto the inner walls and floor. His long shadow spilled out over the ground as the light from his welding equipment flickered and darted. The Surfman rolled large pipes from the back of the factory and collected them together by the pump. Then he started bolting them together.

At the end of his night shift, he would stagger home, tired and drained, but he always opened the store, regular as clockwork, at nine o'clock, even though no one had ever seen a customer go in.

I began to really feel for him. He reminded me of my late dad, always working hard and no one giving him any thanks.

One evening, the Surfman erected scaffolding in front of the two giant storage tanks and, with cutting equipment, began burning into the metal. Every night something new was added or changed, and in the light of day the two gangs would check out the Surfman's progress. Occasionally, the gangs would take turns flexing their muscles and knocking something down. But their hearts weren't really in it, and when the Surfman repaired the damage, they just shrugged and let things stand.

They, like me, wanted to see the Surfman complete his work. We were all enthralled. We were trembling with anticipation. We all knew what the Surfman was building, but nobody put it into words. The Surfman jokes had died away, and a certain grudging respect was apparent. He might be a weird guy, but he was a weird guy who was making something for us. Something we had wanted all our lives.

One night, I was woken by the sound of running water. The Surfman was standing by the metal pipes turning a large wheel tap. He was wearing swimwear. As he pressed a switch, the pump started throbbing and vibrating. The Surfman picked up his surfboard and climbed high up the metal ladder to a position overlooking the empty factory below. He leaned forward and pulled a lever. The doors of the two storage tanks sprang open, and WATER gushed out with all the ferocity of a giant surfing wave! The Surfman was swept from his perch, only to reappear with his surfboard under his feet and his arms stretched out on either side. *The Surfman was surfing!* He rode the wave all the way to the end of the factory, was carried up the metal slope, and then plummeted ski-slope-style onto the piled-up car tires below.

The Surfman retrieved his surfboard and clambered down the tires. With his surfboard under his arm, he walked over to his store and went in. The wave machine wheezed and coughed, then spluttered to a halt. I always knew what it was going to be, but now I screamed the words out loud: "It's a WAVE MACHINE!" My voice echoed out of the window and ricocheted around the neighborhood. I heard whoops and cries of joy from Hammerhead and Nailhead, who had witnessed it too.

Tomorrow was going to be a great day.

In the morning, the two gangs were there early, clutching bits of wood and anything else they thought might do for a surfboard. When the wave machine started up, the gangs clambered up the ladder and, mixing together like one happy family, launched themselves and their bits of wood onto the wave. I just stood and watched. This was going to be fun. None of them had the slightest idea of how to surf, so they sank with their bits of wood and came up with furious faces, spurting water.

I had been saving up money for some time, not quite sure what to do with it. Now, I *knew!* As my dad used to say, "To do the job right, you need the right tool."

I walked over to the SURFING SUPPLIES store and put down my money. The Surfman handed me a real beauty of a board. He wasn't a talkative sort of guy. But as I left, he turned and said, "Have a good day."

I walked over to the wave machine and climbed up the stairs. The gangs stood back to watch. I waited until I heard the crash of water, and as the wave came, I stepped off. All the skateboarding had been good training. I held my balance and rode the crest of the wave for all it was worth. It was the best day of my life. The gangs tried to follow my example, but they had no balance, and their boards were rubbish. They knew what they had to do.

Nailhead led his gang in first. They all bought surfboards and walked proudly out of the Surfman's store. Next, Hammerhead led his gang into the store. When the Hammers came out, Nailhead was there to confront them. He swallowed hard. The words did not come easy to him.

"You wanna have a truce?" he asked.

Hammerhead looked back at his gang. They all nodded their heads. "Okay," said Hammerhead. "We surf alternate days." He held out his hand to shake.

"Done," said Nailhead.

The two gangs beamed at each other.

Nailhead took out a coin. "Heads or tails?"

Nailhead and his gang won the toss, and cheering, they ran over to the wave machine to try out their boards.

I put on my blue bandanna and joined them. The next day, I put on my red bandanna and joined the Hammers.

After a week, they found me out. I was thrown out of both gangs, and my surfing days were over. All I could do now was watch. I felt bored and depressed. Without surfing, life felt almost not worth living.

One day, I was enviously watching one of the gangs surfing when the pump suddenly ground to a halt. A cry of pain went up from every gang member's throat. The wave machine had broken down.

That evening, the Surfman came out of his shop and called me over. He handed me his tool kit, and I walked behind him over to the wave machine. I handed him each tool as he requested it, and when the job was finished, he turned to me and said, "Okay, try it out." I ran home and got my surfboard. I couldn't believe my luck. I tried one wave, curling down its crest and zigzagging in front of it.

"How is it?" called Surfman.

"Almost right," I answered. "I'll just check it out again." And this way I got to surf a second time—a long time—until I felt I was stretching the Surfman's patience and finally called out, "Yeah, it's fine now!" And the Surfman closed it down until the next day.

Fortunately, the wave machine broke down quite regularly, and I was always on hand to carry the Surfman's tool kit. As he worked, he talked to me, explaining what he was doing and why. He named each tool I handed to him as if he wanted me to remember what it was for the next time. The Surfman really did remind me of my late dad: *he* always liked to have me stand by him when he was fixing things. But I did the same thing now that I used to do with my dad. I humored him. I nodded and said "Yeah" a few times as if I were paying attention. But my mind wasn't there. It was focused on surfing and silently crying out for that moment when the Surfman would turn to me and say, "Okay, it's fixed. Go try it out." Then life for me would begin. Floating on those short-lived waves was everything to me.

On their enforced day of rest, while one gang surfed, the other spent its time jogging to the health food store in the next neighborhood for more supplies or sitting around watching surfing movies they had rented from the Surfman's store, analyzing and discussing good moves.

Then the truce broke down. The wave machine had been out of action for a whole day, so the Hammers felt they should surf the next day. The Nails insisted it was their turn, and fighting broke out. The Hammers, anticipating trouble, had come prepared. They had hidden their own surfboards, and producing axes and sledgehammers, they rushed over to the Nails' surfboards and began smashing them.

The result was catastrophic. The Nails let out agonizing screams of pain and doubled over on the ground, hugging the remains of their surfboards. They clutched them like babies and went home broken-hearted to try and fix them. The Hammers felt powerful—they had never been happier. They surfed all that day, confident that they would be surfing every day from now on.

But somehow I knew that would not be the end of it.

That night, I was woken by the sound of banging and crashing. Looking out of my bedroom window, I saw the Nail gang wielding axes and sledgehammers. They were smashing the wave machine. I quickly dressed and ran out to try and stop them. But it was too late. The Hammer gang was there too, and a big battle was taking place. I shouted and tried to reason with them, but no one took any notice of me. Water was spurting out of the pipes, and sparks were flying everywhere.

The following day, the two battle-weary and dejected gangs stood in front of the wave machine and looked at the damage they had caused. Their eyes looked over toward the Surfman's store. He had fixed things before. Surely he would fix things again.

Later that evening, I watched the Surfman walk out of his store and across to the battered wave machine. He stood for some time, just shaking his head. Then he walked home and into his store.

The next morning the Surfman had gone. His store was empty and the wave machine unrepaired. The two gangs stood in silence. Big tears rolled down their faces.

I ran back home to get my late dad's tool kit. The two gangs stepped aside to let me work. I tried various tools, pulling this way and that. But I knew in my heart it was hopeless. I couldn't remember what the Surfman had told me. I hadn't been listening. The gangs' hopeful eyes narrowed.

"Stupid kid," they said and walked away.

Things have gone pretty much back to normal here, the gangs once again fighting each other. Neither of them is interested in my joining them now, which is fine with me.

On bad days, I think about my father a lot and all the things I could have done with him if he were still alive. On good days, I feel sure that the Surfman will return, and this time I know I'll be ready and really listen to what he says and really watch his big hands as he works away at the rusting hulk of the wave machine, restoring it to good working order.

From the *Philadelphia Daily News*

AWARD WINNING

Newspaper

Art Show Draws Upon Ex-Graffiti Scrawlers

By Joseph P. Blake

THERE SEEMS TO be a well-stocked storehouse of creativity deep in the minds of the kids who belong to the city's Anti-Graffiti Network.

From it flows an almost-limitless supply of ideas for murals and paintings that now grace the walls of abandoned buildings and underpasses throughout the city.

These works of youthful art have turned gray and dingy surfaces into eye-pleasing scenes, with images such as waterfalls, sailboats at sea, forest scenes and similar sights not encountered in the drab city streets.

They also have instilled in the budding artists, many of whom are former graffiti scrawlers, a sense of pride that comes from the birth and execution of artistic ideas.

"Every time I look at one of my paintings," said Greg Turner, 18, "I think someone else has done it, because people go crazy over it."

Turner is just one of about 20 members of the Anti-Graffiti Network whose individual works, plus several mural-size paintings done by two or more of the group, are on exhibit through April at the Free Library's main branch on Logan Square in Center City.

Turner not only helped out with a few of the murals in the show, but has eight of his own works on display, including one colorful impression of Hong Kong harbor and another of an Indian temple.

Other themes run the gamut from abstract impressions of still-life figures to pastoral pastels of tropical islands boasting a single palm tree beneath a setting sun.

Many of the teens in the program still view exterior walls as nothing more than inner-city canvases waiting for some color. However, since they've joined the network, their spray-painting attacks are now done in conjunction with the community where the brick or cement walls stand.

"I used to write on walls," said Billy Leach, 15. "But not anymore. Since last summer I've worked on painting murals, and I've done my own paintings, too. My art teacher recommended me to the (anti-graffiti) program. If I wasn't in this, I'd probably still be out writing on walls."

Leach's painting, *Figure Study*, is on display at the library.

Young artists beautify city walls.

It captures with sensitivity and warmth the image of a man deep in thought at his desk. It's Leach's first painting to be displayed in a formal setting, and the idea of someone actually standing back and admiring his work, he said, has made him decide on a career in commercial art.

But you don't have to be a wall-scribbler to join the network. The only criteria are an interest in art and a desire to do something for the community.

Darnell Powell, 17, who says she has never defaced a wall with spray paint or anything else, is just as proud of her black-and-white abstract piece she calls "The Thinker" as Leach is about his art.

Her work, she said, was inspired by Richard Wright's novel *Native Son*.

It is a haunting, angular painting of a man's face that stares back at viewers with square, sad eyes that seem to be contemplating his life.

Powell says she didn't even realize she had a talent for painting until she joined the Anti-Graffiti Network two years ago.

"It's like something inside of me just started coming out," she said. "Like the abstract shapes. When I draw them, it's very peaceful."

According to Jane Golden, artistic director for the mural program, the participants have painted more than 600 murals over the past five years.

"We've done them from small walls to the sides of four-story buildings," she said.

The network is usually contacted through someone in the community who wants work done on a particular wall, or the wall is picked by the network, which, in turn, works with people in the surrounding area in regard to ideas for the wall.

The network was started by Mayor Goode in 1984 to combat the proliferation of graffiti that scarred walls all across the city.

Golden said that many of the murals are of quiet, relaxing scenes such as waterfalls and deer wandering in a forest because that's what the people want.

And the Anti-Graffiti Network is more than willing to oblige.

FROM

Maniac Magee

By
Jerry Spinelli

Illustrated by
Ken Spengler

For most of his life, Jeffrey Lionel Magee had a home. But when his parents died and his life changed, he had to learn to survive on his own. In the city of Two Mills, Jeffrey meets Amanda Beale, a friend who might be able to help him with his problem. But Two Mills has some special problems of its own, and "Maniac" Magee finds himself in the middle of them.

The town was buzzing. The schools were buzzing. Hallways. Lunchrooms. Streets. Playgrounds.

West End. East End.

Buzzing about the new kid in town. The stranger kid. Scraggly. Carrying a book. Flap-soled sneakers.

The kid who intercepted Brian Denehy's pass to Hands Down and punted it back longer than Denehy himself ever threw it.

The kid who rescued Arnold Jones from Finsterwald's backyard.

The kid who tattooed Giant John McNab's fastball for half a dozen home runs, then circled the sacks on a bunted frog.

Nobody knows who said it first, but somebody must have: "Kid's gotta be a maniac."

And somebody else must have said: "Yeah, reg'lar maniac."

And somebody else: "Yeah."

And that was it. Nobody (except Amanda Beale) had any other name for him, so pretty soon, when they wanted to talk about the new kid, that's what they called him: Maniac.

The legend had a name.

But not an address. At least, not an official one, with numbers.

What he did have was the deer shed at the Elmwood Park Zoo, which is where he slept his first few nights in town. What the deer ate, especially the carrots, apples, and day-old hamburger buns, he ate.

He started reading Amanda Beale's book his second day in town and finished it that afternoon. Ordinarily, he would have returned it immediately, but he was so fascinated by the story of the Children's Crusade that he kept it and read it the next day. And the next.

When he wasn't reading, he was wandering. When most people wander, they walk. Maniac Magee ran. Around town, around the nearby townships, always carrying the book, keeping it in perfect condition.

This is what he was doing when his life, as it often seemed to do, took an unexpected turn.

John McNab had never in his life met a kid he couldn't strike out. Until the runt. Now, as he thought about it, he came to two conclusions:

1. He couldn't stand having this blemish on his record.

2. If you beat a kid up, it's the same as striking him out.

So McNab and his pals went looking for the kid. They called themselves the Cobras. Nobody messed with them. At least, nobody in the West End.

The Cobras had heard that the kid hung around the park and the tracks, and that's where they spotted him one Saturday afternoon, on the tracks by the path that ran from the Oriole Street dead end to the park. He was down by Red Hill and heading away from them, book in hand, as usual.

But the Cobras just stood there, stunned.

"I don't believe it," one Cobra said.

"Must be a trick," said another.

"I heard about it," said another, "but I didn't believe it."

It wasn't a trick. It was true. The kid was *running* on the rail.

McNab scooped up a handful of track stones. He launched one. He snarled, "He's dead. Let's get 'im."

By the time Maniac looked back, they were almost on him. He wobbled once, leaped from the rail to the ground, and took off. He was at the Oriole Street dead end, but his instincts said no, not the street, too much open space. He stuck with the tracks. Coming into view above him was the house on Rako Hill, where he had eaten spaghetti. He could go there, to the whistling mother, the other kids, be safe. They wouldn't follow him in there. Would they?

Stones clanked off the steel rails. He darted left, skirted the dump, wove through the miniature mountain range of stone piles and into the trees . . . skiing on his heels down the steep bank and into the creek, frogs plopping, no time to look for stepping rocks . . . yells behind him now, war whoops, stones pelting the water, stinging his back . . . ah, the other side, through the trees and picker bushes, past the armory jeeps and out to the park boulevard, past the Italian restaurant on the corner, the bakery, screeching tires, row houses, streets, alleys, cars, porches, windows, faces staring, faces, faces . . .

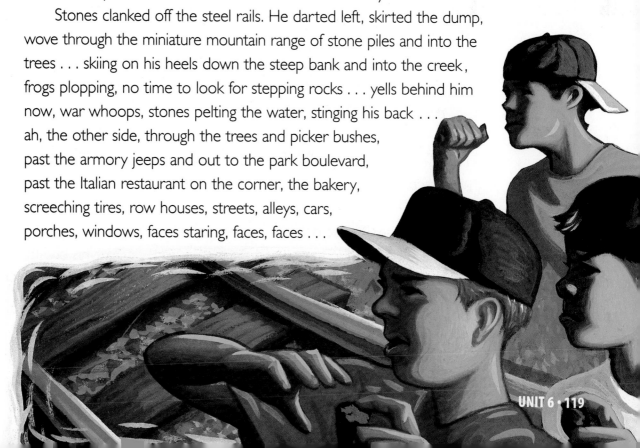

the town whizzing past Maniac, a blur of faces, each face staring from its own window, each face in its own personal frame, its own house, its own address, someplace to be when there was no other place to be, how lucky to be a face staring out from a window . . .

And then—could it be?—the voices behind him were growing faint. He slowed, turned, stopped. They were lined up at a street a block back. They were still yelling and shaking their fists, but they weren't moving off the curb. And now they were laughing. Why were they laughing?

The Cobras were standing at Hector Street. Hector Street was the boundary between the East and West Ends. Or, to put it another way, between the blacks and whites. Not that you never saw a white in the East End or a black in the West End. People did cross the line now and then, especially if they were adults, and it was daylight.

But nighttime, forget it. And if you were a kid, day *or* night, forget it. Unless you had business on the other side, such as a sports team or school. But don't be just *strolling* along, as if you *belonged* there, as if you weren't *afraid*, as if you didn't even *notice* you were a different color from everybody around you.

The Cobras were laughing because they figured the dumb, scraggly runt would get out of the East End in about as good shape as a bare big toe in a convention of snapping turtles.

Of course, Maniac didn't know any of that. He was simply glad the chase was over. He turned and started walking, catching his breath.

East Chestnut. East Marshall. Green Street. Arch Street. He had been around here before. That first day with the girl named Amanda, other days jogging through. But this was Saturday, not a school day, and there was something different about the streets—kids. All over.

One of them jumped down from a front step and planted himself right in front of Maniac. Maniac had to jerk to a stop to keep from plowing into the kid. Even so, their noses were practically touching.

Maniac blinked and stepped back. The kid stepped forward. Each time Maniac stepped back, the kid stepped forward. They traveled practically half a block that way. Finally Maniac turned and started walking. The kid jumped around and plunked himself in front again. He bit off a chunk of the candy bar he was holding. "Where *you* goin'?" he said. Candy bar flakes flew from his mouth.

"I'm looking for Sycamore Street," said Maniac. "Do you know where it is?"

"Yeah, I know where it is."

Maniac waited, but the kid said nothing more. "Well, uh, do you think you could tell me where it is?"

Stone was softer than the kid's glare. "No."

Maniac looked around. Other kids had stopped playing, were staring.

Someone called: "Do 'im, Mars!"

Someone else: "Waste 'im!"

The kid, as you probably guessed by now, was none other than Mars Bar Thompson. Mars Bar heard the calls, and the stone got harder. Then suddenly he stopped glaring, suddenly he was smiling. He held up the candy bar, an inch from Maniac's lips. "Wanna bite?"

Maniac couldn't figure. "You sure?"

"Yeah, go ahead. Take a bite."

Maniac shrugged, took the Mars Bar, bit off a chunk, and handed it back. "Thanks."

Dead silence along the street. The kid had done the unthinkable, he had chomped on one of Mars's own bars. Not only that, but white kids just didn't put their mouths where black kids had had theirs, be it soda bottles, spoons, or candy bars. And the kid hadn't even gone for the unused end; he had chomped right over Mars Bar's own bite marks.

Mars Bar was confused. Who *was* this kid? *What* was this kid?

As usual, when Mars Bar got confused, he got mad. He thumped Maniac in the chest. "You think you bad or somethin'?"

Maniac, who was now twice as confused as Mars Bar, blinked. "Huh?"

"You think you come down here and be bad? That what you think?" Mars Bar was practically shouting now.

"No," said Maniac, "I don't think I'm bad. I'm not saying I'm an angel, either. Not even real good. Somewhere in between, I guess."

Mars Bar jammed his arms downward, stuck out his chin, and sneered. "Am I bad?"

Maniac was befuddled. "*I* don't know. One minute you're yelling at me, the next minute you're giving me a bite of your candy bar."

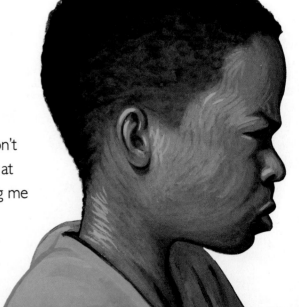

The chin jutted out more. "Tell me I'm bad."

Maniac didn't answer. Flies stopped buzzing.

"I said, tell me I'm bad."

Maniac blinked, shrugged, sighed. "It's none of my business. If you're bad, let your mother or father tell you."

Now it was Mars Bar doing the blinking, stepping back, trying to sort things out. After a while he looked down. "What's that?"

Before Maniac answered, "A book," Mars Bar had snatched it from his hand. "This ain't yours," he said. He flipped through some pages. "Looks like mine."

"It's somebody else's."

"It's mine. I'm keepin' it."

With rattlesnake speed, Maniac snatched the book back—except for one page, which stayed, ripped, in Mars Bar's hand.

"Give me the page," said Maniac.

Mars Bar grinned. "Take it, fishbelly."

Silence. Eyes. The flies were waiting. East End vultures.

Suddenly neither kid could see the other, because a broom came down like a straw curtain between their faces, and a voice said, "*I'll* take it."

It was the lady from the nearest house, out to sweep her steps. She lowered the broom but kept it between them. "Better yet," she said to Mars Bar, "just give it back to him."

Mars Bar glared up at her. There wasn't an eleven-year-old in the East End who could stand up to Mars Bar's glare. In the West End, even high-schoolers were known to crumble under the glare. To old ladies on both sides of Hector Street, it was all but fatal. And when Mars Bar stepped off a curb and combined the glare with his super-slow dip-stride slumpshuffle, well, it was said he could back up traffic all the way to Bridgeport while he took ten minutes to cross the street.

But not this time. This time Mars Bar was up against an East End lady in her prime, and she was matching him eyeball for eyeball. And when it was over, only one glare was left standing, and it wasn't Mars Bar's.

Mars Bar handed back the torn page, but not before he crumpled it into a ball. The broom pushed him away, turned him around, and swept him up the street.

The lady looked down at Maniac. A little of the glare lingered in her eyes. "You better get on, boy, where you belong. I can't be following you around. I got things to do."

Maniac just stood there a minute. There was something he felt like doing, and maybe he would have, but the lady turned and went back inside her house and shut the door. So he walked away.

Now what?

Maniac uncrumpled the page, flattened it out as best he could. How could he return the book to Amanda in this condition? He couldn't. But he had to. It was hers. Judging from that morning, she was pretty finicky about her books. What would make her madder—to not get the book back at all, or to get it back with a page ripped out? Maniac cringed at both prospects.

He wandered around the East End, jogging slowly, in no hurry now to find 728 Sycamore Street.

He was passing a vacant lot when he heard an all-too-familiar voice: "Hey, fishbelly!" He stopped, turned. This time Mars Bar wasn't alone. A handful of other kids trailed him down the sidewalk.

Maniac waited.

Coming up to him, Mars Bar said, "Where you runnin', boy?"

"Nowhere."

"You runnin' from us. You afraid."

"No, I just like to run."

"You wanna run?" Mars Bar grinned. "Go ahead. We'll give you a head start."

Maniac grinned back. "No thanks."

Mars Bar held out his hand. "Gimme my book."

Maniac shook his head.

Mars Bar glared. "Gimme it."

Maniac shook his head.

Mars Bar reached for it. Maniac pulled it away.

They moved in on him now. They backed him up. Some high-schoolers were playing basketball up the street, but they weren't noticing. And there wasn't a broom-swinging lady in sight. Maniac felt a hard flatness against his back. Suddenly his world was very small and very simple: a brick wall behind him, a row of scowling faces in front of him. He clutched the book with both hands. The faces were closing in. A voice called: "That you, Jeffrey?"

The faces parted. At the curb was a girl on a bike—Amanda! She hoisted the bike to the sidewalk and walked it over. She looked at the book, at the torn page. "Who ripped my book?"

Mars Bar pointed at Maniac. "He did."

Amanda knew better. "*You* ripped my book."

Mars Bar's eyes went big as headlights. "I did *not*!"

"You *did*. You lie."

"I *didn't*!"

"You *did*!" She let the bike fall to Maniac. She grabbed the book and started kicking Mars Bar in his beloved sneakers. "I got a little brother and a little sister that crayon all over my books, and I got a dog that eats them and poops on them and that's just inside my own family, and I'm *not* — gonna have *nobody* — else *messin'* — with my *books*! You under-*stand*?"

By then Mars Bar was hauling on up the street past the basketball players, who were rolling on the asphalt with laughter.

Amanda took the torn page from Maniac. To her, it was the broken wing of a bird, a pet out in the rain. She turned misty eyes to Maniac. "It's one of my favorite pages."

Maniac smiled. "We can fix it."

The way he said it, she believed. "Want to come to my house?" she said.

"Sure," he said.

When they walked in, Amanda's mother was busy with her usual tools: a yellow plastic bucket and a sponge. She was scrubbing purple crayon off the TV screen.

"Mom," said Amanda, "this is Jeffrey—" She whispered, "What's your last name?"

He whispered, "Magee."

She said, "Magee."

Mrs. Beale held up a hand, said, "Hold it," and went on scrubbing. When she finally finished, she straightened up, turned, and said, "Now, what?"

"Mom, this is Jeffrey Magee. You know."

Amanda was hardly finished when Maniac zipped across the room and stuck out his hand. "Nice to meet you, Mrs. . . . Mrs. . . ."

"Beale."

"Mrs. Beale."

They shook hands. Mrs. Beale smiled. "So you're the book boy." She started nodding. "Manda came home one day— 'Mom, there's a boy I loaned one of my books to!' 'Loaned a *book? You?*' 'Mom, he practically *made* me. He really likes books. I met him on—' "

"Mo-om!" Amanda screeched. "I never said all *that*!"

Mrs. Beale nodded solemnly—"No, of course you didn't"—and gave Maniac a huge wink, which made Amanda screech louder, until something crashed in the kitchen. Mrs. Beale ran. Amanda and Maniac ran.

The scene in the kitchen stopped them cold: one little girl, eyes wide, standing on a countertop; one little boy, eyes wide, standing just below her on a chair; one shattered glass jar and some stringy pale-colored glop on the floor; one growing cloud of sauerkraut fumes.

The girl was Hester, age four; the boy was Lester, age three. In less than five minutes, while Mrs. Beale and Amanda cleaned up the floor, Hester and Lester and their dog Bow Wow were in the backyard wrestling and tickling and jumping and just generally going wild with their new buddy—and victim—Maniac Magee.

Maniac was still there when Mr. Beale came home from his Saturday shift at the tire factory.

He was there for dinner, when Hester and Lester pushed their chairs alongside his.

He was there to help Amanda mend her torn book.

He was there watching TV afterward, with Hester riding one knee, Lester the other.

He was there when Hester and Lester came screaming down the stairs with a book, Amanda screaming even louder after them, the kids shoving the book and themselves onto Maniac's lap, Amanda finally calming down because they didn't want to crayon the book, they only wanted Maniac to read. And so he read *Lyle, Lyle, Crocodile* to Hester and Lester and, even though they pretended not to listen, to Amanda and Mr. and Mrs. Beale.

And he was there when Hester and Lester were herded upstairs to bed, and Mrs. Beale said, "Don't you think it's about time you're heading home, Jeffrey? Your parents'll be wondering."

So Maniac, wanting to say something but not knowing how, got into the car for Mr. Beale to drive him home. And then he made his mistake. He waited for only two or three blocks to go by before saying to Mr. Beale, "This is it."

Mr. Beale stopped, but he didn't let Maniac out of the car. He looked at him funny. Mr. Beale knew what his passenger apparently didn't: East End was East End and West End was West End, and the house this white lad was pointing to was filled with black people, just like every other house on up to Hector Street.

Mr. Beale pointed this out to Maniac. Maniac's lip started to quiver, and right there, with the car idling in the middle of the street, Maniac told him that he didn't really have a home, unless you counted the deer shed at the zoo.

Mr. Beale made a U-turn right there and headed back. Only Mrs. Beale was still downstairs when they walked into the house. She listened to no more than ten seconds' worth of Mr. Beale's explanation before saying to Maniac, "You're staying here."

Not long after, Maniac was lying in Amanda's bed, Amanda having been carried over to Hester and Lester's room, where she often slept anyway.

Before Maniac could go to sleep, however, there was something he had to do. He flipped off the covers and went downstairs. Before the puzzled faces of Mr. and Mrs. Beale, he opened the front door and looked at the three cast-iron digits nailed to the door frame: seven two eight. He kept staring at them, smiling. Then he closed the door, said a cheerful "Goodnight," and went back to bed.

Maniac Magee finally had an address.

How to
Make an Action Plan

Work to get something *changed* in your community.

Making an action plan is one way to bring about community improvement. An action plan is a written proposal, stating what it is the writer wants to do, why he or she wants to do it, and how it can be done. The proposal should also include evidence that supports the writer's position. This evidence can be photos, articles, and surveys. Together, the proposal and the evidence make up an action plan.

Dear mayor

I would like a baseball

field built in the

space

SPORTS

other cha

nother

BOSTON ST.

BLEACHERS

BLEACHERS

BLEACHERS

WHITFIELD ST.

1 Choose and Support an Issue

What is one thing in your community you want to change? Check out local news reports to see what other people think your community needs. Pick an issue you feel strongly about, but not one that's too big to tackle. Perhaps you feel that your neighborhood needs a dog run where dogs can exercise safely or that your community needs a new public softball diamond. If you did a needs assessment survey, you may want to use that issue. Write a short proposal telling about your idea.

Once you choose an issue, collect evidence to support your idea. Start a file of newspaper clippings. As you collect information, take notes. Support for your position can come from many sources. Talk to people you know. They may be willing to sign a petition or write letters in support of your idea. Local or national newspapers, TV stations, and radio shows may have covered your issue.

TOOLS

- paper and pen
- markers, crayons, or pencils
- folder
- camera (optional)

2 Making a Plan

Any good action plan includes ideas for how the plan might work. For example, if you think your community needs a public dog run, you might find out how much land must be set aside for it. You might research available public areas. You may want to include information about how much the project is likely to cost the community.

Decide what information you need to explain how your idea could work. Then, research that information.

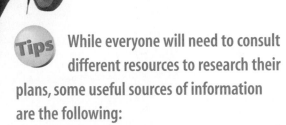

Tips While everyone will need to consult different resources to research their plans, some useful sources of information are the following:

- local Historical Society
- school or public library
- City Hall
- Chamber of Commerce

How Am I Doing?

Before you begin your action plan, take a minute to ask yourself these questions:

- Can you state the idea for your action plan briefly and clearly?

- Do you have at least three pieces of evidence that support your idea?

- Have you collected enough information to explain how the idea could work?

3 Write Your Action Plan

Write a proposal for action. Begin by briefly stating what it is that you want to build or change. Continue the proposal by giving at least three reasons explaining why your idea is a sound one. Finally, explain how the idea might be put into action. Be sure to list the evidence you have collected to support your idea and to show how it could work. Reread your proposal to be sure that it is clear and complete.

If You Are Using a Computer...

Draft your action proposal using the Report format. Then write the letter for your proposal in the Letter format. Create your own stationery by choosing from the selection of letterheads.

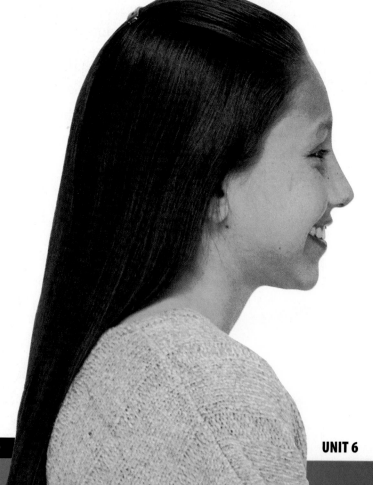

4 Present Your Action Plan

Now it's time to put your action plan together. Put your proposal in the left-hand pocket of your folder. Gather together all of the evidence you have collected. Put the evidence in the right-hand side of the folder. Are you going to mail your action plan to the mayor or a community leader? Write a brief letter stating your idea and explaining that you have included an action plan to describe the idea in detail. Put everything in a mailing envelope and address it clearly and neatly. Include a self-addressed, stamped envelope so the material will be returned to you. Remember to keep a copy of the letter and evidence for yourself. You might want to put your copy of the action plan on display in your classroom.

CONGRATULATIONS

Now you know what an urban planner does. Next time you're in a city, think about all the planning that's needed to make things run.

Karen Heit
Urban Planner ▶

Glossary

al·ley
(al´ē) *noun*
Narrow passageway behind or between buildings.

ar·mory
(är´mə rē) *noun*
Place where weapons are stored.

bi·o·de·grad·a·ble
(bī´ō di grā´də bəl) *adjective*
Something that decays easily and naturally with the help of living organisms like bacteria.

bou·le·vard
(bool´ə värd) *noun*
A wide city street.

bound·a·ry
(boun´də rē) *noun*
A line or other thing that marks a border or limit.

ca·ble car
(kā´bəl kär´) *noun*
A railroad car pulled along the rails by an underground cable.

can·ti·le·ver bridge
(kan´tl ē´vər brij) *noun*
A cantilever is a structure, supported at one end, that is anchored to a wall or a pier. A cantilever bridge is a bridge whose span is formed by two cantilevers projecting toward each other, sometimes with an extra section between them.

con·ven·ience
(kən vēn´yəns) *noun*
Anything that makes work easier or adds to one's comfort.

dead end
(ded end) *noun*
A street that has only one way to enter or exit.

de·faced (di fāst´) *verb*
Spoiled or hurt the looks of. He *defaced* the property. ▲ **deface**

cable car

de·fi·ance
(di fī′ əns) *noun*
A resistance to authority or to any opposing force.

de·mol·ish·ing
(di mol′ish ing) *verb*
Tearing down or destroying. ▲ **demolish**

dis·ap·pear·ed
(dis′ə pērd′) *verb*
Stopped being seen. Vanished; went away.
▲ **disappear**

Thesaurus
disappeared
dissolved
eclipsed
melted away

dump·sters
(dump′stərs) *noun*
Large, metal trash bins.
▲ **dumpster**

en·dures
(en dŏŏrz′) *verb*
Continues, or lasts, for a long time. Something that is taken care of *endures* longer than something that is abused. ▲ **endure**

en·vi·ron·ment
(en vī′rən mənt) *noun*
All the things, such as air, water, minerals, animals, plants, and people, that surround one or more living things.

hab·i·tats
(hab′i tats′) *noun*
Places where animals or plants naturally live and grow. ▲ **habitat**

ha·rass·ing
(hə ras′ing) *verb*
Bothering or troubling over and over again. ▲ **harass**

Fact File

Over 70% of our trash ends up in landfills.

in·ter·sec·tions
(in′tər sək′shəns) *noun*
Places where two or more things cross each other.
▲ **intersection**

intersections

land·fills
(land′filz′) *noun*
Areas of land that have been filled in with garbage and covered with layers of dirt. ▲ **landfill**

a	add	ŏŏ	took	ə =
ā	ace	ōō	pool	a in *above*
â	care	u	up	e in *sicken*
ä	palm	û	burn	i in *possible*
e	end	yōō	fuse	o in *melon*
ē	equal	oi	oil	u in *circus*
i	it	ou	pout	
ī	ice	ng	ring	
o	odd	th	thin	
ō	open	th	this	
ô	order	zh	vision	

Glossary

pier

land·mark
(land′märk) *noun*
An easily seen object, such
as a building, tree, or
statue, that helps one to
find or recognize a place.

ped·dler (ped′ lər) *noun*
A person who sells things
from door to door or from
a cart or stand on the
street. We each bought an
apple from the *peddler*.

pier (pēr) *noun*
A structure built out over
water on posts, used as a
landing place for ships.

pre·dic·a·ment
(pri dik′ə mənt) *noun*
A difficult or troubling
situation.

push·cart
(poŏsh′kärt′) *noun*
A light cart on wheels that
can be pushed by hand.

reck·less
(rek′lis) *adjective*
Not careful.

row hou·ses
(rō houz′es) *noun*
A series of houses in which
neighboring units share a
wall. ▲ **row house**

sar·cas·tic
(sär kas′tik) *adjective*
Witty, in a mean way;
meant to hurt or humiliate.

sew·age (sōō′ ij) *noun*
Waste that is carried off from sinks, toilets, and other devices by sewers and drains.

sin·gle-mind·ed (sing′gəl mīn′did) *adjective*
Having only one aim or purpose.

sour·dough (souər′ dō′) *adjective*
Made from a type of dough that contains an actively fermenting yeast. San Francisco is known for its *sourdough* bread.

stuck-up (stuk′ up′) *adjective*
Snobbish or conceited.

sur·veil·lance (sər vā′lens) *noun*
Close observation.

sus·pen·sion bridge (sə spen′shən brij) *noun*
A bridge held up by large cables or chains that are strung between a series of towers.

Fact File

The longest suspension bridge in the world is the Akashi-Kaiko bridge in Japan, which spans 6,496 feet!

town·ship (toun′ship) *noun*
A division of a county, which has local powers of government over schools, roads, and other aspects of the community.

traf·fic co·or·di·na·tion (traf′ik kō ôr′dnā′shən) *noun*
The planning of vehicle movement in a populated area.

truss bridge (trus′ brij′) *noun*
A bridge held up by a framework of beams or rods.

ur·ban (ûr′bən) *adjective*
Of, living in, or having to do with a city.

van·dals (van′dlz) *noun*
People who destroy or damage things on purpose, especially works of art or public property. ▲ **vandal**

ve·hi·cles (vē′i kəlz) *noun*
A means of carrying people or things, especially over land, sea, or air. Subway trains are efficient *vehicles* for carrying large numbers of people through cities. ▲ **vehicle**

suspension bridge

a	add	ōō	took	ə =
ā	ace	ōō	pool	a in *above*
â	care	u	up	e in *sicken*
ä	palm	û	burn	i in *possible*
e	end	yōō	fuse	o in *melon*
ē	equal	oi	oil	u in *circus*
i	it	ou	pout	
ī	ice	ng	ring	
o	odd	th	thin	
ō	open	th	this	
ô	order	zh	vision	

Authors & Illustrators

Tricia Brown *pages 10–21*

Tricia Brown has traveled throughout Latin America and Southeast Asia, but she is always glad to return home to San Francisco. She is well known for the photo essays she has written about kids in different California neighborhoods. *The City by the Bay* is special to her because she wrote it to help the people of her hometown. Brown donates her earnings from the book to organizations that help children in San Francisco.

Peter Collington *pages 94–113*

Peter Collington's career in picture books began with *Little Pickle*, a book that grew from pictures he had drawn to amuse his small daughter. *The Coming of the Surfman* is also a first for Collington—his first book with words. All of his other books have been wordless fantasy stories.

Jean Merrill *pages 54–69*

Since 1951, Jean Merrill has written more than 20 books for kids, but *The Pushcart War* is probably her most famous book. This city tale has been made into a television play and was also performed on the stage and on the radio. Surprisingly, Merrill lives in the country. She grew up on a farm and loved to spend time out of doors. "Books were the only things that could keep me indoors," Merrill says.

Jerry Spinelli *pages 116–129*

When he was sixteen years old, Jerry Spinelli dreamed of being a major-league shortstop. Then his high school football team in Norristown, Pennsylvania, won a big game. Swept up in the excitement of the event, Spinelli wrote a poem about it. A local paper published the poem, and Spinelli has been writing ever since.

"Experiences are not really complete until I write about them."

Walt Whitman *page 46*

Although his writing was first published over one hundred years ago, Walt Whitman's words still ring true today. Born in 1819, Whitman did not start writing poetry until he was thirty years old. At that time, he took his first trip to New Orleans, Louisiana. The people and places he saw there inspired him. By 1855, Whitman had written enough poetry to put together a collection called *Leaves of Grass*, which he published himself. Today, *Leaves of Grass* remains Whitman's most popular book.

Vera B. Williams *pages 26–45*

This author/illustrator grew up in the Bronx, but considered all of New York City to be her neighborhood. Her family walked everywhere, rode ferries, ice-skated in public parks, and visited city libraries. One of Williams' childhood paintings was included in an exhibit at New York's Museum of Modern Art. Williams said she was "thrilled to be a citizen of so grand a place as New York City."

Books &

Author Study

Walt Whitman

I Hear America Singing
by Walt Whitman
illustrated by Robert Subuda
In his most famous poem, Whitman celebrates America and its people.

Walt Whitman
by Catherine Reef
This biography includes photos of Walt Whitman, along with excerpts from his poems and other writings.

Walt Whitman

Fiction

A Girl Called Al
by Constance Greene
Two girls who live in the same city apartment building become best friends, sharing good times and bad.

The Great Smith House Hustle
by Jane Louise Curry
Cisco and Poppy Smith have just moved to Pittsburgh, where they've stumbled on a mystery that threatens their community. With the help of friends and neighbors, they may be able to solve it.

Mop, Moondance and the Nagasaki Knights
by Walter Dean Myers
T.J. and his friends love the city park where they play baseball. But they soon discover that for some people, the park is a place to live.

Nonfiction

City! San Francisco
by Shirley Climo
photographs by George Ancona
Climo and Ancona take their readers on a tour of a great California city.

The Building of Manhattan
by Donald A. Mackay
In this carefully researched book, Mackay uses words and pictures to show how New York has grown since its beginnings as a Dutch colony over 300 years ago.

The Great Fire
by Jim Murphy
Newspapers described the Chicago fire of 1871 as the great calamity of the age. This book puts readers in the middle of one of the most devastating fires in U.S. history.

&Media

Videos

Software

Magazines

Daniel and the Towers
Public Media Video
Daniel, a Los Angeles boy, helps a street artist build a beautiful tower out of old junk, in this story based on a real event. (55 minutes)

Recycling
Library Video Series
All across the United States young people are improving the quality of life in their communities by working on recycling projects. In this video, you'll meet some of these real-life environmental heroes. (26 minutes)

Taking Care of Terrific
WonderWorks
Family Movie Series
On their daily journeys to the Boston Common, a small boy named Terrific and his teenaged baby-sitter meet with interesting characters and incredible adventures. (58 minutes)

Decisions, Decisions: Urbanization
Tom Snyder Productions
You're the mayor of Alpine, and you must decide how your community will grow.

Immigrant: The Irish Experience in Boston
Wings/Sunburst
Many immigrants came from Ireland to Boston in the 1800s. This program allows you to join one such family and to make the same kinds of decisions that real-life Irish immigrants had to face.

MacUSA
Broderbund
Go on-line and use this atlas to learn about cities in all 50 states and in Puerto Rico. The atlas includes facts, pictures, and terrific maps.

3-2-1 Contact
Children's Television Workshop
This science and technology magazine often includes articles about how technology helps solve city problems.

Scholastic News
Scholastic Inc.
Articles in this classroom news magazine focus on current events that affect kids from a variety of cities.

A Place to Write

How can you help your neighborhood? For information about publications and activities in your area, write to

United Neighborhood Centers of America, Inc.
4801 Massachusetts Ave. NW
Washington, D.C. 20016

Acknowledgments

Grateful acknowledgment is made to the following sources for permission to reprint from previously published material. The publisher has made diligent efforts to trace the ownership of all copyrighted material in this volume and believes that all necessary permissions have been secured. If any errors or omissions have inadvertently been made, proper corrections will gladly be made in future editions.

Front cover: Illustration from CITY BY THE BAY by Tricia Brown and Elisa Kleven, copyright © 1993. Published by Chronicle Books, San Francisco. Used by permission.

Back cover: Top: Illustration of "Doug®" copyright © 1993 Viacom International, Inc. All rights reserved. "Doug®" is a registered trademark of Viacom International, Inc. Used by permission. Middle: © Edward S. Curtis/Odyssey Production. Bottom: "Looking Along Broadway Towards Grace Church," 1981, copyright © by Red Grooms, Marlborough Gallery.

Acknowledgments

Grateful acknowledgment is made to the following sources for permission to reprint from previously published material. The publisher has made diligent efforts to trace the ownership of all copyrighted material in this volume and believes that all necessary permissions have been secured. If any errors or omissions have inadvertently been made, proper corrections will gladly be made in future editions.

Unit Opener: Illustration of "Doug®" copyright © 1993 Viacom International, Inc. All rights reserved. "Doug®" and all related titles and characters are trademarks of Viacom International, Inc. Used by permission.

Interior: "From Miss Ida's Porch" from FROM MISS IDA'S PORCH by Sandra Belton with illustrations by Floyd Cooper. Text copyright © 1993 by Sandra Belton. Illustrations copyright © 1993 by Floyd Cooper. Reprinted by arrangement with Simon & Schuster Books for Young Readers, Simon & Schuster Children's Publishing Division.

"The Homecoming" and cover from THE RAINBOW PEOPLE by Laurence Yep. Text copyright © 1989 by Laurence Yep. Reprinted by permission of HarperCollins Publishers.

The cover of the brochure from the National Storytelling Festival is used by the kind permission of the National Storytelling Association, Jonesborough, TN 37659.

"How the Coyote Gets His Name" by Jerry Tello is now available under the title COYOTE, HOW HE GETS HIS NAME by Jerry Tello. Copyright © 1993 by Jerry Tello. Published by Sueños Publications. Notes are used by permission of the author.

"La Bamba" from BASEBALL IN APRIL AND OTHER STORIES by Gary Soto. Copyright © 1990 by Gary Soto. Reprinted by permission of Harcourt Brace & Company. Book cover illustration by Barry Root, copyright © 1990 by Barry Root. Reprinted by permission of the illustrator. "La Bamba" (Ritchie Valens) copyright © 1958 Picture Our Music. Administered by Warner-Tamerlane Publishing Corp. All rights reserved.

"School Play" from REMEMBERING AND OTHER POEMS by Myra Cohn Livingston. Copyright © 1989 by Myra Cohn Livingston. Reprinted by arrangement with Margaret K. McElderry Books, Simon & Schuster Children's Publishing Division. Cover illustration by Neil Waldman. Illustration copyright © 1989 by Neil Waldman. Reprinted by permission of the artist.

"Doug Can't Dig It" television script from Nickelodeon/MTV Networks. Text and illustrations from Jumbo Pictures, copyright © 1993 Viacom International, Inc. All rights reserved. "Doug" is a registered trademark of Viacom International, Inc., "Doug®" and all related titles and characters are trademarks of Viacom International, Inc. Used by permission.

Selection from an adaptation from "Vanessa's Bad Grade," an episode of the NBC-TV series The Cosby Show. Written by Ross Brown. A Carsey-Werner Production in association with Bill Cosby. Copyright © 1985. Used by permission. All rights reserved. Adaptation originally printed in Scholastic SCOPE® magazine, Volume 36, No. 4, October 2, 1987.

Selection and cover from DINAH FOR PRESIDENT by Claudia Mills. Text copyright © 1992 by Claudia Mills. This edition is reprinted by arrangement with Simon & Schuster Books for Young Readers, Simon & Schuster Children's Publishing Division. Cover illustration by Eileen McKeating copyright © 1992 by Eileen McKeating. Reprinted by permission of the artist.

Selection and cover from YOU MEAN I HAVE TO STAND UP AND SAY SOMETHING? by Joan Detz. Text copyright © 1986 by Joan Detz. Cover illustration copyright © 1986 by David Marshall. Reprinted by permission of PMA Literary Agency & Film Management for the authors.

"A Few Appropriate Remarks" from Cobblestone's July 1988 issue: "The Battle of Gettysburg," copyright © 1988, Cobblestone Publishing, Inc., 7 School Street, Peterborough, NH 03458. Reprinted by permission of the publisher. Cobblestone logo is a registered trademark of Cobblestone Publishing, Inc. Used by permission.

Cover illustration by William Lahey Cummings from THE ABRAHAM LINCOLN JOKE BOOK by Beatrice Schenk de Regniers. Illustrations © 1965. Reprinted by permission of Scholastic Inc. Cover illustration by Joyce Behr from HUMOROUS MONOLOGUES by Martha Bolton. Copyright © 1989 by Martha Bolton. All rights reserved. Originally published by Sterling Publishing Co., Inc. Used by permission of Martha Bolton. "Dinosaurs" from Scholastic News®, March 3, 1995. Copyright © 1995. Published by Scholastic Inc. Used by permission.

Cover from DEAR DR. BELL . . . YOUR FRIEND, HELEN KELLER by Judith St. George. Illustration copyright © 1992 by G. P. Putnam's Sons. Published by G. P. Putnam's Sons, a division of The Putnam & Grosset Group.

Cover from KOYA DELANEY AND THE GOOD GIRL BLUES by Eloise Greenfield, illustrated by Jan Spivey Gilchrist. Illustration copyright © 1992 by Jan Spivey Gilchrist. Published by Scholastic Inc.

Cover from SCHOOL SPIRIT by Johanna Hurwitz, illustrated by Liana Somana. Published by William Morrow & Company, Inc. Illustration copyright © 1995 by Scholastic Inc.

Cover from THAT'S A WRAP!: HOW MOVIES ARE MADE by Ned Dowd, photograph by Henry Horenstein. Photograph copyright © 1991 by Henry Horenstein. Published by Simon & Schuster Books for Young Readers, Simon & Schuster Children's Publishing Division.

Photography and Illustration Credits

Photos: © John Lei for Scholastic Inc. all Tool Box items unless otherwise noted. p. 2: © Valerie Santagto for Scholastic Inc. pp. 2-3 background: © Valerie Santagto for Scholastic Inc. p. 3 br: © Valerie Santagto for Scholastic Inc.; tc: © Maxwell MacKenzie/Tony Stone Images. p. 4 c: © Ana Esperanza Nance for Scholastic Inc.; tc: © Maxwell MacKenzie/Tony Stone Images. p. 5 c: © Lee F. Snyder/Photo Researchers; tc: © Maxwell MacKenzie/Tony Stone Images. p. 6 c: © Michael Newman/PhotoEdit; tc: © Maxwell MacKenzie/Tony Stone Images. p. 44 tc: © Larry Maglott for Scholastic Inc.; c, bc: © Tom Raymond/Fresh Air Photographics. p. 46 br: © Jerry Jacka/Courtesy Gallery 10. bl: © Chris Marona/Photo Researchers, Inc. p. 47 br: © David McGlynn/FPG International Corp. p. 48 bc: © Stanley Bach for Scholastic Inc. p. 49 tr: © John Lei for Scholastic Inc.; bl: © Stanley Bach for Scholastic Inc.; br: © Valerie Santagto for Scholastic Inc. p. 80 c: © Maxwell MacKenzie/Tony Stone Images, Inc.; all others: © Valerie Santagto for Scholastic Inc. pp. 80-81 c: © Valerie Santagto for Scholastic Inc. pp. 81-83: © Valerie Santagto for Scholastic Inc. p. 84 © Photo Courtesy of NBC. p. 86 br, bc: © Stanley Bach for Scholastic Inc. p. 87 br: © Valerie Santagto for Scholastic Inc. p. 112 cl: © Brown Brothers. p. 114 tc: © Stock Montage, Inc. pp. 116-117 c: Courtesy of the Division of Rare and Manuscript Collections, Cornell University Library. pp. 118-121 border: © Joe Sohm/The Image Works. p. 119 tr: © FPG International Corp.; tl, cr: © The Granger Collection; bc: © National Museum of the American Indian. p. 120 tr: © Brown Brothers; cl: © Stanley Tretick/Sygma; br: © Bob Adelman/Magnum Photos. p. 121 tr: © J. Tiziou/Sygma; c: © O. Franken/Sygma; br: © Wally McNamee/Sygma. pp. 122-123 c, tc: © John Lei for Scholastic Inc. p. 123 c: © Stanley Bach for Scholastic Inc. p. 124 bc: © Stanley Bach for Scholastic Inc.; br: © John Lei for Scholastic Inc. p. 125 bl: © John Lei for Scholastic Inc.; tr: © Stanley Bach for Scholastic Inc. p. 126 tr: © Stanley Bach for Scholastic Inc.; br: © John Lei for Scholastic Inc. p. 127 c: © John Lei for Scholastic Inc.; cr, bl: © Stanley Bach for Scholastic Inc.; br: © Valerie Santagto for Scholastic Inc.; p. 128 tl, c: © Art Gingert/ Comstock, Inc. p. 130 tc: © Jon Feingersh/The Stock Market. p. 132 tl: Scholastic Photo Library; bl: Diane Guthrie; cl: © Courtesy of Myra Cohn Livingston. p. 133 cr, br: Scholastic Trade Department; tr: Hans Neleman; br: Scholastic Photo Library. p.134 bl: © Courtesy of Scholastic Photo Library. p. 135 br: © Stanley Bach for Scholastic Inc.

Illustrations: pp. 8-9: Keith Bendis; pp. 10, 11, 16, 18, 19, 22, 24, 28, 30, 32, 33: Jans Evans; pp. 33-34, 39, 40, 42-43: Chi Chung; pp. 50-51: Keith Bendis; pp. 53-54, 57-59: José Ortega; pp. 60-61: Curtis Parker; pp. 88-89: Keith Bendis; pp. 90, 93, 97, 100: Michael Steirnagle; pp. 106-109: David Garner; pp. 110-111, 113-115: Stephen Alcorn; pp. 144-148, 150-151: Chi Chung.

Acknowledgments

Grateful acknowledgment is made to the following sources for permission to reprint from previously published material. The publisher has made diligent efforts to trace the ownership of all copyrighted material in this volume and believes that all necessary permissions have been secured. If any errors or omissions have inadvertently been made, proper corrections will gladly be made in future editions.

Unit Opener: © Edward S. Curtis/Odyssey Production.

Interior: "The Way West" from THE WAY WEST: JOURNAL OF A PIONEER WOMAN by Amelia Stewart Knight, illustrated by Michael McCurdy. Text adaptation copyright © 1993 by Simon & Schuster. Illustrations copyright © 1993 by Michael McCurdy. Reprinted by permission of Simon & Schuster Books for Young Readers, Simon & Schuster Children's Publishing Division.

Satanta, Kiowa Chief's speech and cover from I HAVE SPOKEN: AMERICAN HISTORY THROUGH THE VOICES OF THE INDIANS, compiled by Virginia Irving Armstrong, introduction by Frederick W. Turner, III. Copyright © 1971 by Virginia Irving Armstrong. Reprinted by permission of Ohio University Press/Swallow Press.

"An American Hero" and cover from COWBOYS by Martin Sandler. Copyright © 1994 by Eagle Productions, Inc. Reprinted by permission of HarperCollins Publishers.

"Cielito Lindo" and cover from SONGS OF THE WILD WEST by The Metropolitan Museum of Art. Commentary by Alan Axelrod, arrangements by Dan Fox. Copyright © 1991 by The Metropolitan Museum of Art. Reprinted by permission of Simon & Schuster Books for Young Readers, Simon & Schuster Children's Publishing Division.

"Robert Gard" selection from HARD TIMES by Studs Terkel. Copyright © 1970, 1986 by Studs Terkel. Reprinted by permission of Pantheon Books, a division of Random House, Inc.

"At Home" and cover from IMMIGRANT KIDS by Russell Freedman. Copyright © 1980 by Russell Freedman. Reprinted by permission of Dutton Children's Books, a division of Penguin Books USA Inc. Quotation within "At Home" by Leonard Covello from THE HEART IS THE TEACHER by Leonard Covello with Guido D'Agostino. Copyright © 1958 by Leonard Covello. McGraw-Hill Book Company. Reprinted by permission of Blassingame Spectrum Corp.

Selection and cover from TOLIVER'S SECRET by Esther Wood Brady. Text copyright © 1976 by Esther Wood. Cover art copyright © 1993 by Dan Andreasen. Reprinted by permission of Crown Publishers, Inc.

Cover and illustrations for "Paul Revere's Ride" from FROM SEA TO SHINING SEA, edited by Amy L. Cohn. Cover copyright © 1993 by Scholastic Inc. Illustrations by Anita Lobel, copyright © 1993 by Anita Lobel. Reprinted by permission of Scholastic Inc.

Selections from "The Top News Events of 1993-94" from *Junior Scholastic*, May 6, 1994. Copyright © 1994 by Scholastic Inc. Published by Scholastic Inc. Used by permission.

Selection and cover from THE HOUSE OF DIES DREAR by Virginia Hamilton. Text copyright © 1968 by Virginia Hamilton. Cover art by Eros Keith, copyright © 1968 by Macmillan Publishing Company. This edition is reprinted by arrangement with Simon & Schuster Books for Young Readers, Simon & Schuster Children's Publishing Division.

"A Long and Hungry War" and cover from THE BOYS' WAR by Jim Murphy. Text copyright © 1990 by Jim Murphy. Reprinted by permission of Clarion Books/Houghton Mifflin Co. All rights reserved.

Cover from VOICES FROM THE CIVIL WAR by Milton Meltzer. Copyright © 1989 by Harper & Row, Publishers Inc. Reprinted by permission of HarperCollins Publishers Inc.

Cover of BEN AND ME by Robert Lawson. Illustration copyright © 1939 by Robert Lawson, renewed 1967 by John W. Boyd. Published by Little Brown & Company, Inc.

Cover of THE CAPTIVE by Joyce Hansen, illustrated by John Thompson. Illustration copyright © 1993 by John Thompson. Published by Scholastic Inc.

Cover of CHILDREN OF THE WILD WEST by Russell Freedman, photograph by the Denver Public Library. Hand-tinted by Joan Menschenfreund. Photograph copyright © 1983 by Houghton Mifflin Company. Published by Clarion Books, a division of Houghton Mifflin Company.

Cover of MORNING GIRL by Michael Dorris, illustrated by Ellen Thompson. Illustration copyright © 1994 by Ellen Thompson. Published by Hyperion Books for Children.

Photography and Illustration Credits

Photos: © John Lei for Scholastic Inc., all Tool Box items unless otherwise noted. p. 2 bl, cl: © Andrew M. Levine for Scholastic Inc.; tl: © Andrew M. Levine for Scholastic Inc./Library of Congress, National Park Service-USDI, Library of Congress, Jacob A. Riis Collection, Museum of the City of New York. pp. 2-3 background: © Bob Krist/Black Star. p. 3 br: © Andrew M. Levine for Scholastic Inc. p. 4 c: © Ferguson & Katzman/Tony Stone Images Inc.; tc: © Ana Esperanza Nance for Scholastic Inc. p. 5 c, tc: © Ana Esperanza Nance for Scholastic Inc. p. 6 c, tc: © Ana Esperanza Nance for Scholastic Inc. p. 31 c: Courtesy of Smithsonian Institute Indian chief Satanta. p. 34: © Leib Image Archives. p. 35: © Library of Congress. pp. 36-39: © The Erwin E. Smith Collection of the Library of Congress on deposit at the Amon Carter Museum, Ft. Worth, TX. p. 40: © Library of Congress. p. 41 tr: © Library of Congress; bl: © Erwin E. Smith Collection of the Library of Congress on deposit at the Amon Carter Museum, Ft. Worth, TX. p. 42 bc: © Erwin E. Smith Collection of the Library of Congress on deposit at the Amon Carter Museum, Ft. Worth, TX. pp. 43-44: © Library of Congress. p. 45: © Library of Congress. p. 46 tc: © The Metropolitan Museum of Art, Rogers Fund, 1979. p. 47: © "Singing Vaquero" by Emanuel Wyttenbach/The Metropolitan Museum of Art, The Elisha Whittelsey Collection, The Elisha Whittelsey Fund, 1949. p. 50 car: The Bettmann Archive. pp. 50-51: Reuters/Bettmann. p. 51 br: © John Lei for Scholastic Inc. pp. 52-53: © Jeff Isaac Greenberg/Photo Researchers, Inc. p. 53 br: © Andrew M. Levine for Scholastic Inc. p. 56 c: © National Park Service. pp. 56-57 background: © The Bettmann Archive. p. 58: © The Library of Congress. p. 59: "Orchard Street on New York City's Lower East Side," 1898/© The Byron Collection/Museum of the City of New York. p. 60: "Room in an Immigrant Family's Tenement Apartment," 1910/ © Jessie Tarbox Beals/The Jacob A. Riis Collection, #502/Museum of the City of New York. pp. 61-62, 64-65: Lewis Hine/George Eastman House. p. 66: © Gift of Tenement House Dept./Museum of the City of New York. p. 67: © National Park Service. p. 68 tc: © Ana Esperanza Nance for Scholastic Inc.; all others: © Andrew M. Levine for Scholastic Inc. pp. 69-71: © Andrew M. Levine for Scholastic Inc. except for p. 71 bc: Library of Congress, Wide World Photos, Courtesy of Bancroft Library, University of CA, Berkeley. p. 96: © Tom Van Sant/The Stock Market. p. 97 Mandela: © AP/Wide World Photos; Clinton: © Les Stone/ Sygma; Jansen: © Dallas Morning News/Liaison/ Gamma-Liaison. p. 98 bc: © Stanley Bach for Scholastic Inc. Reagan: © Bettmann Archive; Lewis: © Kennerly/Gamma Liaison; Statue of Liberty: © Bettmann Newsphoto; Sullivan: © Benson/Gamma Liaison. p. 99 br: © Andrew M. Levine for Scholastic Inc. p. 110 c: Detail of "Harriet Tubman as a Baby" by Jacob Lawrence/Courtesy of Jacob Lawrence and Francine Seders Gallery, Seattle, WA. p. 111 cl: "Runaway Slaves Asleep in a Barn" by Jacob Lawrence/Courtesy of Jacob Lawrence and Francine Seders Gallery, Seattle, WA. p. 112: "Harriet Tubman Leads Runaway Slaves Across the Snows of the North" by Jacob Lawrence/Courtesy of Jacob Lawrence and Francine Seders Gallery, Seattle, WA. p. 113 cr: "Slaves Escape in a 'Chariot' Driven by Harriet Tubman" by Jacob Lawrence/Courtesy of Jacob Lawrence and Francine Seders Gallery, Seattle, WA. pp. 114-115: "Harriet Tubman Guides a Group of Escaped Slaves Through the Woods" by Jacob Lawrence/Courtesy of Jacob Lawrence and Francine Seders Gallery, Seattle, WA. p. 116: © The Bettmann Archive. p. 117 cr: © David J. Eicher/Well-Traveled Images. p. 119 bc: © Leib Image Archives; tr: © Library of Congress. p. 120 c: © The Bettmann Archive. p. 121 tr: © Library of Congress. p. 122 tl: © Library of Congress. p. 123 bc: © Leib Image Archives. p. 125 tr: © Library of Congress. p. 126 cl: © The Bettmann Archive; cr: © Leib Image Archives. p. 127 cr: © Leib Image Archives. p. 127: © Halley Ganges for Scholastic Inc. p. 128 cl: © Library of Congress. pp. 128-129: © Halley Ganges for Scholastic Inc. p. 129 cr: © Brown Brothers. p. 130 tr: © NASA; cr: © Bettmann Archive. p. 131 c: © NASA/Photo Researchers. pp. 132-133: © Stanley Bach for Scholastic Inc. p. 134 bl: © AP/WideWorld Photos; cr: © Stanley Bach for Scholastic Inc. p. 135 br: © Andrew M. Levine for Scholastic Inc. p. 136 br: © John Eastcott/Yva Momatuk/The Image Works. p. 138 cr: © Thomas Zimmerman/FPG International Corp.; bc: © Bob Daemmrich/The Image Works.
p. 139 bl: © R. Lord/The Image Works; tr: © Pedrick/The Image Works. p. 140 Lincoln: © Stock Montage Inc. p. 141 cl: © The Granger Collection; br: © Stanley Bach for Scholastic Inc. p. 142 cl: Carlo Ontal; bl: © UPI/Bettmann Archive. p. 143 tr: © Dan McCoy; cr: © courtesy of Clarion Books.

Illustrations: pp. 30-31: Paul Breeden; p. 46: Steve Meeks; pp. 72-73, 75-82, 84-89: Paul Schmid; pp. 102-107, 109: Keaf Holliday; pp. 127-128: Mary Keefe.

Acknowledgments

Grateful acknowledgment is made to the following sources for permission to reprint from previously published material. The publisher has made diligent efforts to trace the ownership of all copyrighted material in this volume and believes that all necessary permissions have been secured. If any errors or omissions have inadvertently been made, proper corrections will gladly be made in future editions.

Unit Opener: © "Looking Along Broadway Towards Grace Church," 1981, Red Grooms, Marlborough Gallery.

Interior: Selections and cover from THE CITY BY THE BAY published by Chronicle Books, San Francisco. Copyright © 1993 by The Junior League of San Francisco, Inc. Written by Tricia Brown and The Junior League of San Francisco, illustrated by Elisa Kleven. Reprinted by permission.

Text, art, and cover from SCOOTER by Vera B. Williams. Copyright © 1993 by Vera B. Williams. Reprinted by permission of Greenwillow Books, a division of William Morrow & Company, Inc.

Selection from BACK TO THE CITY: PITTSBURGH! Copyright © 1992 NeighborFair Pittsburgh Inc. Used by permission.

Selection from THE PUSHCART WAR by Jean Merrill. Text copyright © 1964 by Jean Merrill. Reprinted by permission of HarperCollins Publishers. Cover illustration by Carl Cassler. Cover illustration copyright © by Carl Cassler. Used by permission of Dell Books, a division of Bantam Doubleday Dell Publishing Group, Inc.

Selection and cover from GARBAGE! by Evan and Janet Hadingham. Copyright © 1990 by Evan and Janet Hadingham and WGBH Educational Foundation. Reprinted by permission of Simon & Schuster Books for Young Readers, Simon & Schuster Children's Publishing Division.

"50 Can-Do Kids" by Kathy Love. Reprinted from the March 1993 issue of RANGER RICK® magazine with the permission of the publisher, the National Wildlife Federation. Copyright © 1993 by the National Wildlife Federation.

"Cornerstone Pool Customer Satisfaction Survey" used by permission of the Town of West Hartford, CT, Department of Leisure Services .

"The Coming of the Surfman" from THE COMING OF THE SURFMAN by Peter Collington. Copyright © 1993 by Peter Collington. Originally published in Great Britain in 1993 by Jonathan Cape Ltd., an imprint of Random House UK Ltd. Reprinted by permission of Alfred A. Knopf, Inc.

"Art Show Draws Upon Ex-Graffiti Scrawlers" from *Philadelphia Daily News*, March 29, 1989, p. 14. Reprinted by permission of Knight-Ridder Tribune News Service.

Selection and cover from MANIAC MAGEE by Jerry Spinelli. Copyright © 1990 by Jerry Spinelli. By permission of Little, Brown & Company.

Cover from CITIES: CITIZENS & CIVILIZATIONS by Fiona Macdonald, illustrated by John James. Illustration copyright © 1992 by The Salariya Book Co. Ltd. Published by Franklin Watts.

Cover from A JAR OF DREAMS by Yoshiko Uchida, illustrated by Kuniko Craft. Illustration copyright © 1981 by Kuniko Craft. Published by Atheneum Books for Young Readers, Simon & Schuster Children's Publishing Division.

Cover from TAILS OF THE BRONX by Jill Pinkwater, illustrated by Brian Pinkney. Cover illustration copyright © 1991 by Brian Pinkney. Published by Simon & Schuster Books for Young Readers, Simon & Schuster Children's Publishing Division.

Cover from WHERE THE RIVER RUNS by Nancy Price Graff, photograph by Richard Howard. Photograph copyright © 1993 by Richard Howard. Published by Little, Brown & Company.

Photography and Illustration Credits

Photos: © John Lei for Scholastic Inc., all Tool Box items unless otherwise noted. p. 2 bl: © John Lei for Scholastic Inc.; tl: © Maryellen Baker for Scholastic Inc.; cl: © Frank Cruz for Scholastic Inc. pp. 2-3 c: © Ann Summa for Scholastic Inc.; background: © Tom McHugh/Photo Researchers, Inc. p. 4 c: © Tony Freeman/PhotoEdit. p. 5 c: © Ana Esperanza Nance for Scholastic Inc. p. 6 c: © Tony Freeman/PhotoEdit. pp. 8-9 c: © *The City by the Golden Gate*, painting by Jane Wooster Scott/Superstock. p. 23 tl: © Richard Laird/FPG International Corp.; bl: © Rafael Macia, Photo Researchers, Inc.; tc: © J.D. Cuban/All Sport; bc: © Joseph Nettis/Photo Researchers, Inc.; br: © FPG International Corp.; tr: © Andre Jenny/Stock South Inc.; cl: © Rafael Macia/Photo Researchers, Inc. p. 24 c: © Alain Thomas/Photo Researchers, Inc.; tl: © Barry Durand/Odyssey Productions; Sears Tower: © Steve Elmore/Tom Stack & Associates; Zoo: © Robert Frerck/Tony Stone Worldwide; tc: © J.D. Cuban/All Sport; bc: © Hank Morgan/Photo Researchers, Inc.; c: Alain Thomas/Photo Researchers, Inc.; tr: © Steve DiPaola/All Sport; cr: © Ron Thomas/FPG International Corp.; br: © Bernard Wolff, Photo Researchers, Inc. p. 25 tl: © Sam C. Pierson, Jr./Photo Researchers, Inc.; bl: © Comstock, Inc.; tc: © Mike Powell/All Sport c: James Blank/Tony Stone Images; "HOLLYWOOD" sign: © Tom McHugh/Photo Researchers, Inc.; bc: © Whitby/NST/FPG International Corp.; tr: © David Bartruff/FPG International Corp.; cr: © Rich Buzzelli/Tom Stack & Associates; br: © Comstock Inc. pp. 46-47 c: © *Study for Grand Central* Red Grooms/Courtesy, Marlborough Gallery. pp. 48-49 bl: © NeighborFair Pittsburg, Inc. p. 51 bl: © Stanley Bach for Scholastic Inc.; br: © Ann Summa for Scholastic Inc. pp. 52-53 c: © Detail of *Union Square Station 1992* by Edith Kramer MTA Arts for Transit. p. 70 all: © Ann Summa for Scholastic Inc. p. 71 c: © Ann Summa for Scholastic Inc.; br: © Pete Saloutos/ The Stock Market. p. 72 all: © Ann Summa for Scholastic Inc. p. 73 cr, bl: © Ann Summa for Scholastic Inc.; tl: © Maryellen Baker for Scholastic Inc. pp. 74-75 c: The Bettmann Archive. p. 75 bl (rabbit): © Elwood H. Smith; cr: © John McGrail; br: © The Bettmann Archive. p. 76 tl: © Elwood H. Smith. p. 77 c, br: © The Bettmann Archive. p. 78 c, tl, br: © John McGrail; bl: © WGBH. p. 79 cr, bl: © John McGrail. p. 80 cl: © Elwood H. Smith. p. 81 cl, cr: © Elwood H. Smith. p. 82 bc: © WGBH. p. 81 tr: © Elwood H. Smith. pp. 84-85 © Paul Childress. p. 86-87 bc: © Paul Childress. p. 87 tl: © Paul Childress. pp. 88-89 © LuisCastañeda/The Image Bank. p. 89 c: © Stanley Bach for Scholastic Inc. p. 90 bl: © John Lei for Scholastic Inc.; bc, cl: © Stanley Bach for Scholastic Inc. p. 91 bl: © John Lei for Scholastic Inc.; br: © Ann Summa for Scholastic Inc. p. 115 cl: Courtesy of Anti-Graffiti Network. p. 131 all: © John Lei for Scholastic Inc. p. 132 br: © Stanley Bach for Scholastic Inc. p. 133 tr: © Bie Bostrom for Scholastic Inc.; br: © John Lei for Scholastic Inc. pp. 134-135 c: © Stanley Bach for Scholastic Inc. p. 134 br: © John Lei for Scholastic Inc. p. 135 tr: © Stanley Bach for Scholastic Inc.; br: © Ann Summa for Scholastic Inc. p. 136 bl: © David Weintraub/Photo Researchers, Inc. p. 137 c: © Georg Gerster/Comstock, Inc. p. 138 © Frank Pedrick/The Image Works. p. 139 bl: © Snider/The Image Works. p. 140 tl: courtesy of Tricia Brown; cl: courtesy of Peter Collington; bl: courtesy of Jean Merrill; p. 140 tr: courtesy of Scholastic Trade Department; cr: The Bettmann Archive; br: courtesy of William Morrow & Company. p. 142 br: © M.E. Warren Photography/Photo Researchers, Inc.; bl: The Bettmann Archive. p. 143 br: © Stanley Bach for Scholastic Inc.

Illustrations: p. 22 t: Donna Ingemanson; pp. 22-25: Steven Stankiewicz; pp. 54-69: Beata Szpura; pp. 80-81: Elwood Smith; pp. 92-93: Andrew Boerger; pp. 114-115: Danuta Jarecka; pp. 116-129: Ken Spengler.